Psychodrama

of related interest

Focus on Psychodrama
The Therapeutic Aspects of Psychodrama
Peter Felix Kellermann
Foreword by Jonathan D Moreno
ISBN 1 85302 127 X

Imagination, Identification and Catharsis in Theatre and Therapy
Mary Duggan and Roger Grainger
ISBN 1 85302 431 7

Essays in Drama Therapy
The Double Life
Robert Landy
Foreword by Gavin Bolton
ISBN 1 85302 322 1

Shakespeare Comes to Broadmoor
'The Actors are Come Hither':
The Performance of Tragedy in a Secure Psychiatric Hospital
Edited by Murray Cox
Foreword by Sir Ian McKellen
ISBN 1 85302 135 0 hb
ISBN 1 85302 121 0 pb

Psychodrama

Group Psychotherapy as Experimental Theatre

Playing the leading role in your own life

Eva Røine
Foreword by Finn Magnussen

Jessica Kingsley Publishers
London and Bristol, Pennsylvania

The right of Eva Røine to be identified as author of this work has been asserted by her in accordance with the Copyright, Designs and Patents Act 1988.

First published in the United Kingdom in 1997 by
Jessica Kingsley Publishers Ltd
116 Pentonville Road
London N1 9JB, England
and
1900 Frost Road, Suite 101
Bristol, PA 19007, U S A

An earlier version of Chapters 1–4 was published in 1978 by Artemis Forlag in Norwegian as: Psykodrama – Psykoterapi som eksperimentelt teater (Aschehoug)

Copyright © 1997 Eva Røine
Translation by Ann Zwik

Library of Congress Cataloging in Publication Data
A CIP catalogue record for this book is available from the Library of Congress

British Library Cataloguing in Publication Data
A CIP catalogue record for this book is available from the British Library

ISBN 1-85302-494-5

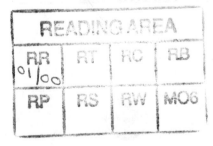

Printed and Bound in Great Britain by
Athenaeum Press, Gateshead, Tyne & Wear

Contents

'Truth is only for the Individual,
in that he Himself brings it forth in Action.'

Søren Kierkegaard,
The Concept of Dread, 1844

Foreword[1]

Human beings play out their lives on earth as if they were on a stage which is sometimes directed far too rigidly, and sometimes in wild chaos. We change our roles as time and place change, and although some play mostly major roles, others barely manage to portray the main role in their own lives.

Psychiatrists have made little therapeutic use of drama and role-playing in their work with human conflicts. The theatre is a world of its own and therapists have been trained to follow a different path. The stage might be considered the private domain of dramatists. Having a poetic ability to condense, uncover and explain conflicts is not included in the daily life of a clinic.

However, the idea of using dramatic techniques in therapy is certainly a good one. The inhibited can benefit by acting out pent-up feelings; those without control can experience the limitations of the role as well as the value of viewing the world from the perspective of different roles, that is, understanding other people. Just as it can be useful to express feelings to others, making them more tangible and binding, it can also be useful to act out impulses (in a safe setting) in order to clarify them.

In recent decades a number of techniques have appeared that more or less loosely make use of the ability of role-playing to provoke and process feelings. J.L. Moreno's psychodrama is the oldest and most reliable of these techniques from the 1920s. Although it grew directly from psychoanalytic theory 'catharsis', it found its own special form.

Eva Røine has worked within the Morenian tradition. With her dual background in theatre and psychology, she has added new dimensions to the proud traditions from Greek antiquity in a fascinating way. She gives us a sense of how the early protagonists presented themselves on stage, not to entertain or instruct an audience but to articulate problems and to find clarity in the wake of ecstasy and anxiety.

Both within and outside the realms of theatre and psychiatry, everyone gains by examining the dramatic traditions of our Western culture in relation

---

1   This Foreword was first published in the Norwegian edition of 1978.

to psychodrama's attempts to help patients to be more true to themselves as human beings. The circle is completed here. Once again, theatre has become the individual's dramatic struggle with fate.

Eva Røine's book also makes an important contribution to establishing a professional platform for the use of theatre in psychotherapy. It is a form of therapy that is certainly at least as effective as regular psychotherapy and, therefore, filled with at least as many problems. She never loses sight of the necessity for formal training in psychotherapy before practising psychodrama. To the extent that psychodrama can be learned from a book, experienced clinicians could use this as a textbook. It also provides valuable inspiration for using psychodrama as a form of therapy.

We live in an era in which societal pressures split our lives into increasingly numerous and changing roles. This makes it difficult to be a whole person. Paradoxically, the many settings and roles that appear in a psychodrama contribute to rediscovering a feeling of wholeness because they affect the entire person. In the field of psychiatry, which is in the process of understanding the social forces that shape the patient role, psychodrama can give the therapist a new instrument for influencing the damaging roles that people play.

Finn Magnussen, *Senior Psychiatrist, National Centre for*
Child and Adolescent Psychiatry
Oslo, December 1977

Preface

The theoretical background for this book is based on my studies in theatre, criminology and psychology at the University of Oslo. These three different fields have conflict as their common denominator.

In the theatre a genuine drama cannot exist without a conflict, which is either solved or projected to the audience as a challenge to its fantasy. Criminology is concerned with people who are in conflict with laws and norms, written or unwritten rules that separate certain individuals or groups from established society. Psychology involves intra-psychic conflicts, or people in conflict with one another. In this context, psychodrama creates a sort of superstructure by offering a forum or a stage or simply a room where an individual in a particular group can try out the entire range of human conflicts. Psychodrama does not lead to psychiatric or legal consequences by classifying a person as a patient or a criminal. In this sense, psychodrama can be seen as a synthesis of the theatrical and social sciences in that it meets the individual on a level of fantasy as well as social reality. The role concept is central in all three fields – the human being as an actor, an executor and an experiencing individual.

Most of the examples in Section IV are from institutions in the United States (US Veteran Hospital, Mimonedes Hospital, Eagleville Hospital and St. Elisabeth's Hospital). Some of the empirical material is from Germany, from the Department of Psychiatry at the National Hospital in Aachen. I am indebted to Professor Andreas Ploeger for allowing me to observe and participate in group sessions involving analytical psychodrama in group psychotherapy. In Section V I present theoretical and practical experiences from my past 15 years as a therapist and teacher.

My theoretical and practical studies in the USA were carried out in 1971 and 1972 at the Moreno Institutes in Beacon, New York, and New York City. I am grateful for the opportunity to thank Dr J.L. Moreno and his wife Zerka Moreno who made it possible, also financially, to study psychodrama so intensively and fully. Meeting Dr Moreno and being able to converse with him personally about many subjects was a special privilege. Hearing about the 1920s in Vienna and his work with children, patients and professional actors was particularly interesting. Although there is reason to name many of my psychodrama teachers, I will mention only one. I would like to name Hannah Weiner because she was especially gifted and because she allowed me to work with her as an assistant in numerous stimulating and instructive psychodramas. Hannah Weiner died far too early, before the age of fifty.

The GROW Institute in New York also gave me a theoretical and practical introduction to psychodrama and group therapy. Here Dr H.E. Smith and his wife Mildred Smith were particularly accommodating. I was given an observer's card allowing entrance into all courses, on the condition that I would not only observe but also participate. This provided experience in many therapeutic forms, including Gestalt therapy, primal therapy, client-centred therapy, various types of encounter groups and psychodrama. Most of the students at the GROW Institute were academics specializing in their fields by working with psychiatric patients, substance abusers and prison inmates.

Among others, I studied modern theatrical forms using techniques closely associated to those used in psychodrama in a workshop led by Alec Ruben for the Encounter Theatre. The Open Theatre, the Liquid Theatre and the Responsive Theatre also provided convincing impressions about the relationship between therapy and theatre as therapeutic tools. Whether these innovative theatrical forms called themselves street theatre, guerilla theatre or spontaneous acting, they all had a politically radical, democratic attitude in common that sought a spontaneous meeting between the actor and the public, that is, one recalling the origins of European theatre, a dialogue between an individual and a group that might have originally been conceived as a therapeutic process.

The immediate reason for studying in the United States was a scholarship from the Norway–America Foundation in 1971. Without this invaluable help, my work would not have been possible. In connection with the theme of my studies in the United States, I spent some time at Daytop Village in New York and its branches in Staten Island and Swan Lake. This therapeutic community is for drug addicts and is based on a specific psychiatric ideology developed by Dr Daniel Casriel, who permitted me to participate in some of his special groups. Daytop Village also uses theatre as a form of therapy (psychodrama as well as more traditional forms) and is known for its guest performance in Europe of *The Concept*, a play written for and by persons addicted to drugs. Charles Devlin, the Programme Director at Daytop

Village, worked out a varied programme so that I could take part in confrontation groups – all-night marathons of group therapy with parents of drug addicts. I was also able to observe testing in connection with admissions and releases, in compliance with the rules of Daytop Village.

The decision to make use of drama as a therapeutic form stems from my previous studies in London at the Webber Douglas School of Dramatic Art. Part of this school's programme was to require its students to dramatize their own texts. After learning about Moreno's psychodramatic techniques, I became aware of how much easier this task would have been if we had used psychodramatic methods rather than the prescribed traditional theatrical techniques. As a teacher at Oslo's Hartvig Nissen School, all of my instruction in improvisation and role-playing was based on psychodramatic techniques. This method of approach encouraged spontaneity and reduced 'stage fright' more effectively than traditional drama instruction. In this school setting I did not make use of psychodrama in its entirety.

However, I have been able to use psychodrama in Section XVI at Ullevål Hospital, where Chief of Staff Henrik Bauge was positive about this relatively unknown form of therapy in Norway. From January to June 1974 I worked with the section's personnel (during this period, psychodrama was introduced as a replacement for traditional supervision). A regular group of 11 to 15 persons volunteered to meet for one day a week. After the group had been meeting for some months, patients also joined the group. In September 1976, when I was employed as a psychologist in this section, these meetings were reinstated. Today, a psychodrama theatre is situated in the basement of the psychiatric ward and is as similar to Moreno's classical stage model as possible. Unfortunately, this stage has not been used since 1984, when I left the hospital.

Moreno's books are comprehensive, but they are difficult when the reader has no practical knowledge of psychodrama. I have chosen to limit myself to the portion of his theory that I think presents the most concrete illustration of psychodrama. To a great extent, Moreno has also developed his own terminology. An abbreviated glossary is included at the end of the book.

On the whole, it has been difficult to find a balance in the boundaries between psychological and theatrical concepts. An example is the word 'drama', which is of Greek derivation and means action. Moreno uses the word 'action' in a very broad sense, just as he also uses the word 'actor', which, as well as meaning a stage performer, also means a 'performer of actions' (Jesus as a therapeutic actor). Moreno also makes a rather difficult differentiation between the function of the role and the different meanings of role as a concept. This is clarified, I hope, in the text. In Part V, where I discuss my experiences in psychodramas in Norway, I have focused more on states of mind than roles. I have also tried to differentiate between behaviour, in what can be observed without being part of an interaction, and action, which includes everything that happens in human interaction – such as speech, gestures, pauses, periods of silence and physical posture.

Moreno called the main person in the psychodrama the 'protagonist'. This word originates from the early Greek theatre where the protagonist was the first individual actor, the man who stepped forward from the collective group (the chorus) and started a dialogue with the group. Moreno was not particularly interested in the origin and development of the Greek theatre. Personally, it is just this historical period that I found especially interesting during my studies. Learning about Moreno's psychodrama renewed this interest. I believe that I can trace a direct connection between the original group process that was the forerunner of both the Golden Age of Greek theatre and modern psychodrama. The word protagonist consists of two prefixes, 'pro' and 'agon', that is in front of, or first, in battle. The protagonist is the person who leads the action. But 'agon' also connotes the pain and anxiety associated with death (agony). The protagonist is the main character in the drama who describes a painful and angst-filled experience in his own life.

The categories of techniques and additional methods are my own, since I find it more systematic and understandable to differentiate between the *techniques*, which are used throughout the whole psychodrama (role-playing, role reversal, etc.), and supplementary methods. These methods can be thought of as scenes that are inserted in order to give more depth to the drama. When combined, there are about 100 different techniques and additional methods – many of which have been developed by Moreno's students. I have chosen to describe the most important ones that I think are most effective. Further, I will not limit myself only to Moreno. It is important to define the borderline between classical psychodrama and how it became what it is today through the originality and lifework of one person. When I go beyond Moreno's publications and look for support in other psychological models and theatrical history, it is because I think that they make a valuable contribution to clarifying psychodrama from other perspectives.

All of the examples of psychodramas are authentic and I have participated in them myself in one way or another. Most of the protagonists from America have been persons marked by some form of societal disapproval: drug addicts, soldiers unable to adjust after returning from Vietnam, psychiatric patients and prison inmates. The examples from Norway are slightly changed to disguise the identity of the protagonists. A protagonist can enact his or her drama on the psychodramatic stage time after time in an attempt to find alternative solutions. Psychodrama addresses all human beings who need to experience imagined actions and unfulfilled needs.

This manuscript was first presented in slightly different form as my doctoral thesis at the University of Oslo in the Spring of 1976. I am deeply thankful to Associate Professor Per Mentzen's supervision and for acting as an 'auxiliary ego' in my attempt to describe psychodrama and how it functions. In addition, I would also like to express my gratitude to my other supervisor, Magister Carl Fredrik Engelstad, who provided invaluable literary assistance, and to my external examiner, Professor Per Rommetveit, who was a source of indispensable encouragement.

In this edition I have also chosen to concentrate on psychodrama as a separate method, even though both sociodrama and sociometry are part of Moreno's triadic model. In my opinion, sociodrama and sociometry are more technical skills that have to be learned, preferably even studied, as specialities. I still think that Moreno covers these social aspects by focusing on psychodrama as development of the individual from the collective, which then leads to human relationships and interaction.

In conclusion, it is important to establish that psychodrama is a creative method that has therapeutic results. It is a method that must be learned and practiced under defensible conditions. Directing a psychodrama is a task for professionals and is subject to the same ethical and professional requirements as any other form of psychotherapy.

Eva Røine
Oslo, October 1997

CHAPTER 1

Theory

Jacob Levy Moreno

Jacob Levy Moreno's exact date of birth is uncertain. Many dates have been suggested, but he was probably born in May, and recent research suggests the year 1889. His national background is obscure: Moreno is an Italian name, but it is said that he was born in Budapest to Rumanian parents who came from the Iberian Peninsula through Turkey to Vienna. He was born in Budapest and moved to Vienna as a four-year-old. We know that Moreno was a citizen of Austria when he emigrated to the United States in 1925. He died on 14 May 1974 in Beacon, New York.

It is rather symbolic that Moreno established his institute and psychiatric hospital on the site of an earlier psychiatric hospital in a town called Beacon, a name that calls to mind a 'lighthouse'. Like the intense, intermittent flashes of light from a lighthouse, knowledge about psychodrama has reached the outside world only periodically, but in a steadily expanding circumference. The United States was first and, in many states, psychodrama is currently used in hospitals, health-care institutions, universities and the police force. The police took part in a psychodrama training programme because an insurance company wanted to reduce the number of fatal or disabling accidents that so often resulted after intervention in family quarrels. Statistics had proven the effectiveness of psychodrama in tense and critical situations.

Psychodrama was created in Vienna in the early 1920s and returned from the United States for a new period of growth in Europe in the early 1950s. Dr Moreno visited Norway in 1956, but the scant recognition he received was a great personal disappointment. He could not understand why Norwegians, with their deep tradition of Ibsen dramas, had so little interest in the dramatic elements of psychodrama. Norway was firmly entrenched in a strong psychoanalytic tradition.

More recently, in the 1970s and 1980s, Europeans have been inclined to think that American psychodrama tends to overact (perhaps especially when compared to the German). It may be that psychodrama in the United States is still under the influence of Moreno's 'magical' power. Despite being small in stature, he projected the physical and vocal presence of a giant – even after the age of eighty. His special style can be studied in old films, and one's immediate reaction is to wonder how this figure of authority managed to liberate so many spontaneous feelings. As a client expressed it in a filmed interview: 'He made my soul soar so it could return in greater strength'.

Psychodrama did not originate as the therapeutic theatre that we know today. As a young student, Moreno used to sit in parks and play areas and watch children at play. He noticed how spontaneously they expressed themselves, often without being bound by prescribed social behaviour or cultural patterns. He began to try out different roles with them and, after a while, he invited any adults who were passing by to join in a spontaneous dialogue. In 1914 Moreno created the expression 'Begegnung', his very personal meaning of the word 'Encounter'. However, encounter groups, as they are known in the United States, have little in common with Moreno's original meaning.

The key to Moreno's deep, although highly individualized, affinity to Existentialism can be found in the word 'encounter'. It was in the unconditional meeting of the minds of humans in psychodrama, one without prejudice, diagnosis and subjective interpretation, that Moreno hoped to lift the barrier and close the gap between 'I' and 'You'. Indeed, he also wanted to close the gap between 'I' and 'God'. There is more than a communication of spirit between the two Jewish men Moreno and Martin Buber, author of *Ich und Du*. From 1918 to 1920 Buber was co-editor of *Daimon*, a periodical published by Moreno. Moreno's all-encompassing and universal definition of the concept 'I-God' created a great deal of resentment. However, Moreno maintained his composure, saying: 'It is the I-God with whom we are all connected. It is *I* which becomes the *We!*' (1970a, p.21).

In keeping with his lifelong contradictory and curious nature, Moreno was simultaneously studying psychiatry, medicine and philosophy, playing out roles with children and laying the groundwork for voluntary self-help groups for prostitutes. His involvement with this last group was neither to reform the girls nor to analyze them, but to help them see their opportunities in life from a different perspective. In the 1930s, in the United States, he continued with this form of group therapy with relatively homogenous and stigmatized clients who were inmates at Sing Sing. Moreno is credited for having been the first to introduce the concept of group psychotherapy.

Moreno's ideas were in keeping with the avant-garde of his era and, in the fields of modern theatre, philosophy, psychiatry and psychology, inno-

vation flourished. Interestingly, psychodrama and the avant-garde th
simultaneously anticipated the newest schools of thought in philosoph'
psychiatry in the mid-1920s under the influence of Martin Heidegger's
fundamental ontology of human being, 'Daseinsanalytik' (1976). Advocates
of Dasein Analysis concentrated on understanding the human experience of
reality in its three dimensions: the surrounding world, the interpersonal
world and the personal world of the individual. These concepts are not far
from the three dimensions of reality that are used in psychodrama: objective,
subjective and personal (outer, inner, surplus). Both psychodrama and the
professional avant-garde theatre started in the early 1920s. While Moreno
was establishing his 'Stegreiftheater' in Vienna, poet and dramatist Antoin
Artaud was dreaming about a theatre that could reproduce 'the most secret
perceptions of thought':

> In this theatre there is a deep buzzing of instinctive realities, but they
> are brought to the point of transparency, intelligence and
> adaptability where the purely physical seems to repeat to us some of
> the most secret perceptions of thought…on this closed and limited
> globe which is the stage (Artaud 1967, p.62).

Moreno was an in-depth researcher as well as a behaviourist. He has no
hesitation about following the protagonist into the dark chambers of
childhood and he follows him just as patiently into simple learning situations.
In both instances he believes in the individual's own ability to find solutions.
Therefore, Moreno's psychotherapeutic viewpoint is closely aligned to
existential analysis as expressed, for example, by the Austrian psychologist
Victor Frankl, who maintains that human beings can leave their state of
flowing with the currents of life and arrive at a state of being able to make
decisions. This approach to psychotherapy was first presented by the German
philosopher Karl Jaspers (1955) in his description of the human condition
as an 'existence of decisions'.

The wave of ideas expressed by Kierkegaard, Heidegger, Jaspers, Medard
Boss and Frankl, among others, inspired a new belief in the 'prospect of an
existence of choice' as opposed to the ideas of the determinists. But this was
a more demanding viewpoint in terms of assuming personal responsibility
for one's own destiny. In what the American psychiatrist William Glasser
(1965) calls a 'new approach to psychiatry', he revokes the use of set
diagnoses in describing illnesses. Instead, he categorizes people into two
groups: those who take responsibility for their actions and those who do
not. Glasser maintains that the ability to take *responsibility* is acquired through
a process of learning. This theoretical approach is closely related to Moreno's

practical work, allowing clients to try out different roles in order to be better prepared for future situations. Moreno calls this 'role training for the future.'

Moreno's optimistic belief in the unrecognized resources and decision-making abilities of human beings was based on his firm conviction that in the final analysis, a human being is his own saviour. A human being is an actor in the sense that he carries out or performs his own personal drama. The great therapeutic actors were Jesus, Mohammed, Josiah and Francis of Assisi, to whom Moreno had a close feeling of indebtedness and personal attachment. Socrates was his ideal as the *redeemer* in the Socratic concept of spiritual birth (*majevtik*) and as the *teacher* who gives human beings knowledge of themselves.

Moreno's personal and significant psychodramatic experience occurred when he was four years old. While playing with friends, he assumed the role of God the Father and gave his friends roles as angels. However, 'God's' attempt to soar into heaven from a chair that had been placed on a table resulted in a broken arm. This hubris, to use the Greek term for insolence against the gods, may have had a permanent influence on Moreno. There is no record of Moreno playing the role of protagonist in a psychodrama. He wanted to be the instrument of redemption and the teacher, and he could portray both gods and devils. But he was always the leader, the director who set the stage, insisting that the innate godliness in all human beings made self-redemption possible.

Although Moreno lived a few blocks away from Sigmund Freud in Vienna, they met on only one occasion.[1] Moreno attended a lecture by Freud and, when Freud completed his analysis of a telepathic dream and the students were filing out of the auditorium, Freud must have noticed Moreno's intense demeanour and stopped him to ask what he was involved in. Moreno replied:

> Well, Dr. Freud, I start where you leave off. You meet people in the artificial setting of your office, I meet them on the street and in their homes, in their natural surroundings. You analyze their dreams. I try to give them the courage to dream again. I teach the people how to play God (Moreno 1970a, p.6).

Moreno's therapeutic theatre arose from his interest in the conflicting roles within each individual; his first project was to study the female in the roles

---

[1] Moreno sets the year of his meeting with Freud as 1912, but it was probably later. Both 'Psychoanalysis and telepathy' (Freud, Vol.xviii, 1963a) and 'Dreams and telepathy' (ibid.) were written after 1919.

of whore and madonna. He began combining professional theatre and therapy in Vienna while working with adult actors at the Stegreiftheater which he founded in 1922. Initially, he planned to stage improvisations based on current topics gleaned from newspapers. This special theatrical form was called 'Die lebendige Zeitung' ('The Living Newspaper'). 'Stegreif' actually means 'suspension bridge' but, as a slang expression, it refers to anything insecure or changing, so that 'auf dem Stegreif' could be translated as 'playing it by ear' and 'auf dem Stegreif dichten' would be 'improvising.' And this is precisely what Moreno's actors were doing. They literally played a text by ear and dramatized it on stage.

The primadonna in this ensemble specialized in portraying meek and modest females, and she herself had been the very incarnation of femininity until the day she accepted the marriage proposal of a suitor who had been so beguiled by her that he became a permanent member of the front-row audience. After they were married, the man realized that her off-stage personality was aggressive, hot-tempered and hysterical. When Moreno heard this, he assigned the actress a role as a vulgar and violent streetwalker. The effect was practically immediate. The role seemed to enable her to gain control of her whole emotional life. Moreno concluded that many persons have unfulfilled or even 'undigested' roles within themselves and that they should be able to play them out in free surroundings. Only in this way could the individual have control over them in social settings.

Moreno emigrated to the United States in 1925, joining the flow of gifted Jewish scholars who came to have such a strong influence on American psychology and psychiatry. His improvisational theatre, The Impromptu Group Theatre, gave its first performance in Carnegie Hall in 1929. 'The Living Newspaper' developed into a fresh and innovative theatrical form that often attracted an angry and unruly audience in this era of economic depression. As in Vienna, famous actors were willing participants during the initial period of enthusiasm, until Hollywood and Broadway lured them away and left Moreno with a feeling of disappointment.

The exodus of the professional actors was a decisive factor in Moreno's future work with psychodrama. In Vienna he had envisioned a 'theatre for the masses' that would motivate the general public toward the idea of group psychiatry. At one point he placed an elaborate throne in a market-place in Vienna and challenged onlookers to come and have a seat. No one accepted the challenge. Furthermore, Moreno made provocative remarks, stating, for example, that the country had no real leader. This was in the wake of World War I and, in the ensuing era of social and political unrest, Moreno must have realized the danger of making such a statement. At least he refrained from making similar experiments. He found his ultimate form in psycho-drama. Involving actors in his therapeutic theatre was never anything other than what he later came to call 'theatrotherapy'. There is no real drama until an individual acts out his own life on a stage. In Moreno's words: 'Play yourself as you never were, so you can begin to be what you could have been. Be your own inspiration, your own author, your own executor, your own therapist and finally, your own Creator' (personal notes for Moreno's speech at International Psychodrama Congress, New York, 1972).

The stage – the magical space

Let us imagine a theatre packed with people. The curtain rises on an empty stage. The audience is presented with a challenge that is bound to horrify some and create anxiety in others. Many frightening and dramatic creatures lurk in the dark corners of the mind and the members of the audience are told that they can place their own fantasy figures on the stage. Without a responsible director, this situation could end up in chaos or panic. But still, the stage is a special magical space where it is possible to create the dramatic characters that are needed for solving latent conflicts.

Experienced dramatic artists can easily envision how imaginary figures appear and assume a life of their own on the stage, since this is an integral part of their profession. A director populates the empty stage with all of the characters of the play even before rehearsals are under way. Just as the empty stage challenges the playwright, it also challenges the director's artistic skills.

Similarly, it is not difficult for a child to imagine the existence of all sorts of fantasy creatures that can appear at any time on their own inner stage. While working with persons under severe emotional stress, we often neglect the ability of most people to create spontaneous fantasies. The fantasies usually represent conflicts with people and events from the past that were not understood, and therefore never fully resolved. In a controlled situation, a stage becomes a sanctuary where people can literally tackle their unresolved conflicts from the past, the present and the future.

The background for this book came from my work with patients between the ages of 13 and 19 who were in a Norwegian psychiatric institution. I had not yet studied psychodrama in the United States. Despite my limited experience in modern methods for using drama in institutions, I was allowed to form a volunteer theatre group. We met in an old chicken shed that had previously served as an isolation ward. Nearly all of the patients, 13 boys and girls, signed up.

The object of the experiment was to use role-playing to understand the patients' own experience of their daily lives. After a year, the results were compared with the therapeutic help that the regular staff members could give to nearly the same client group. This experiment will not be included here because of the transparency of Norwegian case studies and because I became enmeshed in the network of written and unwritten laws that dictate the working procedures of an old-fashioned institution with only few professional employees. The patients' experience of their own lives was irreconcilable with the opportunities for self-expression the institution could offer. During the experiment I was alone with the patients in a small chicken shed on a distant field, surrounded by the darkness of winter days. The following year we were a team of four adults supervising seven girls. In contrast to working in the main building, where broken windows and general vandalism were daily events, there were no similar incidents of any gravity in our shed.

It was while I was working in this small, improvised theatre that I first read Ernest G. Schachtel's (1963) book, *Metamorphosis*. I became convinced that the stage was a therapeutic refuge where persons with psychological problems could free themselves from their past and establish a new connection with the present and the future.

Schachtel describes human development as the result of a *conflict* that forces forward movement. The conflict unfolds between the desire to sink into hibernation (*embeddedness*) and the need for greater mobility and satisfaction in the outside world. Human beings are most comfortable when they are still in their mother's wombs. Therefore, the desire to return to this haven of consummate safety is always present. Both the degree and nature of this conflict vary at different stages of maturity, depending on the physical and psychological qualifications of the individual.

Further, Schachtel emphasizes that movement, longing, the creative urge and *play* are mankind's strongest motivation for forward movement (*emerge from embeddedness*), in spite of the anxiety of freeing oneself from the safe and the familiar. In this connection, Schachtel refers in particular to Soren Kierkegaard's (1963) book, *The Concept of Dread*, in which I later found the best definition to date of the idea and content of psychodrama: 'Truth is only for the Individual, in that he Himself brings it forth in Action' (p.185). Kierkegaard sets freedom up against truth and lack of freedom against the demonical.

Subjective truth exists within the human mind. The place of refuge or the magical space the stage represents encourages action in which the individual himself can set the premises. This is how we as therapists gain insight into the inner workings of the mind. We take part in how the individual sees the world. And this is where the theatre complies with the need in existential psychology to understand how an individual sees 'himself-in-the-world'. Rollo May describes the psychodramatic of inner, or personal, reality thus: ' World is the structure of meaningful relationships in which a person exists, and the design in which he paticipates', (May, Angel and Ellenburger 1967, p.59).

In practical terms, Schachtel's theory on the conflict between the embeddedness-effect versus the activity-effect helped my understanding of why the patients behaved so differently when they were in the institution's living room and when they were in the chicken shed, the 'Theatre.' The contrast was quite alarming. In the living-room, the patients literally sank into cigarette smoke and deafening music, and they had closed off any possibility for contact. In the shed, I had experienced their anxiety, but they also had a strong need to express their feelings in words. In each their own way, every member of the group tried to gain a better understanding of him or herself and the other members of the group. They became involved in their own life situations! Without any previous acting experience, they showed that they were truly searching for their real selves in the theatre. They stepped away from their collective incapability for action and searched for a separate identity.

The Greek expression for 'rising away from' is '*ex-istere*'. In Latin this later came to mean to move one's self forward, to develop. The first actor in the world rose from a group (the chorus) and became involved as an individual. According to Schachtel's theory, we can say that this actor experienced that *a conflict pushed him forward!*

The main tenet of psychodrama is that each individual has an inborn need to be involved in his own life. Psychodramatic techniques are meant to train spontaneity and fantasy in order to break away from, or accept, the limitations of one's own opportunities in a social environment. The stage is the magical space populated by imaginary beings. It provides the venue for situations that have to be mastered. The main difference between traditional theatre and psychodrama is that a play follows a manuscript, while psychodrama plays itself out spontaneously and can never be repeated in the same form.

Psychodrama – an age-old group process

The word 'psychodrama' is composed of two Greek words: '*psyke*' and '*drama*'. Directly translated it means 'soul drama', that is the essence of a person's spirituality put into movement and directed toward someone or something. The result of this is observable behaviour, but psychodrama offers even more. It gives individuals a chance to become the interpreters of their immediate lives. The actor, the executor of actions in his individual life drama, has been doing so ever since birth.

To a great extent, Moreno has created his own terminology. Some of it is based on Greek concepts but he does not consider psychodrama in connection with the dynamic group processes that were probably in force long before the existence of theatres. Moreno states that psychodrama has no historical prototypes. He thinks *commedia dell'arte* is the form that is most similar (Moreno 1970a). This is actually a contradictory statement since *commedia dell'arte* is based on fixed, stereotypical figures who have none of the inner freedom of psychodrama – which allows for interpreting one's own life rather than playing a role in *commedia dell'arte's* pre-arranged gallery of characters. Here, Moreno overlooks the theatrical representations that were introduced in France in the 1700s and referred to in Michel Foucault's book, *Madness and Civilization* (1965). An example of a nearly identical model of psychodramatic theatre from the 1800s is mentioned in this book.

Moreno rarely delves further into Greek history than to Aristotle and his 2300-year-old work, *Poetics*. Aristotle was born after the Golden Age of Greek theatre and far later than the Archaic period (ca.700–550 BC). It was from Aristotle that Moreno borrowed the term 'protagonist' as a designation for the person whose story is being enacted in a psychodrama. But it is within this term that psychodrama and the drama of ancient Greece unite and reflect an almost 3000-year-old group process which is repeated whenever a protagonist leaves the group to enact and speak in front of a group of persons who witness and participate in the action.

Historical sources agree that drama was originally a form of group dynamics. At its most primitive, it may have dealt with seasonal rituals, dedication ceremonies, mourning services for the dead, group invocations for tribal protection or appeals for courage and solidarity. We could look at the first cult of hero worship as a projection of hope for salvation and victory, a celebration of a tribe when it found a leader to guide it through crises. It is reasonable to assume that these earlier heroes were merely legendary figures who had performed miracles, god-like humans from an obscure reality. Since the dream of a Saviour, in one form or another, is deeply integrated into the human psyche, hero worship is a result of a group process. A community unites around a symbolic or real figure which is then given the attributes necessary to ward off surrounding forces of danger. The first step toward social independence was taken when the community assigned a role of leadership to one of its members, and thereby questioned the omnipotence of the gods and demons.

At some point in prehistoric time, a group gathered in prayer or supplication and selected a human leader. One individual was set apart from the group and the development of Greek theatre was on its way. Theatre historian Gerald Else (1965) emphasizes two important historical events: The invention of tragedy by Thespis and the introduction of tragic drama by Aeschylus. Else considers Thespis' creation of the role of the actor so important that if Thespis had not existed, that is if we knew nothing about him, we would have had to make up a fictional founder of tragedy. Thespis provided the transition between the choral group and Greek drama as we know it today. He is the individual who steps forward from the group and becomes the leader and speaker in the drama. Therefore, Thespis is the first recognized protagonist in history, although there were probably a great many others before him.

Returning to theatre history, we can catch a glimpse of the contours of psychodrama in the 700s BC. Moreno's hypothesis that humans have an innate need to bring the unknown under societal control is reflected throughout the entire development of Greek drama. The progression from chaos to conscious mastery begins in the ecstatic orgies of Dionysian intoxication and ends, after only a few hundred years, in a highly developed artistic dramatic form that is still part of the world's finest classic repertoires.

Collective ecstasy can be seen as a primitive process of identification at a time in ancient Greece when humans thought of the deities as close and personal beings. Historian Walter Schubart establishes the relationship between religious ecstasy, eroticism and the primeval Great Mother (the idea of a universal, protective mother). He thinks that the first sacrifices may have been no more than pleas for protection. There was no conscious feeling of religious or social guilt in terms of human sacrificial offerings. The birth of children was an accepted fact. Years of crop failure and starvation were not understood in terms of cause and effect. Schubart describes a person's confrontation with death, seeing a corpse for the first time, as primeval fright: 'The first religious idea that seizes man at the moment when his surrounding world in no longer a matter of course, but a problem' (1969, p.25).

Frenzy, ecstasy and identification with the Great Mother in religious and erotic abandonment represents the unconscious, free-flowing energy associated with the id in Freudian terminology. Women killed their children in drunken ecstasy. The subsequent awakening and sight of mutilated corpses must have inspired the primeval horror described by Schubart.

After intoxication and ecstasy came impotence, apprehension and anxiety. Great Mother did not guarantee eternal safety. She could be dangerous and threaten obliteration. When the forces of nature are released, man is helpless.

In the heavens above, or even inside earth, there were revengeful gods and evil demons. An individual (ego) projects anxiety onto external beings and, at the same time, attempts to form an alliance with them in order to survive. Philosopher and sociologist Levy-Bruhl (1935) states that these 'collective representations' sprang up at the moment when man needed an immediate explanation of a problem in his world. It was not a question of searching for the cause of the phenomenon, but for a 'self-evident truth'. The idea of the world of spirits, gods and demons appeared at the instant of crisis, when man needed this explanation to save himself from the incomprehensible. The ideas became 'truths'.

This very ability of being able to form mental images is the precondition for what we call fantasy, and it is the starting point of all cultures. When animals are frightened, they either take flight or take the offensive. A child, and primitive man, can rewrite a fantasy just as an artist can express an inner world of ideas in musical tones, colours or words. The only difference is that the child and primitive man express themselves more simply. For better or for worse, their worlds have fewer nuances. To be able to control the evil forces, they must ally themselves with the forces of good. But when the exterior world can no longer be controlled, crippling anxiety appears.

Primitive man's invocations and children's play can both be seen as the starting point for a natural psychodrama in which an individual seeks out the dangerous to bring it under control. In Sigmund Freud's study of play when it is not pleasurable, he sees it as an expression of the instinct to master. All that is frightening has to be mastered and all that is still hidden in the world has to be understood in order to maintain equilibrium and tolerate the circumstances of life. According to Freud, even a nightmare is a courageous attempt to enter into forbidden areas in order to gain insight and the ability to survive: 'A nightmare is often the unconcealed fulfillment of a wish – of course, not of an acceptable wish, but of one that is officially kept at a distance' (Freud 1963b, Lecture xiv, Vol.xv p.213).

A nightmare explores the forbidden, the 'dangerous'. Freud defines the word '*unheimlich*' as the opposite of '*heimlich*' (home-like). *Unheimlich* is whatever does not belong. At the same time, he emphasizes an inner relationship between the two words: 'That which does not belong is still something familiar' (*Das Unheimliche ist irgend eine Art von heimlich*), since nothing can actually exist in the human psyche that has not ever been there. The dangerous then becomes something that once belonged but was suppressed because of its problematic nature. The dangerous appears within a certain familiar context and becomes frightening when it is not understood. Whatever turns up is a challenge that must be mastered. In this way, terror, fear and anxiety also become elements in play when it is a mastering instinct. Freud differentiates between terror, fear and anxiety (*Schreck, Furcht und Angst*). An individual experiences terror when faced with a danger he does not expect. Fear presupposes something specific that the individual associates with danger, while anxiety is a state of inner disturbance and anticipates a danger that does not exist in any definite place - 'free-floating anxiety'. Freud's entire psychoanalytical method is based precisely on delving into the hidden darkness of childhood and bringing 'the dangerous' to light – making what was not understood understandable and the invisible visible.

The Austrian-English psychiatrist Melanie Klein (1937) may have the best description of the child's archaic psyche in the psychoanalytical tradition. Basically, she builds on Freud's orthodox psychoanalytical model but has a special way of distinguishing the life of fantasy, attempting to explain how the infant has internalized images of its surroundings. Primarily, these surroundings are parents or parts of parents – such as the mother's breast. The fundamental feeling of basic security, or insecurity, is located in the deepest level of *psychic structure*. Here, Melanie Klein differentiates between the good mother who provides security and the bad mother who wants to destroy. This could be compared with Henry Stack Sullivan's later distinction between the evil mother, who poisons, and the good mother, who eases the child's transition from its haven in the womb to the external, unrelenting stimuli from the surrounding world (1947).

Based on Melanie Klein's model, it is tempting to compare the infant's first experience of closeness to its mother with primitive man's wish to unite with Great Mother, the symbol of security. 'Leaving mother's womb' means changing interactions. Primitive man must have felt that when the sun shone and the soil was fruitful, it was through the kindness of Great Mother. Conversely, when drought or flood ruined a harvest, it was a punishment. The oldest Greek symbol of motherhood is Demeter – to whom Oedipus returned, according to Attic legend, in his hour of death. In his *Oedipus at Colonus*, Sophocles describes his companion Theseus' experiences when Oedipus entered into Mother Earth's sacred hollow. The messenger in the drama describes Theseus' vision: 'Oedipus held a hand in front of his face to protect his eyes, as if he had seen a sight so gruesome that it could not be tolerated by any person...'. Could it have been the evil mother that Oedipus saw?

To understand psychodrama thoroughly, it may be necessary to follow Melanie Klein in her description of the two first stages of the psychological development of a child. She presents important similarities between what a child might experience and what we can imagine primitive man felt in the transition from close identification with Great Mother to anxiety, when separation was unavoidable.

Melanie Klein describes the first two stages in a child's psychological structure as *persecutory anxiety* and *depressive anxiety*. A child experiences persecutory anxiety when it feels it is under direct attack from the outside world. We can find a parallel here to the primitive person when he unconsciously experiences the forces of nature in thunderstorms or natural catastrophes. However, depressive anxiety is fear – perhaps better described as muscular and nervous tension when there is an indefinable feeling of insecurity. In comparison, we can mention the experience of a primitive person when he feels that he has overstepped the rules of the tribe to ensure his own protection by the Great Mother or when the tribe itself is confused as to whether or not it is complying to the rules. The familiar scapegoat arrives in these circumstances and a general feeling of guilt is transferred to an object or a person who will have to bear the consequences.

To understand how psychodrama functions, it is important to accept that internalized projections are also deeply rooted in the psyche of modern man. Only then can we follow, and accept, the grotesque images that a protagonist can experience. These are the images that psychodrama has to dramatize – that is to make concrete and visible in order to break down the myth of the 'dangerous'. Melanie Klein's model is a useful tool for explaining why it is possible to dramatize images that have been constructed in the psyche and for understanding how the primitive person, the child or any other individual under emotional strain has a need to seek out immediate solutions for problems in the external world. Thus the objective of psychodrama is not only to make problems concrete but also to gain insight and self-control.

Melanie Klein presupposes that the psychic structure is focused on two worlds *simultaneously*. The first, the mental world, is a continuation of the past; the second is the material world, an examination of the present. Both worlds contribute to the individual's immediate understanding of situations and persons. The inner (mental) world is composed of correlations to external objects. The difference between children's exterior worlds and their inner visual images (*imagos*) is expressed in play. Melanie Klein found that this inner world was where children formed misrepresentations of their relationships to important persons in their lives. For example, the children's images of their original objects of love, primarily their mothers, were often distortions of the direct impression their mothers gave in similar contexts. Play therapy revealed that children had completely different conceptions of reality. In their inner worlds, mothers were evil and persecutory – despite the fact that they were, in fact, both devoted to their children and concerned about them.

The above is a good parallel to the many imaginary persona that appear on a psychodramatic stage. The protagonist's darkest fantasy can pour out visions that are just as distorted as the figures painted by Hieronymus Bosch in the 1400s – fantastic combinations of animals and people. Both persecutory anxiety and depressive anxiety are captured and portrayed in grotesque pictures which seem to pour from a mind that has long been dominated by hatred and pent-up aggression. In a psychodrama, elements of a person's inner drama can be brought to life separately, for example, by making concrete specific fears – just as it is possible to dramatize dreams of wild and vicious animals, impersonal powers aiming at destruction or amputated hands that want to strangle. To Melanie Klein, the latter represent 'part objects' and are the primitive images in the most basic psychic structure of humans during their three first months of life, a time when children feel a direct threat from exterior sources.

Melanie Klein places the formation of the superego between the age of six months and the second year. The superego covers a multitude of good and bad inner objects. The internalization of the superego – that is the force that both persecutes and punishes – is compared with an *inner environment* in which the ego feels helpless in the shadow of powerful parental figures who, in the deepest levels of the mind, are vicious persecutors. Gradually, these assume the shape of merciless judges who threaten punishment or cause feelings of guilt.

In the first primitive stage of persecutory anxiety, in its struggle to survive, the ego searches for a connection with good object relations. The next stage, depressive anxiety, is dominated by the fear of losing the objects of love. This deep anxiety, in terms of punishment and feelings of guilt, is oppressive because of the overwhelming sense of helplessness. The child and the primitive human react in ways that we cannot judge in terms of our civilization. The deeper levels of consciousness function differently, and if we are to gain any comprehension of this function, we must try to perceive it in other ways. C.G. Jung suggests a pre-logical developmental stage. To analyze all of the stages of development, we have to accept that we have what Jung refers to as 'presupposition':

> In so far as I have been capable of analyzing this, this feeling (of foreignness) stems mainly from the fact that the first suppositions of archaic man are substantially different than ours – that the archaic human lives – if I must say so – in another world. Until we can comprehend this presupposition, he will remain a mystery to us. But when we come to know it, everything will be relatively simple. We

can even say that primitive man has ceased to be a mystery when we have learned about our own previous presuppositions (1933, p.149).

These are precisely the presuppositions that one must decide to meet the protagonist with when streams of bizarre pictures seem to come from chaos and to be searching for a sort of logic. When archaic figures or symbols from deep levels of consciousness that have forgotten hatred, anxiety and guilt turn up in psychodrama, it is tempting to make a hypothetical experiment. The starting point is still Melanie Klein's theory of persecutory anxiety on the deepest mental level and, later, depressive anxiety with the separation anxiety and guilt that follow.

When the protagonist woke up after this Dionysian intoxication and saw the results of man's 'natural aggression' in the mutilated corpses that surrounded him, it was easy to understand that he could consider Great Mother a threat to life itself. Friedrich Nietszche suggested in *The Birth of Tragedy* (1969) that the Greeks' adoration of Apollo, god of the visible and understandable, was a counterbalance for sparing them, literally, from drowning in the Dionysian ecstasy.

In Melanie Klein's primitive battlefield for individual survival, we find the ego in search of good object relations that can provide safety from the powers of persecution and destruction. The protagonist's individual struggle to redeem himself (his ego), can be seen as an initial attack on Great Mother – she who promised safety but who was not to be trusted.

But persecutory anxiety was followed by depressive anxiety, guilt and the fear of punishment. The protagonist rose from his ecstasy (the uninhibited unfolding of the id, among other things, in unconscious sexual intercourse and in many perversions such as sadism and sodomy). After having compromised with externalized powers (gods) or, according to Freud's model, solved the Oedipus conflict and internalized parental authority as moral law (superego), the individual's laborious development of an ego begins – an ego which must constantly free itself from the past and investigate the future. Dreams, myths, play, development in the Greek drama from subordination to social control and the many imaginary figures from various forms of artistic expression (not least in painting) bear witness to the human struggle to clarify a position and the human will to survive. However, in the lives of most people, as seen in psychodrama, there are many forgotten *dramatis personae* on the stage of our inner world. They are challenges that influence the way we think, experience, feel and communicate. Psychodrama simply makes use of the same dramatic techniques used by primitive people when they began to manipulate the gods in order to find solutions to their crises.

Returning to the original rites, we can glimpse the beginnings of the dramas that represent man's initial attempt to communicate with the gods. And later, when an individual was selected to represent the group, the group dynamics were transferred from the gods to a human being. The leader was required to fulfil the expectations of the group members and to produce answers to their questions.

Theatre historian Benjamin Hunningher (1961) maintains that the initiation of myths brought about a development that distinguished drama from sacrificial offerings. Drama became free when man began to act freely. When man began to ask *why*, he required an answer. This explains the origins of the myths, the harbingers of drama – that is the assignment of different roles. For example, early peoples asked why the sun rises at certain times every day and why it sets just as regularly. Well, they answered, the sun god Helios rides over the heavens every day from east to west. The ranks and names of the gods gradually became important in terms of deciding which magical dramatic technique should be used. In many ways, magic becomes a transitional stage between ritual and drama. Both ritual and magical aspects turn up in psychodrama through imitation, simulation and symbolic actions.

It can be said that ritualistic offerings were the original dramas. The sacrifice and subsequent consumption of the sacrificed were sacred rites which were cultic rather than magical. It is difficult to make a clear distinction between the cultic and the magical since there will always be elements of magic in the cultic and vice versa. But this 'rehearsed magic' has internalized the consciously-experienced primeval fright. It has become a dramatic technique for negotiation with gods and demons. Gerardus van der Leeuw, expert in the history of religion, expresses it this way: 'In a cult there are two who speak together. In magic, in the final analysis, only man speaks; man governs the world by force, and controls it with God's help, that is, ultimately, without God' (1969, p.195). Both gods and demons are assigned names and roles when they have been given a place in the hierarchy: 'There is a reason that the names of the gods are so important in a religion. It is the first form, in which a figure slowly begins to show itself. It is the basis for man to acquire power, the magic word, with which one calls it forth' (ibid., p.85).

Nevertheless, the difference between religion and theatre is that in religion, God continues to rule through substitutes on earth, while in the theatre, man assumes responsibility for himself. Therefore, one can look upon the entire development of the Greek theatre as a reflection of man's process of individualization from subservience and dependence to individual emancipation.

It began at one time or another in the fields, or near the block of stone, the wooden stake or the tree where offerings were made to Dionysius. There was an individual rebellion, a conscious state of mind, when man experienced being separate from the group, alone in the company of the gods. Who he was or how he felt is impossible to ascertain. We do know that the starting point was ecstasy and intoxication – but not unconscious intoxication or uninhibited ecstasy, because then the rebellion could not have taken place. A voice took shape within man and found its form in words. The key figure in the Greek drama is the one who strides into battle and begins to speak and act: the *protagonist*.

Moreno translates the word protagonist as 'madman' or 'a man in a frenzy' (1970a). This is misleading. Such a person would be more comparable to the satyrs in their unarticulated intoxication and ecstasy. Gerard Else (1965), characterizes the satyrs as cowardly and depraved. To qualify as a protagonist, one must have been concerned with a problem, be able to express oneself, even if very primitively, and be understood. The argument is that the protagonists began their reflections *after* intoxication and ecstasy. Some may have also recognized that they literally had to save themselves from assaults on their lives.

No one knows who the first actor was. Officially, Thespis has been given this honour. Thespis appears in history in the year 534 BC when he won a poetry prize in Athens. Thespis came from the district of Icaria in Attica, an area that had deep traditions in the worship of Dionysus. It is said that Thespis angered the Athenian statesman Solon by jumping onto the altar of Dionysus and representing a god. This was hubris, an arrogant act against the gods. However, Solon had no hesitation about representing man in a political and social situation (Else 1965).

Solon is clearly part of the second tradition that is thought to have led to the creation of Greek drama, in which skalds recited the poems of Homer and descriptions of the sagas from the *Odyssey* and the *Iliad*. But Solon was also a protagonist, a messenger of his own words. Gerard Else (1965, p.43) characterizes Solon's relationship to drama as: 'Not one of passion, but of rational insight into man's character and motives'. The tradition passed down from Homer was to present poetry about timely subjects to a discriminating public. These recitations were accompanied by a lyre and aroused deep feelings of sorrow and joy in the attentive and participating public. On that score, the presentation and technique are reminiscent of the actors in Moreno's Stegreiftheater when they improvised dramas about current events from the daily newspapers. A Homeric skald is a protagonist because he is a spokesman who moves an audience. But he also exemplifies a conscious artist who has woven various art forms into one experience – music, song, dance and poetic speech. In other words, he practices a form of dramatic art.

A very different tradition must have preceded the spontaneous protagonists who stepped forward and started an interaction with their groups. They were the human link between the collective group and 'the deities'. The god of vegetation and fertility, Dionysus, was half human, partially brought down to the level of humans from Olympus. He was the son of Zeus and Semele, a woman of the people. Here we see the ancient idea of incarnation in a human son, he who also rises from the dead. Frazer (1963) describes Dionysus as the god of resurrection and the god of vegetation, the symbol of rebirth into a new life. Having a human mother, he is also a son of man. Thespis, as a spontaneous protagonist, does not belong in this category. Archilochus, however, who is mentioned in the history of theatre in 675 BC, does belong because he could 'extract (*exarxai*) the most beautiful stanzas from the chorus'. He was at his best 'when his mind was soaked in wine' (Else 1965, p.13).

Of course, one can only speculate as to what inspired Archilochus to use a group to further his own needs, to find confirmation of himself. He may have had special musical talent. We know that the Phrygian flute played a major role in rituals. The Phrygian flute had a more driving tone than any other instrument of that time. In fact, its tone was far less civilized than the Homeric Lyre. Ritual song and dance preceded the dithyramb, a poetic text sung to music, which evolved into a sort of festival cantata. By the time this developed, drama had also begun to appear in set forms in which the role of the protagonist is especially interesting.

Whatever the motive, whether it gave personal pleasure to present beautiful stanzas in antiphonal song or to receive answers to urgent questions, the protagonist is the person who steps from the gathering of people and initiates a dialogue between himself and the group. He becomes the catalyst of the group process. One of his experiences may have been so overwhelming that he captures the attention of the group. Further, he must have the ability to express himself so clearly that the group understands the message.

This interaction between the protagonist and the group can be compared to jazz, when a soloist introduces a theme which the orchestra then plays, answers, repeats and develops. The first protagonists may have considered themselves the spokesmen of the group, as many persons later looked upon their vocations as writers. But, regardless of how one perceives the person who breaks away from the feeling of loneliness after intoxication, the chorus of antiquity or the protagonist in a psychodrama, there is always reciprocal influence between the group and the individual in which the latter directs the speech and the action. Although we know very little about the training of a Greek chorus, it is still possible to compare the protagonist of antiquity and the main person in a psychodrama. They are both individuals who take it upon themselves to interpret a situation or a destiny, either voluntarily or through group pressure. Both elevate the spiritual content so that it is beyond the level of general discussion and break through the everyday frame of reference. This becomes a *drama*, which triggers an understanding of the universal human condition.

Historical sources relate that vocal quality was an important consideration for the selection of the protagonist. As drama developed and became more complex with both second and third leads – a deuterogonist and a tritagonist – vocal quality continued to be an important consideration. The protagonist was preferably a tenor since he would also play female roles, while the second and third parts were respectively a baritone and a bass. This was during the Golden Era of Greek drama, in the time of Aeschylus and Sophocles. Before this time, vocal quality may have also been a deciding factor in choosing a group leader. Archilochus may have been chosen on this basis. However, one must remember that the theme was equally crucial. Sometimes the issue discussed by the protagonist might have been so urgent that the group paid attention to him regardless of the pitch of his voice.

As an experiment, it has been possible to study how a group process is initiated, with a natural selection of a protagonist. In a group of twelve members, the warming-up phase of the psychodrama consisted of a guided day-dream – an inserted scene that can be particularly suitable for focusing the group members' attention on an important person in their lives. They can choose freely, but since the guided day-dream ends on a mountain top or in a cave, also by free choice, the persons often appear as archetypes – either old men with beards – or no person at all, just a cave of well-being, as if 'in mother's womb'. After the guided day-dream, each member of the group was instructed to find a theme – the first spontaneous comment or thought that occurred to them – and to say it quietly to themselves. There were both men and women in the group, some with deep voices and others with thin or flat voices. It was expected that the member of the group with the most captivating voice would assume leadership. However, in psycho-dramatic terminology, the atmosphere soon became 'warm' and, above the general hum of voices, some became more distinct and intense. The decisive theme that broke through came from a woman whose voice was neither beautiful nor well-developed. In this way, through a sort of spontaneous process, a protagonist emerged and went through a deeply tragic psychodrama about child abuse. This time it was not a universal theme that won support, such as unfair treatment, unresolved sorrow, fear of authority, aggression toward parents or feelings of guilt.

In principle, this process is repeated before each psychodrama. Neither the most 'interesting' person nor the most captivating voice win the floor. It is the intensity of the theme and/or its universality that channels the group feeling and selects the protagonist. Deep traumas, unfulfilled needs or relatively simple conflicts can all be subjects that evoke group response. The warming-up process itself is the determining factor. A protagonist usually appears relatively quickly, and often there are two or more. This confirms Moreno's hypothesis that incomplete situations and 'undigested' roles within an individual force their way to the surface and need to find release. The same mental pattern of behaviour can be seen in children when, in play, they fearfully seek out the 'dangerous.' Certain games seem to concentrate on this very element by presenting aspects of a child's life that are considered a threat to their safety, even though they led to unpleasurable experiences. Hunningher (1961) equates children's play with the dramatic techniques of primitive people. The point is to ensure protection by entering into a contract, to finally gain control over personal situations by cunning or persuasion. A psychodrama invites a magical atmosphere that includes dramatic techniques for uncovering the unfinished or the unresolved and bringing it under control. These are the underlying dynamic forces that inspire the protagonist to leave the group and play out his own life drama, just as he, in the Archaic period, took the initiative and questioned his fellow men rather than the gods.

If we return to the development of Greek drama, we can find the need to release individuality and to help the person gain control of the situation. The Golden Era of Greek drama reached its height within a period of about 120 years under Aeschylus, Sophocles and Euripides (525–406 BC). All three of these men were actors as well as poets – in other words, they were protagonists presenting their own texts.

The first Greek poets who preceded the three great dramatists brought speech and action into a group (the chorus) and it would be more correct to think of them as carrying on the tradition of the Homeric skald than as being inspired Dionysian protagonists. Although tragedies were originally only staged once, their texts were rehearsed and prepared. Like Homer's texts, they described historic events, myths and sagas. They had none of the spontaneity of the chaotic and haphazard group worship of Dionysus which was never recorded in writing. The development of drama under the three great tragic dramatists also reflects the Greek theatre's gradual conquest of fear, subservience and dependence on the gods by using dramatic techniques to steer a path toward social control.

Aeschylus upholds the ancient Greek belief that the fate of humanity is subject to the gods. The individual learns about the godlike through suffering but also has to accept being subject to outside control. Sophocles sets up a tragic 'I' against the gods. Persons are only partly individuals. They are saga kings and mystical figures who are in rebellion but who have to yield to the power of the gods. King Oedipus is one of these tragic heroes who atones for his unintentional murder of his father and fulfils the fate which he was given at birth. Although Freud and Eric Fromm interpret the figure of Oedipus from different points of view, they agree that he is a symbol of rebellion, but where the 'powers' are, in the end, too strong to conquer. Freud (1941) interprets the Oedipus drama as an unconscious rivalry between father and son, rooted in the issue of incest. Eric Fromm (1970) uses Sophocles' trilogy as a starting point and interprets the theme as a generational rebellion, a struggle between those who are in authority and those who want to destroy it. Euripides, the last of the three great classical dramatists, brings people right down to earth, or the stage, and allows them to play out their conflicts in the context of their daily lives, at the marketplace or in their homes. Euripides is also interested in the female psyche and his *Hippolytus* is the first romantic drama in history. In Euripides' plays, human beings are in control, but by this time the Golden Age of Greek Drama had come to an end. Interestingly, Euripides wrote *The Bacchae* towards the end of his life in an attempt to understand and return to the theatre the ritualistic elements that the tragedies had lost in their struggle to win social control. Similar attempts were also made, in near desperation, in the twentieth century by Antoin Artaud, Jean Genet and Jerzy Grotowski and other independent theatre ensembles. But compelling and unreleased forces in the more traditional, rehearsed theatrical productions of today still can be found, and the theatre public searches for these elements. In a psychodrama, the protagonist fights intensely and directly with the forces of ancient drama. In this sense, a psychodrama is primitive in comparison to today's traditional theatrical productions.

A comparison of the Homeric skald with the spontaneous protagonist from the Dionysian cult of worshippers illustrates the difference between dramatic art and psychodrama. The skald and the poet both present their words in a conscious, artistic form. In the creative process, the poet could probably be compared to the 'untrained protagonist' who rummages around in the chaos of the mind. Henrik Ibsen describes the vocation of a writer as a 'Battle with Trolls in the Vaults of the Heart and the Mind.' Ibsen's trolls can be compared to psychodramatic roles. The writer's talent enables him to master them in his fantasy and to give them subtle expression. In psychodrama, the protagonist also fights against trolls but neither victory nor defeat can be repeated, at least never in the same way. Just as the great writers delve into the depths of the mind and incite humans against one another in interpersonal and social conflicts in the play, the little everyday man demonstrates his life and destiny in a psychodramatic play. A similar comparison has been made between writing and psychoanalysis:

> In his dynamic understanding of *character*, Freud elevated behavioural psychology from a purely descriptive level to a scientific one. Concurrently, he accomplished for psychology what the great dramatists and authors achieved in artistic form: he showed human beings as heroes, because they fight passionately in an attempt to find a meaning in the fact that they are born at all (Fromm 1970, p.50).

The protagonist and the writer both unleash mental power. In terms of tragedy and powerlessness, any man and woman can present material that equates with the themes of literary classics. But it would be just as meaningless to refer to the participants in a psychodrama as actors as it would be to present psychodrama as art. The only similarity is that a psychodrama and its participants document humanity. The special criterion for psychodrama is that it manages to liberate tragedy from real life. Here, psychodrama can also be distinguished from contemporary playwrights who work within 'the theatre of instinct' (Artaud), 'ceremonial theatre' (Genet) and 'ritual theatre' (Grotowski) or the 'communal spirit' of certain ensemble theatres.

However, participation in a psychodrama enables a protagonist to give partial expression to the artistic qualities that live within all human beings: creative powers that were blocked out because playfulness came to an end and was later kept in check by the strong censorship of social standards. This is the inner aspect that Grotowski calls 'the hidden essence of the actor's soul.' He tries to release this essence by using techniques that are different to those of a psychodrama but which are similar to what a protagonist and an actor share when impulses come from the inner mind and repressed forces flow forth and give new dimension to reality. Here, Grotowski is as close as anyone can come to the essence of psychodrama:

> If an actor tells a story or acts something out, it is not a story of the present. It is not *hic et nunc*. There is no doubt that he has to present a certain story. This is the main point. The story has to work like an act of revelation, or more precisely, a *declaration of faith*. He has to

present his actions on the basis of his own life, an action that moves him, exposes him, reveals him and uncovers him. At the same time, he should not be acting, but imbuing his experiences of life into the action. He should rediscover the ambitions that are in the very depths of his body... Then, if the actor can do this, he is the phenomenon *hic et nunc*. It is not telling about something or creating an illusion. It is in the present time (1973, p.66, author's translation from the Danish).

It is precisely this spontaneous connection between an inner 'hidden essence' and an outer reality that characterizes the drama of antiquity. It is the individual who demonstrates his own human strength in the struggle to justify his life and actions, just like the protagonist in a psychodrama. But Grotowski, like all playwrights, is bound to the performance which, in spite of everything, still has to be prepared beforehand. In the creative process, the actor can be filled with inspiration that springs from his deepest reserves – what Moreno considers the highest aim: 'the newly created time in the creative moment' (*status nascendi*). However, the actor's tragedy is that once this divine inspiration has been registered, it will, at best, become part of a planned liturgy. The spontaneous can never be repeated!

In a practical sense, Grotowski's work with actors to help them reach into their inner resources, or 'the hidden essence', comes closest to explaining the dramas of antiquity and psychodrama. Theoretically, Antoin Artaud is the playwright who has presented the closest explanation. He envisions the theatre of the absurd in the same way that Moreno puts it into practice, by abolishing logical concepts and limitations in time and space. Like Moreno, Artaud also anticipates modern psychiatry, which tries to understand the individual in a personal reality.

It may seem to be somewhat of a paradox that theatre, which presupposes a script, has become such an appealing medium for investigating the human mind. The motives have also been extremely different. For example, Jean Genet uses disguise, fabrication and a false identity to emphasize the meaninglessness of existence, but as an author he uses them to realize his plans. Genet touches upon psychodrama by allowing the characters in his plays to reach a personal reality through imaginary roles. The play *The Balcony* might be the best illustration of this. The action takes place in a bordello and the customers dress up to look like persons they would like to be, while simultaneously giving free reign to their desires and perversions.

To find genuine points of resemblance between theatre and psychodrama, we have to go back to a period in history when the theatrical medium accepted madness as truth. During French classicism, in the 1700s, 'theatrical representations' were introduced in psychiatric wards. These clearly resemble many of the inserted scenes in psychodrama. The attitude is also similar: the premises of the mentally ill are accepted totally. For example, a patient who thought he was eternally damned was forgiven for his sins by a person dressed like an angel in white linen and carrying a sword. Another patient, who was starving himself to death because he was convinced that he was dead, was persuaded that even dead people eat. A group of people dressed in white sheets and made up to look as pale as corpses enjoyed a delicious meal in the patient's room (see Foucault 1965). Here, as is always the case in psychodrama, the protagonist was able to decide on his own version of the world. Therefore, it is not absurd to see dead people eating or an angel appearing from heaven to offer forgiveness. The aim is to always meet the deepest needs of the protagonist.

A German psychiatrist, Johannes Christian Reil (1759–1831), offers a model that is nearly identical to Moreno's psychodrama:

> Every psychiatric hospital should have a specially arranged theatre with the necessary machinery for portraying different situations. The institution's personnel should be trained to play different roles: judges, executioners, doctors or heavenly angels, or the dead who have risen from their graves – all of the elements that can play a major role in the mental status of the patient and that makes a therapeutic impression on his fantasy. A theatre like this should be equipped to present scenes from a prison, a dungeon, an execution site, and an operating room. Don Quixote should be able to be knighted, women who think they are pregnant without any justification should be released from their burden, repentant sinners should be granted absolution in appropriate ceremonies. In short, this kind of a therapeutic theatre would help individual cases in a number of sicknesses, reawaken fantasy and wonder, bring forth the most contradictory feelings such as fear, anxiety, surprise and tranquillity in accordance with the patient's need to eliminate his fixed ideas or his feelings that have gone astray. (Mezurecky 1974, p.39–40)

Dr Reil also understood that plays should be written especially for the patients, plays they could perform themselves. The roles should be assigned according to therapeutic need. For example, the fool should be given the role of a fool in order to see his foolishness (see The mirror technique, Chapter 5).

Swedish playwright Kent Andersson's play, *Who are the Crazy Ones?*, is a well-known example of a therapeutic theatrical process. The plot is set in a psychiatric hospital where a play is being written in collaboration with the patients. The starting point was their own experiences. Moreno would probably have protested this and called it theatrotherapy, because the process would have to be marked by repetition and thus lack the necessary spontaneity. In this sense, a role that is created and performed by a patient might have been positive in that it provides a release through spontaneous reduction of stress but, after a number of performances, there would be a gradual risk of fixation. In this case, the process would have an anti-therapeutic effect and be completely different from the free development that springs from man's innermost sources and finds expression in the here and now.

The spontaneous drama of antiquity and therapeutic psychodrama are processes which distinguish themselves from any other organized performance in that they represent unique experiences in a person's life and can never be repeated in the same form. Even though psychodrama is rooted in the drama of antiquity and Dionysian intoxication, and often takes the form of pure absurd madness, it is still a method of therapy for persons who need help in solving inner and outer conflicts.

The structure and dynamic composition of psychodrama

The basic structure of a psychodrama is simple, but its construction is wise and varied in terms of the content of each of its three main stages: the warming-up stage, the psychodramatic enactment stage and the concluding stage of sharing. The three stages are equally important, although the relative length of time used for each stage can vary. Sometimes the warming-up stage is the longest. The director can make use of different techniques during this stage (see Additional methods, Chapter 3). Other psychodramas can proceed directly into the enactment stage if a protagonist has been selected with an immediate problem that has united the group. The group proceeds to the next level and the transition is made into the enactment stage. The psychodrama is always in the second stage as soon as the protagonist is chosen.

Although all three stages are equally important, the conclusion (or sharing phase) of the psychodrama must be seen as the most essential stage – one which must never be pushed aside because of a time schedule or weak response in the group. The leader is responsible for protecting the protagonist who has presented his life situation. It is also important that everyone participates in supporting the protagonist. If a person will have to leave the group during a psychodrama, this should be reported ahead of time (excluding side trips to the toilet). The concluding stage is practically a ritualistic act which strengthens the ties among the group members and helps them from talking about the psychodrama with outsiders.

The group always binds itself to the following pledge of secrecy:

> I commit myself on my honour not to discuss what has happened in this room with any outsider. I can tell as much as I want about my own experiences but not about those of others, and I will never mention anyone by name.

The protagonist

As defined earlier, the protagonist is the leader of the enactment and the dialogue. Protagonists are usually selected by the group after they have presented their problems. In institutions that work with psychodrama on a daily or weekly basis, a psychodrama with one person usually sets a process in motion that is carried over into the next psychodrama session. This is because the theme is usually of such universal appeal that it awakens fresh and different responses. The theme could be unresolved grief after losing a close friend, opposition to an authoritarian guardian or superior or a lack of self-confidence and inability to assert oneself.

In a psychodrama a protagonist presents his version of a personal conflict which is either intrapsychic or related to important persons in his life. He presents his burden to the members of the group, who are both witnesses and participants. While the drama is being played out, the group should share the protagonist's burden and help him to bear it without any pity or judgement. If the protagonist's fate is not one that the group can identify with, it is at least some consolation that it is a human fate. Interpretations are not allowed and advice should be kept to oneself. Participation involves sharing personal experiences or contributing non-verbal expressions of sympathy. A psychodrama is amoral. It does not judge and it does not try to find easy solutions. It accepts a situation as it is experienced by the protagonist. It offers the possibility of finding different solutions and new perspectives through members of the group who have had similar experiences. This sharing takes place in the final stage of the psychodrama, but it is fully permissible to bring in stage three whenever a situation in the psychodrama requires clarification. On these occasions, the third stage can be compared to an inserted scene. The protagonist is always the central figure.

The director

Although the protagonist leads the enactment in accordance to his deepest needs, the director is responsible for keeping the situation under control.

The direction a psychodrama takes is largely dependent upon the ability of the director to make rapid decisions. Naturally, this requires theoretical insight and training in the use of psychodrama's many techniques and inserted scenes. The director has to enter into an interaction (ordinary role-playing and other methods) but, at the same time, he must remain separate and look for ways to find alternative solutions in difficult situations. Also, he must have the authority to break into the drama and focus on understanding and insight into the 'here and now'. The enactment should be stopped when the group's influence on the protagonist becomes too dominating. This would be an intrusion on the whole purpose of the psychodrama, *which is the individual's right to give an account of, and justify, one's own personal experience of reality.*

Indeed, there will always be strong forces – conscious and unconscious opposition – at work between the individual and the group. Intangible insinuations often arise between the individual and the director, between the whole group and the director, or between individuals in the group, the director and the individual in focus.

If the protagonist tries to manipulate the director, the situation has come to a critical point. In this case, the director must use his authority to interrupt and draw attention to what is happening. The director's assessment of this situation is of utmost importance. Interrupting too quickly can be interpreted as an act of revenge from the director. At worst, the entire group could turn against the director and the protagonist would gain support for his actions. This would make it difficult to gain any new insight into the habitual behaviour of the protagonist. However, if the interruption is made at just the right moment, while the manipulative behaviour is visible and the protagonist is 'caught in the act', then both the protagonist and the group will gain insight that will be helpful in the interaction that follows.

The director plays a double role in the last stage of a psychodrama. First, he must step down and become a regular member of the group and contribute personal experiences. At the same time, he must follow the rule about refraining from giving interpretations and 'good advice'. The ideal director should act as a catalyst for feelings in the group and channel them in appropriate doses back and forth between the protagonist and individual group members. Any exaggerated identification from members of the group can upset the protagonist's enactment and 'steal the show'. The protagonist must always be the most important person; the experiences of the protagonist must never be explained away, minimized or depreciated. The director must use tact and discretion and never presume to play the role of 'redeemer'.

Since there are a number of misunderstandings about the role of the director in a psychodrama, this function must be carefully defined. Many myths are associated with this role, a fact that can be partially blamed on Moreno. At the very beginning of the warming-up stage, an ordinary director – one without hypnotic powers or a magical personality – should make it clear that he is there as a helper and a deliverer as a person who is responsible by virtue of his special knowledge and who, therefore, has the right to stop the production. The interaction in the group also requires definition, including the fact that each individual is responsible both for himself and for the other members of the group. It is helpful if the director has an assistant or co-therapist. In institutions that regularly use psychodrama as a form of therapy it would be common practice to train its personnel so that there will always be staff members who understand the special language and functions of a psychodrama. Doing this will help avoid unnecessary communication problems.

In recent years there have been discussions of principle in terms of the protagonist's co-responsibility during the enactment stage of a psychodrama. The Norwegian Institute of Psychodrama has taken the viewpoint that the protagonist owns his own reality as long as the enactment lasts. In the concluding stage responsibility is returned to the protagonist and the members of the group. They must all return to objective reality and to the outside world. The fact that no one can change another person is a fixed rule. Only by understanding oneself and one's own behaviour patterns is it possible to have constructive interaction with others. There is no sense in reacting like the happy and enthusiastic protagonist who said after his psychodrama: 'Now I'm going home to get that guy'. 'How old is he?' asked the director. 'Ninety years old', answered the man, simultaneously seeing the humour in the situation.

Auxiliary egos

The protagonist chooses his auxiliary egos from the group. These are persons he needs as deputies from real life. That is, their function is to join in an experimental drama based on the premises set by the protagonist in order to clarify a conflict: 'The first function is that of portraying a role of a person *required* by the subject; the second function is that of guiding the subject by warming up to his anxieties, shortcomings and needs, in order to guide him towards a better solution of his problems' (Moreno 1970a, p.59).

Any member of the group can be an auxiliary ego without any previous training. Often, coincidental and external factors influence the choice. For example, a protagonist might need a deputy mother. A woman in the group speaks in an unusual way, there may be something special about her, the style of her hair or something as trivial as the colour of her dress. The strange thing is that the woman, having left the group and joined the protagonist, actually manages to reproduce glimpses of the past. Of course, special techniques help, particularly reversing roles with the protagonist. And more surprising things can also happen in the most unexpected ways. For example, a meek and shy woman, when attacked by a protagonist as his mother, can suddenly present opposition that was never thought possible. A *psychodrama à double* occurs, and the group witnesses two protagonists in a symbolic fight for survival. According to the rules of psychodrama, the original protagonist must always be allowed to continue.

The auxiliary ego represents various psychodramatic roles – portraying either ordinary figures from public life, such as a father, mother, teacher, doctor, etc, or supernatural beings, such as witches, madonnas and abstract concepts like the world or the conscience. Psychodramatic roles consist of undigested material in the protagonist's life. They are brought to life to be replayed in scenes from the past or to be tried out in hypothetical scenes in the future. The supernatural beings represent 'dangerous areas' or 'powers'. In a psychodrama the protagonist is always encouraged to seek out dangerous areas and to start up a dialogue with the threatening powers. It is also important that the protagonist reproduces unresolved social situations. The aim is to gain control, to 'master the situation'.

An example of the above could be the protagonist who vaguely remembered a place where 'something' happened – a forest, a bedroom or maybe just a place in a dream. As long as this place represents danger and causes anxiety it will continue to dominate the individual's behaviour and emotional reactions. The psychodrama encourages the protagonist to make contact with the vague outlines and to find their true contours in order to de-mystify 'the dangerous'.

Dreams are often puzzling myths carrying important information from the entire history of our lives. Dramatization of dreams can be a fantastic adventure into the unknown, into both the appealing and the repugnant. Moreno describes an integrated personality as a person who can bring out the child in himself and, with the help of fantasy, overcome the unknown (flexibility in unfamiliar situations) and thus feel more secure within his own social domain. Moreno presents the same theory time and time again: Man can only redeem himself by expressing himself through action. The royal road to victory is spontaneity, and this is the true precondition for psychodrama. Therefore, one never speaks in the past tense. A fifty-year-old man can never be younger, but he can dare to enter into the kingdom of childhood and speak in the present. In this way, he works with his whole self and traces the furrows of the past that are entrenched in his psyche forward to a here and now. The creative moment, *status nascendi*, is the point where the longitude and latitude of a human life merge:

> In the spontaneous-creative enactment, emotions, thoughts, processes, sentences, pauses, gestures movements etc. seem first to break formlessly and in an anarchistic fashion, into an ordered environment and settled consciousness. But in the course of their development it becomes clear that they belong together like the tones of a melody; that they are in relation similar to the cells of a new organism. The disorder is only an outer appearance; inwardly there is a consistent driving force, a plastic ability, the urge to assume a definite form; the stratagem of the creative principle which allies itself with the cunning of reason in order to realize an imperative intention (Moreno 1970a, p.36).

In this way we can observe a protagonist – an ordinary man or woman – in heroic justification of the personal dramas of their lives. Auxiliary egos function as deputy roles in the protagonist's personal drama.

The double

The double plays a third role. This function has to be learned, although some persons seem to have an inborn ability for empathy. Doubling is a very profound technique in psychodrama. The danger here is that the person who plays the double can easily project his own problems onto the protagonist or interpret a situation in his misunderstood desire to help. Here again, the director has to make decisions about the use of doubles. If it turns out that the double is trying to manipulate according to personal needs, he should be removed from the drama. The protagonist might also go along passively with all of the double's recommendations and allow himself to be dominated. The strategy then has to be changed by adding special techniques or inserted scenes.

The classical use of the double requires quite a lot of training. The double either follows or sits next to the protagonist, set slightly in the background so that he will not be a distraction. He studies the slightest movements of the protagonist and imitates them. It is important that he perceives the protagonist's body language and rhythm in order to capture the small signs that give voice to what is not being communicated verbally in the drama. The double speaks out loud, expressing what he thinks the protagonist does not dare say. He brings thoughts that are slumbering beneath the protagonist's threshold of consciousness to the foreground. The protagonist must always remember that he can disagree with the double's suggestions. The director must always make certain that the double is right by asking the protagonist. The doubling contract states that the function of the double offers very personal help, but that it can be mistaken. If the double is on the wrong track, the protagonist corrects him. However, if the double is doing a passable job, the protagonist follows up and moves on to a deeper level:

PROTAGONIST: I...I...don't want to say any more to Mother.

DOUBLE: I am always so afraid of hurting her.

PROTAGONIST: No, it's not that. I'm thinking more about Father.

DOUBLE: Father seems to tolerate less.

PROTAGONIST: That's it. I...

DOUBLE: ...I feel guilty.

PROTAGONIST: I feel that it's my fault that Father doesn't speak up to her. ...I should talk back to her.

Of course, there is no rule that the double and the protagonist should have a dialogue similar to the one above. Sometimes the double just adds a key word or a single sentence. Note that the protagonist rejected the double's first suggestion. The double responded by using the word 'guilty' and then the protagonist continued by expressing the reason for his guilt feelings. We make a distinction between depth doubling, as shown above, and provocation doubling. The latter should only be carried out by the director, who always reminds the protagonist that he is being provocative on purpose. Provocation doubling is used to help the protagonist express himself more clearly or bring his defence mechanisms to the surface. Here too, the protagonist has the right to object and, if he does, the director will stop.

Another doubling technique is simpler and therefore more primitive and arbitrary. It is easy to learn, and group members seem to be very willing to use it. When a member of the group comes upon an idea that he thinks is important, he can walk over to the protagonist, stand behind him and express his 'thought.' Sometimes there are two or three doubles behind a protagonist. This method seems to activate the group strongly, but it should be used with caution since it can trigger too many opposing impulses at once. When this method is used, it could become more of a trial and error session than the classical method, which requires deep concentration and insight.

The group

The last role function is assumed by the group as a co-existing element. The group can be directed and used collectively. For example, it can be trees in a forest, singing birds or pounding sounds; it can represent unidentified creatures in dreams, create caverns or act like a symbolic force – such as pressing a protagonist down into nightmarish situations, forming a ring that has to be broken through or rocking the protagonist on outstretched hands as if he were a child. Protagonists can often play out most of their psychodramas with the group as a whole. It is not unusual for young drug addicts to interpret their experiences for the group rather than in individual interaction.

When using the group in this way, the director must use authority and keep individuals from taking off on their own 'ego trips'. Also, some members of the group might have original ideas and imaginative remedies that they pass on to the director. It is up to the director to decide whether or not these are better solutions than the ones he is considering. The interaction between the group and the director must be open and visible at all times – no whispering in the corners! One of Moreno's many pieces of advice to psychodrama directors is: Don't forget the protagonist, but never lose the group! Reduced concentration in the group will always lessen the intensity of the whole drama. *Group intensity is essential for the protagonist.* The following is an example of how a group can be used collectively.

A man sees himself crawling through a long tunnel (the group creates a tunnel). He feels that he has to 'press forward through a sewer pipe' (the group's hands form an opening which they force him through). Since it is equally important for the body to remember as it is for the brain, all details are carefully followed. The man comes into a small basement room (the group forms walls around him). There is a table in the basement (two persons make a table by crouching on their knees and elbows). The man says that the table is larger (four persons make the table). We now have a man and a table. The man can go no further. After reversing his role with the 'table', he says that he is waiting for blood – sacrificial blood, *his own* blood. In a psychodrama a role reversal always means an expansion of the protagonist's personal field of experience. The director asks the four persons to form the table again. The man kneels in front of the table. We are witnessing a man who is willing to sacrifice his life!

At times like this, when one sees genuine self-abandonment, perhaps especially with suicidal persons (see Suicidal try-out, Chapter 3), it is important to go along with the protagonist's premises, to stretch the imagination as far as possible, even right into a symbolic death. In this scene the director stood behind the protagonist and proclaimed, with a judge-like, authoritarian voice, that the man could have one wish fulfilled before his sacrifice. Suggestions of a hike in the mountain wilderness, a deep forest, a meeting with a wise man and similar ideas that are often made to people who are drawn toward Eastern philosophies met with no reaction. Then the 'judge' said that it was time to initiate the sacrificial act and, since a sacrifice was a ritual ceremony, he would be carried in a procession. The protagonist was carried around the room on outstretched hands and then placed on the 'table'. After a pause in deep silence, the protagonist was asked to open his eyes. The group had witnessed the action and it was accepted. The scene later became the basis of a dream psychodrama about guilt and submission to an authoritarian father.

The above demonstrates how a psychodrama often uses drastic measures, even in a Kafkaesque process like this one. A second example demonstrates how the group function can be unnecessary in the last stage of a psycho-drama.

A young girl acted out a dream in stage two. In the dream she saw a person kneeling over a small child. She herself was a spectator. She did not understand the meaning of what she saw. The director asked her to exchange places with the kneeling person. Then she saw that the child had a face. After reversing roles with the child she whispered: 'But it's me!' The girl was asked to return to her position as a spectator. From there, she said that she felt as if she were stuck in a swamp. The director asked some of the group members to hold her. At a given signal they released her, and she ran over to the kneeling person and pushed her away violently. She herself was so overwhelmed that she burst into tears – a purely spontaneous reaction, without any understanding. She just cried. The director gave her a piece of chalk and asked her to draw the child's face on a blackboard. With difficulty, she began to draw in thin, careful strokes. She drew a small, detailed face, a neat and tidy picture. She finished the drawing with a smile which cut off any form of sharing in the concluding stage. Instead, the group remained in deep silence, but it did not feel like oppressive silence. It was not necessary to say anything. Some may have thought that there had been a problem about an abortion or sexual identification, but there was simply no more to talk about.

It is tempting to use this example as an illustration of Moreno's appeal to people to be their own creators and redeemers. The girl had created and given life to a symbolic face that had not been there.

Role systems and role functions

The word 'role' originated in the theatre. It appears as 'rôle' in medieval France, derived from the Latin *rotula*. Scripts, or often scores, were written on large rolls. Assigning individual scripts for public performances was not common until the sixteenth and seventeenth centuries. It was then that a scene, or a part of a play, was referred to as a role.

Today, both 'part' and 'role' are used in English. English was also the first language to introduce the concept of roles into sociology and psychology. Moreno was the first to launch role reversal as a term in psychiatry. This was in 1934, nearly one year before the social psychologist George Herbert Mead. The theatre has adopted the word 'part', as in playing a part, while sociology uses the terms 'role' or 'role-playing', which involve prescribed activities, attitudes and behavioural patterns in conformance to social positions. William Aubert defines the concept of role as 'the sum of the norms that are associated with a definite task or position. A role lies like a circle of expectation around the Ego' (1964, p.46).

In psychology the role concept is far more complicated and comprehensive. In psychoanalysis the ego is the core of the individual, the 'mediator' between the id and the superego – although this model also admits that the ego has different environments and worlds. Social psychology, on the other hand, concentrates most of its attention on the ego's roots in a social structure. Here the ego experiences itself both as a self, based on its own expectations and, as Mead expresses it, 'A self based on the viewpoint of another'. Mead (1952, p.366) also states that the ability to 'take the role of another' presupposes sympathy: 'The attitude that we characterize as sympathy springs from the same ability as taking the role of another part...' The ordinary term for this is 'putting oneself in the other's place.' Moreno does not consider the presence of sympathy when he uses role reversal. To Moreno, the primary consideration is that something happens, that either a positive or negative transference takes place (see also 'Transference, empathy and tele', p.74). In concrete terms, this is exactly what Moreno accomplishes with the technique of role reversal.

However, role expectations and role experiences bring us into many complicated relationships, especially because one and the same person often has to fulfill many different expectations and norms that are, in turn, associated with different roles. The more complicated modern society becomes, the greater will be the demands on an individual's ability to adapt and be flexible – or at least to be able to give the impression of managing to play a role. Often this is only accomplished through standardized status symbols used to keep up with a neighbour. The American sociologist Erving

Goffman describes this in terms that are often borrowed from the theatrical world. In *The Presentation of Self in Everyday Life*, Goffman (1959) uses many analogies to the language of the theatre – how people arrange their *performances* and prepare the *image* they want to create for the public. Goffman is also concerned with what he calls *staging a performance*, and the crushing blow it can be when *the performance falls flat*. Goffman is especially concerned with how people try to *maintain* a drama, in contrast to Moreno who is most interested in how he can *change* it (through creativity and spontaneity). At the same time, society is increasing its demands for specialization and this can become too much of a burden for one or more of the role functions that an individual has to assume in the course of a day. Roles conflict with one another. In serious pathological cases, in R.D. Laing's (1960) terminology, 'false self systems' can develop. In this case, we find ourselves with roles that seem to play themselves autonomously with no connection to the conscious mastering of the individual (in Laing's terminology, 'un-coupling').

Like the concept of conflict, psychodrama also creates a superstructure over the dramatic and technical viewpoints of the theatre and sociology by considering a role as both a cognitive and intrapsychic process.

Moreno uses the role concept in different perspectives and, in turn, these perform different functions in a psychodrama. In terms of behaviour, a role has more dimensions than meet the eye: partially developed (for example, the child who cannot master the adult role), over-developed (the 'perfect', or the person who seems to be wearing a mask), normally developed (here the concept of normality is flexible in terms of the ego's position in the social environment – for example primitive man, persons in unusual local communities, etc.), nearly or totally absent (a working person who cannot master the role of mother or father) and distorted into a hostile attitude (for example opponents in a political duel).

A role is also seen in a perspective of time: has never existed (for example, for many women, the role of motherhood), undeveloped or latent (Gauguin did not discover that he could paint until he had reached the age of 42), existing in relation to some persons but not to others (sympathy or antipathy) and was once present but, due to unfortunate circumstances, was suppressed, erased or transformed into its opposite (among other examples, this can apply to persons who switch from heterosexuality to homosexuality).

A role, or interaction between roles, is also an intrapsychic process. Here Moreno postulates a set of role systems divided into three levels. Each level builds on the former one in a chronological development, but in continual interaction. Moreno's three divisions within the concept of a role are: the psychosomatic roles, the psychodramatic roles and the social roles.

Psychosomatic roles

Psychosomatic roles are dispositions which the individual has acquired at a very early age. Primarily, these are established as a result of what the relationship to a mother or a person who has acted as a mother has been (the first extension of the self). Therefore, psychosomatic roles become the basis for the individual's relationship to his environment in the broadest possible sense, in terms of security, or inner tensions as a result of insecurity in the first months and year of a child's life (compare to Eric H. Ericson's concept of basic trust and R.D. Laing's ontological insecurity).

A psychosomatic role (or disposition) could be, for example, an individual's eating habits. We have the compulsive eater, the person with no appetite, or the one who eats in moderation. Further, there is the insomniac, the person who is always tired, and the one who sleeps regularly and normally. Or we could take a person's sexuality: the impotent, the promiscuous or the one who knows how to give and receive on a healthy basis. Naturally, when we look at a person from these perspectives, we do not consider acute life situations. Dispositions are relatively permanent types of behaviour. Therefore, the psychosomatic roles are the most integrated and the most difficult to identify. From a negative perspective, they can be compared to Medard Boss' 'confined melodies of life', that is conditions on a deep mental level when the individual once came to a halt in anxiety or uncertainty. Boss (1963) is interested in the connection between the psyche and the soma and sees a direct relationship between a neurosis and the organ the neurosis chooses to express itself in. Blockage occurs when the individual does not have the opportunity to express himself completely in his surroundings. Often, when a blockage is not strong enough on an external level, it moves into deeper levels, 'from the periphery inward into the body, a change that results in it becoming even more hidden' (p.165). The 'melody of life' stopped playing, or at least it became hushed. The individual did not dare to make use of the entire orchestration offered by life. These persons can have severe pain and repressed hatred or guilt, tightly tangled knots beneath a seemingly smooth façade. An experience on the level of a psychosomatic role would touch upon these tangled knots. Here a combination of psychodrama and bioenergetic techniques can be most useful.

Since Moreno respects the fact that the body has its own language, he also includes the first preverbal stage. Therefore, a psychodrama often unfolds on a non-verbal and symbolic level. As a rule, if necessary, a person can play the role of an infant. In this case, it is not unusual to see a protagonist clinging to a deputy mother (auxiliary ego) and sucking a finger. After these experiences, many protagonists have been able to say that they seemed to recognize scents from a distant childhood and that these made them do certain things almost as reflex reactions. When critical, intellectual control was switched off, the body 'remembered'. Some protagonists recall experiencing caresses or blows that had long been forgotten.

Psychodramatic roles

Psychodramatic roles include all sorts of fantasy figures from the protagonist's world (the total extension of the self). These can include perfectly ordinary persons from real life, for example, the protagonist's boss. In this connection, the boss becomes a psychodramatic role because he is surrounded by surplus reality. The protagonist has projected a personal fantasy picture onto the boss. The protagonist attaches qualities and attitudes to this person that are not the ones he actually has or represents in his social role. The result is a conflicting relationship and, often, a breach in communication (refer to the concept of transference in psychodrama, p.74) This raises the important distinction between the use of a social role and the function of the role. About the latter, Moreno says: 'The function of the role is to enter the unconscious from the social world and bring shape and order into it' (1970a, p.v).

Let us return to the protagonist's boss who clearly represents a *social* role in objective reality, but whom the protagonist thinks of as a *psychodramatic* role in the psychodrama. Bringing the real boss onto the stage would accomplish little or nothing. This could be done in other kinds of groups, such as an encounter group. It may seem to be a paradox but, in psychodramatic terms, solving a conflict on the fantasy level is more beneficial than a confrontation. A confrontation forces verbal explanations, discussions, accusations and justifications, and none of these belong in a psychodrama. An auxiliary ego is a deputy from real life, *as the protagonist experiences him*. The auxiliary ego plays a social role (as in the case of the boss) but this only functions as a model to reflect what the protagonist experiences on the fantasy level.

Psychodramatic roles are subjective fantasy pictures that may have been stored for many years. Maturation and personal development are defined according to how well or poorly an individual has managed to master psychodramatic roles over the years. Many people have brought developmental defects upon themselves because they have not managed to free themselves from a dominating mother or an authoritarian father. Feelings of guilt and inferiority can be rooted in problems that have never been solved, either consciously or unconsciously. A father may have died before a reconciliation or perhaps a man has never realized that he was obsessed with an continual desire to compete with each and everyone because he is, in fact, still competing with an older brother.

In extreme cases, a psychodramatic role can be so strong that it lives its own life within an individual. It then becomes a completely disassociated part of a personality. Robert White (1948) describes certain aspects of this in his chapters on dissociated conditions, amnesia for personal identity, and multiple personality. The behaviour of persons characterized as psychopaths, or sociopaths, can also be far from having a reasonable relationship to accepted norms. Here special reference is made to Hervey Cleckley's comprehensive work, *The Mask of Sanity* (1964). In his interest in the psychopathic personality, H.S. Sullivan (1947), who created the expression 'the not me', refers to Eugen Kahn (1931) and his different categories that fall under the psychopath designation. The irresponsible use of the term psychopath, as it has become part of everyday language, should be avoided. In some persons, the disassociated role manifests itself in attempts to come into contact with his environment, often to the despair of family and friends, because the behaviour involved seems impossible to understand. In other people, formidable 'persons' live within the individual and create tremendous anxiety. The auxiliary ego's role function is to come into contact with the protagonist's troublesome psychodramatic roles, while representing, at the same time, their own psychodramatic roles to the protagonist. In these situations, when the scene begins to get dramatic, the auxiliary egos have to keep their wits about them under the firm guidance of a director.

We have emphasized that the adult's degree of spontaneity and flexibility depends upon the extent to which the person has managed to gain insight and mastery over psychodramatic roles, especially in childhood and adolescence. When persons in critical phases of their lives become blocked and come to a standstill in anxiety and fear, or simply give up trying to master their lives, they will become rigid or psychologically inflexible. An incomplete or faulty understanding of psychodramatic roles can be seen in the form of projections, suspiciousness or, perhaps, paralyzing helplessness. A person who is considered adult and 'normal' in daily life might have trouble accepting certain traits in others without knowing why. Those who feel antipathy for other races, religions or alternative viewpoints have inflexible personalities, often with authoritarian traits (see Adorno *et al.* 1950). This does not signal psychiatric disturbance until the psychodramatic roles gain control of the mind and the individual becomes dominated by external creatures, hallucinates or becomes enclosed in his own world, living in isolation with these fantasy figures.

Moreno points out that Goethe was actually the first person to describe psychodrama in literature. In his novel, *Lila*, the main character lives in a world populated by mystical, over-sized beings, but is helped by a doctor who gives her the courage and insight to be freed from them. Dr Fried helps his patient in the same way in Joanna Greenberg's *I Never Promised You a Rose Garden*, one of the few published authentic portrayals of what a mentally ill patient experiences in a world that is completely separate from the one we others live in.

Psychodrama is also used in treating psychotic patients and one can come into real contact with pent-up imaginary persons that seem to lead a life of their own. Fantastic fabulations can appear and the director and the group try to see the whole picture and find a relationship. A psychotic person always tries to communicate something, no matter how strange and seemingly confused it is. By taking part in this world, which is 'real' to the patient, it becomes possible to understand its 'reality' for as long as the patient thinks it is important to sustain his drama. The psychotic's way to relate becomes a kind of role-playing, perhaps in a desperate attempt to take hold of and understand what we call objective reality.

Social roles

Social roles are the third type of role within Moreno's system. These are behaviour models which the individual has understood, expressed and brought under control. Moreno always includes all of the role dimensions in the individual's experience of the moment. Psychosomatic, psycho-dramatic and social roles are also phases that are built on experiences.

The first phase provides the basis for the individual's feeling of security in the world. In the second phase, the child transforms security or insecurity into ways in which to meet the world. It is in this phase that the psycho-dramatic roles should be brought under control. The child and teenager must learn how to master 'the dangerous' and challenging in new situations. Not until the third phase does the adult personality manage to master what is expected of him in social situations. However, when Moreno discusses good social functioning, he does not mean the greatest possible adjustment to the expectations of other people or societies. To the contrary, Moreno thinks that the individual should have all of his resources at hand, from all phases of his personality and at all times. The individual should 'live his own social role' by using his whole self as defined by Moreno's definition of an integrated personality, that is a person who not only duplicates but who moves forward in self-development, regardless of chronological age – *the creative person.*

It is important to emphasize that although a psychodrama may seem unrealistic in the enactment stage, the director can point out opportunities for maturation and growth in the final stage. Primarily, this means that the protagonist must recognize opportunities, as well as possible limitations, himself. The distinction between fantasy and social learning can best be understood through psychodrama's operational use of objective, subjective and personal reality.

Role systems and the role functions in a psychodrama run on a parallel line in a two-sided dynamic process: on the one side is the protagonist's intrapsychic state in the here and now and, on the other, the energy that is stimulated in the group through its interaction with the protagonist. The psychodramatic play can take many and unexpected turns. The 'tools' of the leader are always part of the external structure of the psychodrama, that is the three first stages as well as the techniques and inserted scenes he always has at hand and which must be evaluated in relation to what is happening both to and around the protagonist.

A director always works from the periphery toward the centre, that is from the group toward focusing on the 'dangerous' on the stage (or the floor). Thereafter, the focus is returned to the group and the objective reality that is waiting when the protagonist has played his version of a personally experienced drama.

In other words, the periphery (the physical presence of the group in the room) represents the outer (objective) reality which presupposes a relatively similar frame of reference for social roles. The chosen protagonist is allowed to enter into his personal reality by enacting psychodramatic roles. A psychodrama makes deliberate and maximal use of the protagonist's fantasies, needs, courage and will to tackle the psychodramatic 'undigested' roles in what Moreno calls surplus reality. This enables coming into contact with the psychosomatic roles from the lower levels of the protagonist's personality dispositions. The objective is to gain insight and control over the social roles in objective reality which the protagonist will return to when the drama is completed.

Phases of development and levels of experience

It is often difficult to follow everything simultaneously in a psychodrama: the protagonist's continually new ideas and the unexpected directions a psychodrama can take, whether influenced by the group as a whole or by its individual members. The director must always keep the overall picture in mind and make use of inserted scenes whenever they are called for. It is often necessary to transport oneself back and forth to different places and different time periods in various phases of development and levels of experience. These changes in time and place may be especially frequent when dreams are being presented. While the protagonist is reliving the dream in the enactment, he is also associating it with former events. For example, a protagonist may be presenting a dream that he is a freedom fighter and planning to attack a rural village (his childhood home). Just as this is being enacted (dramatized with the help of the group), he remembers a time when he used to hide with a friend when his mother called for him. This then becomes the starting point for a new scene, which might place us in the midst of the protagonist's current life situation. While he was in the psychodrama's scene, he was simultaneously transporting himself through his dream images, to memories of a long-lost childhood, to an immediate closeness to his conflict-filled present. As strange as it may seem, the protagonist speaks in different ways from scene to scene. Here the director must perceive what the protagonist is attempting to express and interpret it into dramatic language suitable for the participation of the group. That is, the director should assign pertinent roles that will help to move the drama forward. Since the action is constantly shifting back and forth in time and place, it is important to know what is happening and the best way to respond to the protagonist's need to be understood.

In terms of communication processes, the model used by the American psychiatrist Harry Stack Sullivan can be especially useful here. Sullivan's model clearly parallels Moreno's three-role system in his use of three categories to describe an individual's stage of development and level of experience in terms of communication, perception and emotional development. These categories also determine a type of role-playing that parallels the roles in a psychodrama. Sullivan's divisions into prototaxic, the parataxic and the syntaxic phases corresponds to Moreno's psychosomatic, psychodramatic and social role levels.

Like Moreno, Sullivan's starting point is the child's first experience of its mother or the person who is the acting mother (the mother as a proto-role). Here Sullivan uses the concept of empathy in a special sense, as 'a peculiar linkage' which first and foremost transmits the mother's emotional maturity or nervousness, creating feelings of safety or insecurity in the child. Sullivan stresses the child/mother relationship from the time the child is six months until the age of two years and three months. About empathy, Sullivan says that it can be either 'emotional poison or positive interaction'. The poisoning can take place as early as in the mother's womb when the mother does not want to be pregnant and is distressed by her condition. If the mother is also negative in her attitude to the child later on, this will have a decisive influence on the child's development. Their interaction will not result in mutually positive communication.

This is clearly related to Moreno's theory about dispositions as the starting point for psychosomatic roles. A child's first experience of himself in the outside world is in his interaction with his mother. In Moreno's meaning, the ego in interaction with its first auxiliary ego, which exists as clearly as a physical object and as a part of the infant's own mind. We can also find a correlation here to Melanie Klein's internalization of object-relationships and the child's experience of part objects, such as the mother's breast. Sullivan also assigns an important role to the mother's breast in terms of the infant's experience of the mother as good or bad and how this, in turn, influences further development. The initial basis for the 'I-you pattern' (or patterns) is established in what Sullivan refers to as 'the structure of Self' (1947, p.134).

The child's first aim is to strive for satisfaction and security. Here Sullivan brings in a built-in motive which he believes is inborn, called the *power motive* (1947, p.6). This later develops into a quality he calls *power drive* in persons who feel an inner sense of powerlessness. In contrast to the power motive, power drive is a quality that is learned as a result of being frustrated in the need for mastering, but when the mastering has been hindered by overpowering adults.

The child's first self-system, the nucleus of the personality, develops from the need for security and the power motive (which alone can be viewed as a conflict between owning and wanting to own) and it is this system that generates what Sullivan calls the first tool, *anxiety* (1947, p.9). Anxiety is called a tool because the child, and later the adult, consciously or unconsciously listen, to it as a measurement of acceptance or disapproval from their environment. For Sullivan this results in *selective inattention*:

> To maintain a sense of security and avoid anxiety, the child must be careful to register how it makes an impression on others. It becomes important to gain praise and recognition… Therefore it selectively ignores that which does not rouse recognition and in this way, avoids disapproval from important adults (1947, p.131).

The individual's entire experience of self seems to be based on his perception of the reactions of others. These then determine a sort of role-playing in that the individual feels like 'the good me' or 'the bad me' or, when the experience creates so much anxiety that it results in a dissociative reaction that is totally unacceptable, the individual becomes 'the not me'. This last maneuver can be compared to what R.D. Laing calls 'the unconnected self': 'By "unconnecting" he (Peter) meant that he cut out each and every connection between his "true" self and the "false" self which he officially rejected' (1960, p.120).

Sullivan's self-systems, can mean different things within the same individual, for example when he cannot master a situation as a whole. Sullivan also uses *self-dynamism, self-system* and *self* in the same sense: 'The self is not a static entity, but a combination of interpersonal processes. It is necessary to emphasize that the Self is always associated with interpersonal relationships' (1947, p.7).

One of Sullivan's forms of role-playing in psychodrama, in terms of certain ways of being, is determined by how people experience themselves:

> ...only as one respects one self can one respect others... Should one have a satisfactory and realistic attitude toward one's Self, the other will also share this attitude. In fact, it is not 'for with what judgement you judge, you shall be judged' but 'as you judge yourself, so shall you judge others' (1947, p.128).

The prototaxic phase

Sullivan's first phase, the prototaxic, is a state of cosmic entity – a concept Moreno calls the cosmic self. Cosmic entity implies a state of self-sufficiency. The self and the surrounding world are the same. As a cosmic self, the individual experiences 'floating along' as part of a whole. In particular, this applies to an infant. As long as an infant has not learned the dimensions of time and space, it is surrounded by a wholeness.

Prototaxic symbols are perceptions or forms of language that are either undeveloped or seemingly impossible to understand – which adults can also have in certain given conditions. Pathological conditions or deep intoxication belong to the prototaxic phase. Language, feelings and perceptions are distorted or completely blocked. It is tempting to think that the person who seeks for heavy intoxication unconsciously wants to return to a state of security (in Schachtel's terminology: embeddedness). Intoxication is a means of escaping the anxiety that is associated with the desire to detach oneself.

A psychosis can also be seen as a desperate attempt to fight anxiety and search inward to a world promising more security than that which the outer world represents. The psychotic who has lost contact with his environment, or who does not dare take contact with it, may be seeking a security that is different from our definition of the word. Therefore, the therapy we offer must help him work his way through his anxiety back to his surroundings. To do this we have to understand the symbolic language of the psychotic. We have to take part in his world, on his premises. Only then can a psychodrama participate in the psychotic's 'journey through madness' and bring him back from the psychosis with more insight and a more confidence in himself in the world.

As Sullivan (1947) describes schizophrenic conditions, they can also be characterized as prototaxic: 'Schizophrenic conditions...for reasons that are far too complicated to describe here, are conditions where a person has withdrawn to very early stages of development. A common footstool can become God's throne, the footstool of God. The schizophrenic is surrounded by cosmic forces' (p.136). In a psychodrama there is no hesitation about entering into the symbolic world of a schizophrenic. By disregarding the dimensions of time and space, and suspending all common forms of logic, one can catch a glimpse into unknown worlds.

The parataxic phase

Sullivan calls the second phase the parataxic phase. The individual communicates with the world by 'rewriting' it in order to master a situation, for example through wishful thinking, projections and day-dreaming. A person in the parataxic phase makes extensive use of what Sullivan calls selective inattention, that is omitting whatever causes anxiety or discomfort. In Sullivan's terminology, transference distortions are parataxic distortions. These are phenomena that constantly appear in a psychodrama when the protagonist enters into distorted and garbled interaction with auxiliary egos: 'Transference distortions are also a method for a person to show others some of his most serious problems. In other words, transference distortions may be an obscure attempt to communicate something that the therapist really has to understand before it can become an insight for the patient' (Sullivan 1970, p.27). The parataxic person is one who has come to a standstill at one or another stage in development. He is often unnecessarily aggressive, or in a state of constant self-defence, unless he has lost the ability to assert himself.

When a protagonist reacts this way in a psychodrama, one can experience his struggle with many imaginary persons or psychodramatic roles that he has not managed to control. Here the task of the psychodrama is to point out these reactions to the protagonist and to use auxiliary egos to initiate communication with important persons in his life. An experimental drama with deputy persons may enable overcoming the helplessness that, at one point in his development, was the reason for becoming unnecessarily aggressive, being in a constant state of self-defence or having too little self-confidence, etc. In this connection, Sullivan was very aware of the dynamic interaction between the patients in his office and imaginary persons who seemed to influence the patients' experience of the situation:

The psychiatric interview is greatly complicated by the patient replacing the psychiatrist with one or more persons who in reality clearly differ from what the psychiatrist represents... The interviewee's behaviour is influenced by these fictional persons whose presence seems temporarily more imminent and real than the psychiatrists, and he then interprets the psychiatrist's comments and behaviour as if they have come from another imaginary person (1970, p.27).

The syntaxic phase

Sullivan's third phase is the syntaxic stage. This is reached when a person makes use of language, feelings and perceptions which are immediately understood by the other part (consensual validation).

Like Moreno with his three-part role system, Sullivan maintains that each phase builds upon the previous one if the process of development has been relatively stable and taken place under relatively favourable conditions. In the syntaxic phase, an adult integrated personality can solve inter-human conflicts with understanding and tolerance. Moreno's objective is mastering the social role or, in Sullivan's terminology, mastery on a syntaxic level.

The second stage of a psychodrama, the enactment phase, will almost always take place on a parataxic level of experience because the protagonist is struggling to find a relationship and to gain control of the conflict that is being dramatized. In a psychodrama the syntaxic phase is when the protagonist has gained an understanding of his problem and can use his insight and talk about it in relationship to others. When this occurs in stage three, the director's aim is to support the protagonist in his choice, or, perhaps, when he is ready for it, to discuss alternatives which presuppose that the protagonist might have to admit to some mistakes and change his attitudes or accept his life as it is and make the best of it. Sometimes this can happen after only one psychodrama. Other times, many psychodramas are necessary before the conflicts can be brought to light – if, indeed, the subject can have any benefit at all from psychodrama as a form of therapy.

Ego conditions and acting out techniques

Similar to Moreno and Sullivan, Eric Berne, the founder of transactional analysis, categorizes an individual's interactive systems into three parts. His objective is also the same as Moreno and Sullivan's: 'The aim of transactional analysis is *social control*, where the adult maintains the control he exercises over others who (in turn) consciously or subconsciously attempt to activate the patient's ego condition as a child or a parent' (1961, p.86). When Berne capitalizes the words 'Child', 'Parent' and 'Adult', these words designate ego conditions. These have their corresponding psychic organs. The state of a Child ego has its archepsychic organ, a Parent ego has its exteropsychic organ and the Adult ego has its neopsychic organ.

Berne also maintains that each ego condition, with its corresponding psychic organ, builds upon the other in chronological development. Later, these influence one another through mutual interaction. But Berne's model is slightly different from Moreno and Sullivan's models. They build the systems vertically, starting with the infantile stage at the bottom, the 'incomplete personality' in the middle and the integrated adult on the top. In Berne, the Child (with the corresponding archepsychic organ) is on the bottom layer and the Parent is on the highest (with the corresponding exteropsychic organ), but the Adult (with the corresponding neopsychic organ)is in the middle. This resembles Freud's classic tripartite model, where the ego appears as a compromise between the pressure of the id and the superego and becomes a person's instrument of control if the individual is relatively well-adapted.

The condition of the Child ego

The condition of the Child ego is a complex system of feelings, attitudes and behaviour patterns from the individual's earliest infancy. Berne compares the fundamental condition of the ego to a recording cassette or a video. When the child was very young and more or less helpless, it imitated its parents or guardians and gathered arguments and opinions based on 'authorities.' This might be seen as a secret process of learning through observation or magical dramatic techniques. Statements are recorded on an inner cassette and behaviour is copied onto a 'video.' The Child ego condition that later appears in the Adult reflects how the 'authorities' made their mark.

Berne distinguishes between two forms of the Child ego condition, depending on how the child has managed to outgrow childhood: the adapted child or the natural child. In the first, a person is dominated by parental influence even in his Adult ego condition. He is accommodating or withdrawn, but he can also become a tyrannical father or an hysterical mother – a phenomenon often appearing on the psychodramatic stage. The Child dominates, overpowering the Parent and the Adult. This archepsychic organ characteristically displays abrupt reactions that are based on pre-logical thinking and distorted perception.

On the other hand, the natural child has been both independent and rebellious. The harmonious balance that was established in the Child ego condition regulates the Adult and the Parent. Ideally, the Adult internalizes the Child ego condition in the sense of being child-like (inventive, flexible, creative) but not childish (impulsive, moody, uncontrolled).

The condition of the Parent ego

The condition of the Parent ego is a system of feelings, attitudes and behaviour patterns that resemble parents or guardians. An exteropsychic person adheres to borrowed value systems, for example as judgmental, domineering or overprotecting. However, if the guardians have been reasonable instructors, the Parent ego condition in the subsequent adult will be understanding and sympathetic, with the ability to contribute 'digested' experiences.

Berne compares this second ego condition (Parent) with playing back the cassette or the inner video tape that the child used to record behaviour models. If the child has had domineering or judgmental parental figures, the cassette and the video reproduce 'undigested' commands and judgements (in certain situations).

In psychodramas this is often so tangible that it approaches a caricature when, for example, auxiliary egos or protagonists revert to previous role patterns. This is particularly true when the individual is under strong emotional pressure. However, the most amazing is still that they themselves seem to be unaware of their highly irrational reactions and attitudes. They simply 'play back' stored patterns of speech and behaviour as if these have been kept in a reservoir somewhere within themselves.

The condition of the Adult ego

Berne compares the condition of the Parent ego to a computer. An Adult is primarily engaged in converting exterior influences into information, which is then interpreted and classified on the basis of previous experience. In the Adult ego condition, the individual makes calculations, evaluates situations and assumes responsibility. The condition is characterized as an independent system of feelings, attitudes and patterns of behaviour which are adapted to current reality. In this connection, Berne takes into consideration who the person is and which experiences have been available to him in his particular culture: 'The criterion is neither the accuracy of the evaluation nor how the reactions are accepted (depending upon which culture one belongs to), but how the programming itself takes place and the use each individual makes of the available data' (1961, p.68).

Many people believe they are always in their Adult ego condition. Berne thinks this is a dangerous mistake if the aim is simply to maintain an attitude of cool, critical common sense. In this case the spontaneity and impulsive energy from the deeper sources of a personality, where creative fantasy is lodged, are not released. The person becomes a computer. This type of person illustrates the distinction Berne makes between an ego condition and a role because when a person becomes locked into an attitude composed of a standardized pattern for how he thinks he should be, then he has ceased being. He is playing a role. In Moreno's terminology, he has become a role conserve and a 'robot'. He has lost his source of creativity:

> When a therapist plays a role as a therapist, he will not get very far with a sensitive patient. He must *be* a therapist... If he thinks that a certain patient needs fatherly assurance, he does not play a fatherly role. No, he must free the patient from his Parent ego condition...
>
> A patient can play a role in another patient's drama. But as an individual, he is not playing a role when he is a Parent, Adult, or Child; he exists in the condition of the ego of one of these three. A patient in the condition of the Child ego can decide to want to play a role, but it makes no difference which role he plays or whether he shifts from one role to another. In any case, he will remain in the condition of the Child ego. He can even play a role as a certain kind of child, but this is still only one of many possibilities within his repertoire. Just as children play in reality, and assume the role of a mother, a doctor or a baby, they are still just as much children at their individual age levels while they are playing these roles. (Berne 1961, p.258)

Play, pastimes and games

The way in which we manage our ego conditions – well, less well or poorly – depends on which manuscript we have at our disposal and how we manage to correct and 'proofread' it and 'change the text'. Berne uses the term 'manuscript' in the sense of a life situation or life opportunities. In this connection, he differentiates between play, pastimes and games.

Play is the spontaneous experience of investigation and mastery. It also involves a deep emotional engagement. Therefore, play can be serious, even deadly serious, when the engagement is such that the playing oversteps certain socially accepted norms. For example, if a child is caught 'in the act' in sexual play by a judgmental adult, the child's 'manuscript' can be off to a very bad start.

A pastime is an innocent type of social companionship as long as the parts play according to the same rules. Chess and football are examples of social activities that take place within a satisfactory set of rules.

Games turn up when there are differences between the parts. Competition shows itself in subtle manipulations to gain control of the other part. Even stereotyped rituals based on social conventions are a kind of game. An innocent 'How are you?' has an underlying pattern. The person answers, 'I'm fine thank you' (implying: don't think that I'm worse off than you are) or 'Well, things aren't very good' (implying: take some time to talk to me. Poor me. You should have enough time). The person who opened the dialogue might not have the slightest interest in how the other person is and quickly replies: 'Everything will be fine, you'll see'. The little game has come to an end. 'A' lifts his hat and disappears down the road, while 'B' is left behind feeling abandoned and wishing he had not admitted his sorry state of affairs.

Games can just as easily be subconscious or conscious attempts to gain control. Berne points out how married couples often communicate from different ego conditions. The man as the Parent and the wife as the Child, or vice versa. This can be a game that continues throughout their lives and might be the reason for staying married. Conversely, there could be reason for divorce if the woman grew out of the Child ego condition and found her place as an Adult. In this case she would insist on communicating with her spouse as an Adult. A permanent Parent ego condition on his side would be intolerable.

What might be the most unpleasant type of game is called the 'double bind,' where inconsistent and confusing signals are sent from the same person. This is a game that is often played in a family where the weakest part is defined as schizophrenic. Laing and Esterson (1964) describe eleven patients diagnosed as schizophrenic. The study is unique because the authors have brought in all of the patients' closest family members. The study indicates that schizophrenia (in many cases) seems to be determined by social and familial factors in that the patients cannot assert themselves in relation to important persons in their surroundings.

Berne also uses the term 'games' as 'sections of more complicated transactions'. These become parts of the 'manuscript'. The first draft is the protocol:

> ...In an analysis of the manuscript the 'household drama' becomes the way it was first played out with unsatisfactory solutions, a protocol... (1961, p.118).

Obsolete 'hieroglyphics' turn up later in what Berne calls the script proper (temporary and incomplete derivations of the protocol). This impermanent script has to be adjusted to comply to the individual's real possibilities. Berne calls the adjustment, or the compromise, an adaption: 'And adaption occurs precisely when the patient tries to play out in real life, and manipulate the persons around him' (1961, p.118).

Berne unites the protocol, the manuscript and the adaption into one term: the manuscript. In reality, the manipulation of others and adaption (adapting or cutting the manuscript) is not far from the theatre's dramaturgy, the natural enemy of Moreno's creaturgy! When the individual is pressured by his environment, he is forced to manipulate, invent rules and adjust the game to fit the framework (dramaturgy). However, if there had been freedom to negotiate and act, then the individual would have been able to make use of far greater resources and improve his possibilities in life (creaturgy), that is permission to rewrite the weak and incomplete chapters of the 'manuscript.'

Practically speaking, cutting and editing one's lifetime manuscript and assigning the 'roles' one needs in order to rewrite it are the very basis of psychodrama. As with Moreno, the patients in Berne's groups try to present their personal reality and relive their dramas in the attempt to find better solutions:

> Because a patient looks for persons who fit into his special manuscript, he looks upon the members of the group 'through his own glasses'... He has a tendency to pick (for him) the right persons to play roles as mother, father and siblings... When the cast of characters is complete he tries to draw out the answers he needs from them (Berne 1961, p.119).

The difference between Moreno and Berne is that while Berne works with an analysis of ego conditions and attempts to improve the patient's life manuscript (in a group where communication disorders and transference disorders are the basis for analysis), Moreno allows all kinds of impulses to play themselves out in a concretization of conflicts in interaction with deputies who represent the actual persons in the patient's life drama. Here it is extremely important that the director of the psychodrama is constantly aware of the ego conditions of his players.

Moreno's four universal dimensions

Psychodrama does not aim to make diagnoses. It accepts all states of mind as a person's only natural reality of the moment and accepts all of the premises in the psychodramatic enactment. In these, Moreno operates with four universal dimensions as the basis for the psychodramatic techniques he uses in his therapy. These are time, space, reality and the cosmos.

Time

To Moreno, time is a therapeutic concept which is just as three-dimensional as the concept of a role, existing simultaneously within an individual as the past, the present and the future. Nevertheless, time is a concentrated experience where the here and now is more of a deciding factor than a lengthy past and a distant future. The here and now reflects the past and determines the future. The past provides material for understanding previous roles. New roles, trying out roles for an alternative life, prepare for the future. Moreno stresses that in contrast to Aristotle's definition of dramatic talent as mimesis or imitation, psychodrama is the exact opposite of mimesis. He referred to imitations of traditional theatre as 'a cult of death and canned relics of the past' and, although Moreno was a great admirer of the renowned Russian dramatist Konstantin Stanislavsky, he thought that Stanislavsky's techniques could never produce more than reproductions of feelings. In fact, this was not true, but Moreno's statement might be explained by the fact that he himself had never practiced Stanislavsky's techniques.

Moreno takes similar exception to psychoanalysis because he thinks it emphasizes the importance of the past through reproduction and because psychoanalysis 'replaces the mystery of existence by a scheme of unreal transactions, promising self-realization to the patient, but actually depriving him of finding his essence in life itself' (1970c, p.24).

Here Moreno does not seem to stress the importance of a protagonist gaining spontaneous insight by acting out (reproducing) an event from the past. Instead, the 'unreal transactions' in psychoanalysis can be seen as similar to psychodramatic roles where the protagonist fights precisely to seize 'the mystery of existence' and to grasp what is essential in life. However, Moreno is correct in saying that psychodrama in itself is not mimicry, since it is an enactment that can never be reproduced or copied. An event from the past in one psychodrama will always be different in a second one, even though it is the same event. The threads of the past run together and merge into a point where time, as a dimension in itself, can be seen from different perspectives by the protagonist. This is why it is important to be able to look at one's whole life, but not in chronological order or by reliving it systematically. Time is an incessant movement back and forth from the past to the future, with the present as the dramatic point of intersection. In this sense, Moreno shows himself as a 'practical existentialist'. His aim is to grasp existence itself and to do something about it: 'The protagonist is being prepared for an encounter with himself' (1970a, p.xxii).

Moreno rejects the security of being anchored in a concept of time carefully divided into the 24 hours of a day, the days of a week and the months of a year. He encourages the protagonist to avoid clinging to the temporal, that which hinders the growth of all creativity. The concept of time, as it is used in a psychodramatic enactment, frees the protagonist from all of the oppressive concerns of daily life. Moreno offers to trade security within the concrete boundaries of time for the freedom to move beyond all boundaries – to childhood, old age, before birth and after death. Here, in that everything is possible, psychodrama borders on the theatre of the absurd. A man gives birth to children, a woman meets herself after her death. The strange thing is that the protagonist accepts this trade-off naturally, and often covetously, and enters into a new concept of time for as long as the psychodrama lasts.

Space

Mankind has separated time into concrete units to create order and security. For the same reasons, it fills space with objects. The mysterious expanse of space has always been frightening. Like the ostrich that hides its head in the sand in fear, human beings have tried to forget unpleasant things throughout history by creating a small world of familiar and cherished objects. They create their own private spaces and shield themselves from the unknown by establishing an especially intimate relationship with their objects. The material world becomes a refuge from anxiety for death and the unavoidable.

Space also consists of relations with things, from a distance. In the twentieth century, distances have decreased because of modern communication; our knowledge of the universe is steadily increasing. The heavens have become our greatest challenge. We have yet to ascertain whether there are human beings on other planets. Just as primitive man had concrete imaginary figures as superpowers, the film industry shows mystical and threatening creatures from outer space. People report seeing 'flying saucers' and experiencing senseless anxiety. These sensational stories do not desist until the phenomena are registered and explained. Today, sputniks circle the earth as if it were the most natural thing in the world and calculators have replaced the human brain for making minute calculations. Science corroborates the fact that boundaries are constantly pushing forward both in inner and outer space. Moreno's thoughts are not as foreign as they once were in the years between the world wars, when many called him a dreamer, an eccentric and an irrational person who repealed the concept of time while simultaneously expanding space without defining its limits.

Moreno compares man's fantasy journeys into inner space with the efforts of the astronauts and their unyielding desire to conquer new territories. In Moreno's terminology, the astronauts illustrate man as a psychonaut. The mind is the inner space. Therefore, the space of a psychodrama is important as a reflection of the protagonist's experience of reality. The protagonist is always asked to recreate the space as it exists in his memory. On this point, Moreno wholly agrees with Stanislavsky's concentration on emotional memory:

> The kind of memory that helps you reexperience the feelings you once had…is called emotional memory. Just as your visual memory can reconstruct an inner picture of one or another forgotten object, emotional memory can bring back feelings you have already experienced. It can seem as if they are beyond all memory until a sudden idea, thought or familiar object brings it all back in full strength (1937, p.168).

Details are recalled: the table was there, the window is here, outside is the old tree, the cat ate a bird. Emotional reminiscence is experienced subjectively. Details are displaced, action is concentrated. People in the space of reminiscence begin to live their own psychodramatic lives. Material things such as a chair, a table and a clock are no longer lifeless objects but inner images that help the memory and contribute to a complete experience. Things then acquire their own very special and important function. They participate in the drama. The protagonist exchanges roles with them as well, talking to himself as the 'old cupboard' where he had once heard a screaming voice.

Reality

Like his concept of roles, Moreno also works with three divisions of reality: the actual reality, reduced reality, and surplus reality. These correspond to what the author of this book calls objective, subjective and personal reality when explaining what is experienced when changing from one state of mind to another in a psychodrama.

Life or actual reality

Moreno refers to actual reality as the daily experience of our lives as it is at home, at work and in the daily trivialities of our social lives. Trivialities are not meant to imply that there are no problems, but as long as the conflicts can be solved through relatively realistic means, we are functioning in social roles, on a syntaxic level.

But, in the final analysis, we might not be all that skilled at playing our roles. Although relationships with important persons in our lives are incomplete or unsettled, we continue to play our roles inadequately because the thought of a showdown is associated with anxiety or a surplus of energy we do not seem to have. Changing the situation seems threatening. The outcome of a possible confrontation is uncertain, so one lets matters remain as they are. Relationships at the office or in the marriage continue as they were. As long as the crises can be avoided, everything remains in a state of status quo.

This is why Moreno believes in the necessity of a therapeutic framework to shed light on the actual reality of life. Simulating enables trying out new roles and gaining different perspectives of oneself. Absentee persons from actual reality are represented by auxiliary egos and the 'undigested' psychodramatic roles are tried out in ordinary and familiar situations. Trying out alternative reactions in various situations might lead to more suitable behaviour. The protagonist gains insight and knowledge by finding new and better answers to old and inappropriate stimuli without having to worry about the consequences. At worst, the protagonist might have to accept that his behaviour is not getting him anywhere, for example that it is undiplomatic and perhaps even insulting. Simulation is useful as preventive therapy because a failure is not experienced as strongly as it would be in real life. Within the framework of the drama, the situation can be reversed and turned upside down. Since an experience of actual reality is usually closest to the syntaxic level, without serious distortions of the experience, humour can also play a part. Simulation techniques and trying out new roles often release healthy peals of laughter. However, this is not the case when defence mechanisms are so much a part of the individual's reality that he cannot react in more than one firmly established way. In this case, the reality of life itself is experienced from within a rigid protective shell.

In this connection it is interesting to mention Professor Ulf Kragh's Defence Mechanism Test, which is, among other things, used in the air forces of many countries. Ulf Kragh is a professor at the University of Oslo. The method, perception genesis, is, in short, to present two pictures with a central figure (a hero or a figure one identifies with) and one picture with a peripheral figure in a threatening form. These are shown subliminally and repeatedly for extremely short durations of time with a tachistoscope. The time durations are gradually increased and, after seeing each picture, the subject of the experiment has to say and write down what he saw. The test's hypothesis is that subliminal threats lead to an underlying manifestation of anxiety and precognitive defence mechanisms (compare to Freud's terror – anxiety – defence against anxiety). By successively increasing the intensity of stimulus, the precognitive levels are activated in an organized sequence from earlier levels (subjective structures) to later levels (objective structures). The test reveals which precognitive level a certain structure appears in, and in which sequence, quite accurately. This makes it possible to ascertain how the subjects structure their surroundings and which solutions they come to in threatening situations.

The test's results show how persons restructure in different ways, from the first subjective (subliminal) levels to a more objective, realistic level of perception. In the test there are examples of people who cannot overcome their anxiety and who therefore adopt various kinds of defence mechanisms. The test can also point out a parallel in the genesis itself (the series with images of the threatening person) and the frequency of certain kinds of defence mechanisms. Subjects who protect themselves after long periods of exposure by restructuring the situation make maneouvers that can be traced back to Freud's classic defence mechanisms: Defence reaction, that is the threatening person is changed to a kind, sympathetic, protective figure, or identification with the aggressor, or aggression against the 'I', understood here as looking upon the identification figure as a sick, crying or dead person. In some instances total repression has been documented in that the subjects see a white spot or even nothing at all in the area of the picture where the threatening person was placed. Some even see the threatening figure as a face of stone! (Melanie Klein's hypothesis about persecutory anxiety in children in their deepest level of its psychic structure.)

Reduced reality, 'infra-reality'

Moreno's use of the concept of reduced reality, or 'infra-reality,' is especially associated with established social situations where the individuals are assigned roles within an explicit framework which defines them in a specific relationship to one another. Moreno's point of departure is the consultation room where the patient and doctor sit facing each other, limited by a subject-centered discussion and an interpretation. The doctor certainly has the advantage. He is the expert. The contact between the doctor and the patient hardly represents a genuine dialogue between two equals. It is more like an interview, a research session (where the doctor is the researcher), or a projective test (where the patient, not the doctor, is the one being exposed). There is no outlet for whatever might be really happening inside the patient. His most desperate thoughts, perhaps about suicide or escape, are experienced on a level of fantasy and he can only communicate mere fragments of the inner dialogue he experiences so strongly. Reality deteriorates and becomes incomprehensible and absurd because his thoughts contrast strongly to his actions. This could result in a paralyzing fear which intensifies the patient's picture of himself as the weak one.

There are many situations where the power between the respective parts is unequal: The accused who testifies in court, a child facing parents or teachers, an office worker in relation to a boss. The ability to act becomes paralyzed by overwhelming feelings that cannot find expression. Details become distorted; fists are clenched in powerlessness. A psychodrama attempts to free the individual from reduced reality and to give enough time to find adequate expression for his true feelings. Reduced reality differs from the author's subjective reality in that the protagonist has a choice. For instance, he can choose to leave the therapist's office. In the author's terminology, reduced reality is more like personal reality.

Surplus reality

In Moreno's terminology, one dimension that will always exist in any experience of reality is 'surplus reality'. Surplus reality is the invisible and abstract dimension that can change the course of an individual in a matter of seconds. It can be found in the unexpected and in the attempt to grasp meaning in what is unspoken. Many might prefer to call this fantasy but, in this context, fantasy is too transitory. Surplus reality is the individual's personal experience of a situation, with the best of intentions and in complete honesty. Surplus reality comprises both the protagonist, the stage and the actions. In the author's terminology, this is 'expanded reality'.

In the context of a psychodrama, surplus reality has many uses. The whole psychodramatic role in itself consists of surplus reality. As a method, it is used in role reversal. For example, the protagonist might be involved in a heated discussion with an auxiliary ego who represents an important person from real life. In order to understand the protagonist's experience of the auxiliary ego, the leader asks for a role reversal. The protagonist states what he thinks the other part represents. This then becomes the basis for the director's future strategy. The protagonist's way of acting cannot be understood until his personal experiences are understood. 'Surplus reality' makes it possible to perceive the inner world of the protagonist.

Cosmos

Classical antiquity struggled with the problem of cosmos. In Greek, it actually means 'world order'. Plato spoke of the cosmos when referring to an organized whole which was reflected in the city-state. Man's task was to create order and harmony in the city as well as in his inner life. Time was a cosmic dimension, literally referring to movement in the heavenly bodies and harmony in space. Augustine came to represent the opposite of Plato's view of cosmic space because he was interested mainly in the inner space of man, the space of the mind. Augustine also understood time as a human dimension rather than a phenomenon that actually existed in outer space.

In a psychodrama we recognize time as movement (Plato) as well as time as an inner dimension which is subjective and changeable. But rather than the ancient Greeks, Moreno's contemporaries, Sigmund Freud and Karl Marx, were the ones to inspire him to launch such an unusual, often highly personal, terminology. In opposition to Freud's viewpoint that everything in the world was summarized in the individual psyche, Moreno launched the concept 'cosmodynamic'. Turning to Marx, who viewed human beings as products of economic and social conditions, Moreno created the expression 'man as a social atom'.

Moreno maintains that human beings are cosmic creatures without any individual or social limitations. Cosmodynamic implies that mankind possesses a spiritual energy of unknown dimension in time and space. The outer and inner worlds are in intense and constant interaction. Moreno was a true believer in what he called 'a cosmic reality.' Therefore, he found it meaningless to discuss whether or not God existed. Man has the ability to create God in his own image, as seen in the embodiment of Jesus Christ. The most important event in modern religion was when God became replaced by an invisible, cosmic, super power by an individual whom the very poorest in spirit could understand.

Since time immemorial, many different religions have reflected man's deep desire to be born again. Persons with grave mental illness also appear to have an inner desire for salvation. To others, this desire seems like pure madness, but for the individual himself, it seems to have a purpose and to follow a certain course of progress. Anthropologist Gregory Bateson maintains that when a schizophrenic period has started, it is just as reliable as an initiation ceremony – working through a symbolic death to being born again.

> 'Once started, a schizophrenic episode will be as structured as an initiation ceremony – a death and a rebirth – which the individual is thrown into by his family, or coincidental circumstances, but which assumes a fixed course that is determined primarily by endogenous factors…this is merely the final and natural result of a total process. What needs to be explained is why so many who depart on this kind of a journey never return (Bateson 1970).'

R.D. Laing describes the psychotic state as a process of regression. A psychosis is an inner journey and a rebirth (neogenesis) involving an enriched and transfixed sense of 'being in one's self'. Bateson's viewpoint closely resembles R.D. Laing's explanation of schizophrenia as a strategy to maintain a certain form of life.

In Moreno's terminology, catharsis, embodiment and rebirth are closely connected. Moreno accentuates the Eastern interpretation of catharsis (active or primary), as opposed to the Greek (passive or secondary), because the Eastern world's meaning presupposes that man has actively redeemed himself (Grace, which is the opposite of this phenomenon, is more familiar in the West.) On a psychodramatic stage, embodiment occurs when a person takes part in symbolic power. God, or Christ, comes alive and communicates forgiveness or consolation. This too is an active function. If the protagonist needs forgiveness or consolation, he has to call upon the Saviour himself and enter into a dialogue with him.

In psychodrama, catharsis and embodiment lead to rebirth in the symbolic sense. In any form of therapy a successful therapeutic result is a rebirth, because the individual gains renewed strength and opportunities to act. The difference between psychodrama and other therapeutic methods is that psychodrama makes use of ritual actions and magic in its enactments. In this sense, the act of reliving an event is an imitation (mimesis). But since the enactment always occurs in the present and *in situ* (in Moreno's terminology, actually at the place where the thoughts are acted out at the moment), it is not reproducing but creating (Moreno would say anti-mimesis in status nascendi, the creative moment.) Christ becomes a fellow actor on the human stage, or even a comedian! ('Die Gottheit als Komödiant'). Moreno argues that since the image of God exists in all of humanity, he will also be able to form himself according to the conditions of every person: 'The image of God can take form and embodiment through every man – the epileptic, the schizophrenic, the prostitute, the poor and rejected… God is always within and among us, as he is for children. Instead of coming down from the skies, he comes in by the stage door' (1970c, p.22).

This conscious use of 'make believe' drama (Stanislavsky's 'as if') is nourished by man's natural desire for security. Magical wishful thinking has its primitive roots in us all. These roots reach as far into the past as to the 'lost paradise', the protection of mother's womb. By allowing the magical 'as if', the enactment becomes ritualistic. Embodiment becomes an action that leads to a new state of being. In Bulgaria, among the Turks in Bosnia, a birth ceremony is still practiced for the adoption of a child: 'A woman then takes a boy whom she plans to adopt and pushes him into her clothing so that he becomes wrapped in them. After this, everyone thinks of him as her real son and he inherits all his adoptive parents' property' (Frazer 1963, p.19). This description resembles a common practice on the psychodramatic stage. For example, a woman wanted to be born anew as a man. The symbolic birth was both a rebirth and an initiation. The therapeutic aspect here was the acceptance of the group (social recognition) and the person's ultimate acceptance of herself in her new gender.

In his views on embodiment and rebirth, Moreno is showing an extremely tolerant viewpoint of humanity. Prejudice within the group in terms of sacrilege or propriety is not given any room for expression. In a rebirth the drama is turned around and an ordinary man or woman takes part in a symbolic truth that has been granted to humans because they are cosmic beings. In Moreno's opinion, any therapeutic method that overlooks these extraordinary human resources is incomplete. His most important aim in a psychodrama is to replace human anxiety with the strength to explore his own universe and find his own meaning. Here we must see Moreno as a realist, since in these long journeys unlimited by time or space the objective is always to return to this world. Moreno offers an alternative to Laing's goal: the freedom to journey into the inner world. Laing maintains that this 'Metanoia sequence' (a fundamental change of mind or character) cannot be achieved within the individual's original family or in a (traditional) psychiatric clinic.

Laing proposes that a patient is not allowed to travel into the 'inner' but that he remains at a crossroads because the institutional world prevents a journey into madness. 'These people often become more removed from the extremely difficult and mystifying relationships within their families, and they are put into a situation which is at least as difficult and mystifying: the context of a psychiatric institution (Foudraine 1971, p.85).'

Transference, empathy and tele

The term 'transference' stems from psychoanalysis and describes the process that takes place when a patient begins to displace or transfer positive or negative feelings toward the analyst. In a psychoanalytical treatment, transference is an important therapeutic element since it facilitates uncovering latent conflicts from the past. However, transference is a complicated form of communication which occurs just as often in real life as in a therapeutic situation.

Sigmund Freud has the honour of 'discovering' transference and turning it into a psychoanalytic tool. He concluded that transference is an attitude that is rooted in childhood experiences. The patient fears the analyst's disapproval and punishment and resorts to manipulation to gain acceptance. He repeats old behaviour patterns, often pathetic rebellion against authority. In this sense, transference becomes an acting out technique used in an attempt to gain control.

But the classical psychoanalytic situation invited a disproportionate balance of power. Freud called negative transference 'resistance'. Freud himself was certainly an authoritarian figure but this was not his intention, in the negative meaning of the word. Also, the prevalent idea about raising children at the turn of the century was that a loving father was to guide and steer his children toward what he thought was best. This idea has led to traditions that have had negative consequences in treating patients because, in many cases, the patients have been deprived of their own sense of responsibility and autonomy.

Svein Haugsgjerd (1970) discusses a number of viewpoints which are also pertinent in Norway. Among other things, he focuses on traditional medical theory and the doctor's role which creates an 'idyll of security,' but which the doctor and the patient both know in their hearts is false because, in reality, the doctor rejects a patient's personal experience of the situation (pp.36–37). The controversial Dutch psychiatrist Jan Foudraine (1971) strongly criticizes the traditional role of the doctor who looks upon and treats a patient as an object.

Psychodrama is clearly distinct from the psychoanalytic model in that it does not allow any interpretations of transferences or countertransferences. Like Dasein Analysis, questions are not asked about why these transferences occur but, rather, why they do not occur – that is transferences and countertransferences are allowed to play themselves out without interrupting to help the patient understand his behaviour. Psychodrama uses transference as a tool by introducing auxiliary egos on the stage so that the protagonist can fight them there.

In Moreno's terminology, positive or negative transference is acting out, that is taking action and bringing all sorts of thoughts and impulses to life (in this case we are discussing guided acting out, since the rules of psychodrama forbid any form of physical violence.) The term 'acting out' is used comprehensively in modern literature (Lawrence and Weissman 1965) and covers a much greater field than Freud (1963b) originally intended.

Moreno places a therapeutic framework around all initiatives that stem from suppressed impulses and fantasies. Therefore, acting out is not only seen in terms of reproduced material (the past), it is also recognized as the necessary expression of an urgent present.

According to Moreno, countertransference has five main causes: unresolved personal problems in the auxiliary egos, protest against the psychodramatic director, poor portrayal of the roles assigned to the auxiliary egos, lack of faith in and negative attitude toward psychodrama and interpersonal conflicts influencing the therapeutic situation (1970a, p.xviii).

Since the primary rule in a psychodrama is that the protagonist is the leader, any countertransference will interfere with his sovereignty. Interpretations and projections from the group that are rooted in the needs of the group, conscious or subconscious, are not permitted. These group interpretations and projections are defined by the very descriptive term 'acting in', one which has a very different meaning in psychoanalysis. Rosen (1963), who introduced the term acting in, interprets it as a direct assault on the therapist, but one which is, in reality, addressed to another person:

> He (the therapist) might be certain that the behaviour was aimed at him...and say that he *played out* his impulse... But I still see that the therapist is wrong... I firmly maintain that the individual *played in* (acting in), he played in a dream that referred to an inner environment. (Lawrence and Weissman 1965, p.22)

In a psychodramatic context, a person in 'the inner environment' would be an 'undigested' role (a psychodramatic role). In terms of psychodrama, Rosen's example of acting in would be seen more as a 'transference disorder' where the auxiliary ego forgets that he is to be wholly at the disposition of the protagonist.

The expression 'transference disorder' (or 'parataxic distortion' in Sullivan's terminology), stems from the more recent orientation from the 1920s onward and reflects a changed viewpoint of the doctor as an omnipotent person. According to Sullivan's (1970) description of a psychiatric interview, after recognizing the presence of imaginary and irrational persons surrounding the patient – invisible in the consultation room – strategies were changed in order to achieve the required insight and personality change.

Changing from Freud's classical transference situation, viewing the patient's immediate need in the here and now illustrates psychodrama's surplus reality and its inclusion of the past, present and future: 'Transference disorders, whatever they may be, are also reactions to factors that are not only experienced within the analytical situation. The primary focus is on immediate disorders which include the therapist, because here and now experiences are seen as an influential part of personality change' (Wolstein 1964, p.17). Actually, the person whom the patient is struggling to understand (get under his control) is not the psychoanalyst. Therefore, the interpersonal situation is transferred onto a level of fantasy: 'In reality, the other person who arouses and receives a special form of communication with the patient, is not present in this dynamic interpersonal situation. It is in this sense that the distorted attitude is expressed in the personification of the analyst (ibid. p.18).'

From this perspective, the analyst is a psychodramatic figure (a role) and the therapeutic situation can be compared to a monodrama in which the patient and the doctor try out different acting out techniques (note auto-drama and monodrama in terminology). Carl Rogers (1949) takes the consequence of this fact by assigning the doctor and the patient roles as advisor and client. This is also a psychodramatic attitude: 'We have gradually come to place more emphasis on the client-focused aspect of the relationship, because the more fully the therapist is able to understand the client as the client understands himself, the more effective it seems to be' (p.86).

However, the most central concept in psychodrama is still empathy, in the sense of an awareness and understanding of the emotions and feelings of another person. The primary function of a double is to understand with feelings. Some persons are particularly gifted in this ability. They have what might be called an intelligence of feeling. Other persons find this difficult, while others cannot be used in this function at all. What this last group has in common is that their extremely rigid personalities result in their doubling becoming direct projections of their own emotional positions (acting-in).

Freud emphasizes that empathy, *Einfühlung*, seems to be especially diffi-cult for persons with definite narcissistic personalities. He calls attention to four particular types of narcissistic personalities whose love is based on their personal motives: what they are (themselves), what they once were, what they would like to be and persons who were once a part of themselves. The difference between identification and object-love, according to Freud, lies between what one subconsciously wants to be and what one would like to have. We often see this in psychodramas where married couples have trouble taking the other's role. Reproaches or 'warnings' are common techniques here. The desire to change the other person seems more important than understanding the other person. For that matter, spouses are poorly suited as doubles and should not participate in the same psychodrama until they have each been protagonists separately.

In a psychodrama we also make a careful distinction between identifica-tion and empathy. Identification in a psychodrama is a spontaneous tempo-rary fixation which often shows up as an attempt to free the protagonist from his conflict (acting in). On the other hand, empathy in doubles or leaders represents a spontaneous emotional empathy without searching for intellectual solutions. In terms of the helpers, empathy enables total reception of the protagonist's impulses.

In modern psychotherapy empathy is seen as a specific way of understanding another person's subjective experience. As defined by the American psychologist J.R. Dymond (1949), it is 'The imaginary transference of oneself to think, feel and act as the other part does, and in this way, to construct a world as he seems to' (pp.228–233). The German psychologist Theodor Lipps comes closest to an operational use of empathy in terms of its function in a psychodrama:

> An instinctive ability to feel one's way into the nature of objects of others (inanimate and animate), which is made possible through *imitation of their positions and movements.* "The science" of other's subjective experiences also builds on this ability to imitate. More concretely, it is a sensing of the kinesthetic impulses which spring from this physical imitation. (Dragnes 1967, p.41)

In the classic double situation as introduced by Moreno, a double feels his way into the protagonist's 'personal world' by assuming his positions and repeating his movements. By role reversal with inanimate objects such as a table or a typewriter, the protagonist receives 'moods' and 'messages' which seem to speak to entirely different sides of his psyche than the purely intellectual one.

Dymond's definition of empathy applies more to the more primitive doubling method, in which people simply go behind the protagonist and try to express immediate thoughts and feelings. Here, giving structure to the other's 'world' is more haphazard than in the traditional doubling technique (the 'hit and run' technique developed, particularly, by Elain Zachnov).

Empathy is also seen as something other than identification. It has a very special function in a psychodrama and is also separate from intuition, which, in this connection, is more of an immediate presentiment than direct empathy. Intuition is an extremely complicated concept which is kept separate from this relationship. It is closely akin to empathy but it also carries other implications (see Westcott 1968). During the interaction between the double and the protagonist, and between the director and the protagonist, empathy begins to approach what is called 'tele' in psychodramatic terms. This transference of thoughts and emotions between two senders and two receivers is what Moreno calls 'Zweifülung', as opposed to 'Einfülung' (empathy in English). Tele derives from the Greek and means 'far', or 'influence into distance': 'Like a telephone it has two ends, and facilitates two-way communication' (1970a, p.xi). From spontaneous empathy on the emotional level, tele can reach beyond the limits of what is physically comprehensible. We move into an area which, particularly in America, is being studied under the designation ESP (extra sensory perception). In a psychodramatic interaction, tele could be a form of thought telepathy, or perhaps it can be traced back to what C.G. Jung describes as the ability for pre-logical thought.

The stage – a tangible, physical place

The most fundamental connection between psychodrama and theatre is the use of a stage as a sanctuary for growth. The word theatre (in Greek, *teatron*) originally included the stage as well as the spectators' area. The stage and its surrounding area was an organic whole without any separation between the main dramatic characters and those who were pressed into the periphery. Everyone joined in the action. This setting functioned as a meeting-place for communication as well as religious and social interaction.

A circular orchestra (Greek: dance area) was pounded into the earth and an altar for a deity was placed in its centre, providing a mid-point for ceremonial processions. In the Archaic era of Greek theatre (ca. 750–550 BC) there was only one orchestra, but during the Classical era (ca. 550–450 BC) it became common to build a wall on the outskirts of the circle, a skene, behind which the actors could change their costumes and masks. Seating for the public was cut into the hillside and sunshine provided lighting. The Greek theatre reached its height in the Hellenistic era (ca. 450–100 BC). The public and the chorus were two different elements that interacted with the dramatic acting. The public still participated with cries and hoots and shouts of delight but in the Classical era it had already become the chorus' professional function to insert observations or protests. The chorus, placed down in the orchestra, represented the people – common man in joy and sorrow. The main characters, members of royalty, legendary figures and gods acted on the roof of what had originally been a wall but which eventually had an additional structure behind it. In this way man gradually raised himself to the level of the gods and their legendary equals. Then, when the chorus was discontinued, the drama unfolded directly between the actors and the public, between the scene and the auditorium. Over the years (as early as in Roman theatre), the scene was lowered to its current level so that the public could follow the action.

Moreno's classic psychodrama theatre is reminiscent of a Greek orchestra in that the stage is round or oval. An intermediate level leads up to the stage. The director makes conscious use of the height progression, from the floor to the intermediate stage and then to the stage itself, to prepare a protagonist.

When a protagonist is pointed out by the group, or has appointed himself and been given approval by the group and the director, a process representing increasing levels of experience is put into action. It might be important here to refer to Chapter 3, which describes the operational use of the concept of reality as it is experienced by the protagonist in a psychodrama. Of course, even as an ordinary floor, the stage can have all these functions.

Objectively, or statistically, everyone knows that a certain number of people drown each year. In a sense this is not a concern, because it is just the way life is. But the experience would become a subjective one after standing on-shore and hearing a person call out for help. In Moreno's fitting terminology, reality becomes 'reduced'. The outer world shrinks. One is faced with a compelling choice and still has time to think about it: should I run and get help or should I rescue the person single-handedly? This does not become a genuinely personal experience until the individual himself is out in the water, in the process of drowning. He is in the experience. This is a personal reality. Stories have been told about persons who experience their entire lives in a series of brief, fleeting pictures when they are drowning. The person does not return to objective reality until he has been brought ashore and given dry clothing and food.

A protagonist is chosen in objective reality, the structure and lighting of the room, the group members – concrete things. On the intermediate stage he feels separated from the group. Reality changes and becomes 'reduced'. He feels threatened by his surroundings and it is not unusual for a protagonist to make use of different defence mechanisms such as aggression, laughter or various other kinds of attempts to escape.

A common course of procedure is to allow the protagonist to 'think out loud' while walking around on the intermediate stage. Scattered comments describe discomfort or a misunderstood feeling of trying to make himself 'interesting'. Reality has become subjective, close and obtrusive. The level of experience that psychodrama aims to achieve, the protagonist's personal reality, is gradually formed while he is on the real stage. No longer does he think the group is composed of prying spectators. The group has also acquired a different function. Like the Greek chorus that represented the interests of the common people – the collective – the group members of the psychodrama cease to exist as individuals. The sum of the group's intensity and experience is placed at the disposition of the protagonist so that he can present his reality, just as the actors in a stage drama recreate the playwright's inner world according to the playwright's premises.

Moreno's psychodramatic theatre also has a balcony, on which figures from an outer sphere appear (psychodramatic roles on a symbolic level).

These are figures from dreams or persons who are dead, but who still exist in the twilight of memory where anxiety and remorse are lodged. Perhaps God is there, represented by Conscience or the Evil One, threatening punishment. The objective is to bring these more or less undefined figures onto the stage and into communication, just as the professional protagonists (the great tragic authors) in Greek theatre once campaigned against their gods in order to incorporate them into the human agenda and make them more accessible. This was accomplished by communicating with them carefully from a respectful distance (Aeschylus), then by entering into a dialogue with them (Sophocles), and finally bringing them to earth and putting these powers on an equal footing with humans (Euripides). The process that took about 120 years in the first theatrical arena in the Western world is one that today's protagonist is meant to go through within a few hours. All that is un-researched and un-finished has to be put under social control, often as a temporary experience of insight and mastery. Nevertheless, it is a start because the individual becomes engaged in his own life situation.

The Shakespearean stage of the late 1500s also had some similarities to the psychodrama theatre. As well as a balcony and a stage, which was slightly more than a semi-circle, there was an open, suggestive space where everything could take place in the world of fantasy. The action was projected from the inner mind. The stage was the empty space which was populated according to the commands of the director and where anything might happen in agreement with the audience and the actors. The psychodramatic stage can also be compared to the simultaneous scenes of the Middle Ages where the drama moves naturally from one setting to another through simple theatrical strategies – for example by describing the new scene.

Since all probability is abandoned in the Theatre of the Absurd, this genre also has its similarities to psychodrama. Memory and thought have no limitations in time and space. Here psychodramatic roles lead an independent life and are called forth according to the needs of the protagonist. If the enactment calls for it, each and every form of realism is abandoned. In this way, there is nothing comical about seeing God the Father descend from the balcony in a pair of blue jeans. The best description of a psychodrama might be that it is a combination of the realistic and the absurd. Even Jesus as a dramatic character – in Moreno's words, as an 'actor' – is an absurd figure. Johannes Slök discusses this in *Det Absurde Teater og Jesu Forkynnelse* (1963).

There is only one central point where psychodrama can be distinguished from theatre: there is no permanent script with a solution that has been predetermined. Even the formal structure of a psychodrama, with its warming-up, enactment and concluding phases, is quite similar to the traditional stage drama which has an exposition, action and conclusion. The action, whether in a psychodrama or a stage drama, requires an introduction and a presentation of the person and the problem. The action is played out accordingly and it results in a solution, a conclusion or a presentation of a universal question. Just as a theatrical production is not expected to present stock solutions, a protagonist's problem does not have to be solved at the end of the psychodrama. If this were so, it would result in banality. But often, small fragments flicker in the distance and provide hints of possible solutions.

In reconstructions of the protagonist's world, practical facilities are necessary, but there are no traditional stage decorations. However, tables, chairs, a couch, etc. are necessary. Additional stage props are seldom called for, unless an object is a kind of 'main character' in the drama. For example, in a psychodrama where the protagonist was a writer, a typewriter was such an invaluable part of the enactment that it had to be included. By reversing roles with the typewriter, the author rediscovered his desire and pleasure in his work. In another psychodrama a walking stick was so important that the protagonist remained motionless until he was able to hold one in his hand. Indeed, this was only a floor mop but it worked. When fantasy is in extreme need of something, even a pillow can serve as a mother's breast. On the other hand, one must be cautious about including too many everyday props, such as cups and coffee pots, in an enactment. They seldom bring any surplus reality. They are more inclined to hinder the enactment by allowing the protagonist to get caught up in unnecessary details.

However, music and other sounds, such as bird calls, banging effects, sirens, etc. can be extremely useful. Sounds have a direct effect on memory and facilitate changes in mood and atmosphere. When the required machinery is lacking, the group can be instructed to make the sounds. This is just as effective as the real thing.

The classical psychodrama theatre should have lighting equipment, even if it is very simple. Some directors prefer working without lighting on regular floor space, for example in a living room. It may be that they are not experienced in using lighting effects and theatrical equipment, so that it all seems too artificial. This intentional lack of reality has no appeal to some of the more diagnosis-oriented clinics. At one of the psychiatric wards in Aachen, Germany, where psychodrama is practised according to a more analytical model, they were not unwilling to change the atmosphere in a room but felt that using a stage was foreign to them. In these instances, psychodramas often seem rather flat and pale in comparison to those using professional lighting techniques.

Both of Moreno's psychodrama theatres, in New York and Beacon, had coloured lighting systems. At St Elisabeth's Hospital in Washington, D.C., which may have the world's best-equipped theatre with a carpeted stage and a complete lighting system, the light is consciously used as a means of reducing or increasing intensity. The theatre's director, James Enneis, who is now deceased, had his own theory about the use of light. He emphasized an atmosphere with blue light when a protagonist needed to concentrate. When necessary, and justifiable, red light was used to bring forth and strengthen an emotional experience. Green light was suited to provoking impulses when the experience was enacted on the irrational level, for example in hallucinations. At other times a warm, yellow light was softened or strengthened according to the circumstances. When a group has achieved a maximal feeling of safety, it is even possible, and often correct, to set the scene in virtual darkness. Of course, psychodramas can be produced in normal lighting but special lighting certainly distances both the protagonist and his co-actors from the many inhibitions associated with their everyday lives.

Moreno was the first to use the theatre in modern psychotherapy and to extend the individual's enactment possibilities both in the outer world and in the inner spaces of the mind. He was able to realize the dream of the writer and patient Antoin Artaud of 'a stage as a tangible, physical place that can reproduce the most secret perceptions of the mind'. Artaud, diagnosed as a schizophrenic but finally released from his tragic incarceration in a hospital by his friend J.P. Sartre, longed for the place where he could 'seize his thoughts in flight, hold them tightly, and allow him some idea of his own existence'. In an attempt to understand his own condition, Artaud writes:

> I am suffering from a dreadful disease of the spirit. My thoughts forsake me on each and every level. From the very basic, the thought itself, to its outer materialization in words. Words, sentences, inner thoughts, common reactions of intelligence: − I am constantly hunting for my intellectual existence. Therefore when I can seize a form, no matter how imperfect it is, I fixate on it for fear of losing the whole thought... I suffer from this, but accept it in the fear of not dying as a whole person. (Letter to J. Riviere in Artaud 1967, vol.I p.62)

CHAPTER 2

Techniques

We differentiate between the techniques used throughout the entire psychodrama and the additional methods or inserted scenes used by the director to intensify the drama or move it forward.

Apart from its exterior structure and separation into three main phases, there is no predetermined 'recipe' for a psychodrama. It can be compared to a dish composed of many ingredients. If the chef is asked to name them, he can run through a list of his raw materials. But the special talent of a skilled chef is the ability to prepare the dish to perfection, knowing which ingredients are complementary and how to combine them into a successful whole.

The director of a psychodrama works under similar conditions. He cannot simply stand there with an index card and divide the drama into its various parts, he must have an intuitive sense founded in deep knowledge and experience. Like the chef, he can be innovative but, in terms of seasoning and cooking times, he has to be aware of the outer limits. A bad psychodrama director is like a bad cook. They can each fall prey to the temptation to add too many extra finesses and end up with a result that dissatisfies, frustrates or even angers their clients.

More than a detached and scientific attitude, every psychodrama requires a director with a deep sense of empathy and ability to make quick decisions. Many surprises can turn up within a very short time. The very essence of a person's life can be presented within a few hours. However, if a psychodrama is seen as a method that is to be used over a longer period of time, for example those dealing with special problems such as repressed aggression, hysteria dysfunction, or appeasement behaviour tendencies, certain contours and repetitions can be studied more systematically. Relatively little work has been done in this area. Usually, a psychodrama is employed as an immediate solution for an individual in crisis.

Persons who know little about psychodrama often argue that it is dangerous, that it can be taken too far and be harmful for the protagonist. Naturally this is true if the dramas are in the hands of non-professionals. A psychodrama director must have completed a required course of study, had professional guidance and practised under the supervision of experienced professionals. In institutions, at least one experienced assistant who knows the various functions in a psychodrama should assist the director. In terms of psychiatric patients, psychodrama should only be practiced in co-operation with personnel who are familiar with the patients and work with them on the ward.

However, it can also be harmful not to go far enough in a psychodrama. If the protagonist is restrained or held back by an apprehensive director, there is more danger of psychological stress than there is when the protagonist is allowed to investigate his own needs freely. An incomplete psychodramatic enactment results in frustration. The degree of the frustration depends upon the extent of the protagonist's need to go into depth.

The third phase in the psychodrama, the sharing phase, is most critical in terms of the final result. The protagonist will feel vulnerable and exposed if the director is not in complete control and able to use the group as helpers and co-therapists. In a psychodrama one always works from the periphery toward the centre. Having been chosen from the group, after the enactment the protagonist should be returned to the group where everyone shares experiences without any interpretations. The fundamental perspective of the group must be one of tolerance of all that is human, no matter how idiosyncratic it may seem.

In addition, in terms of the psychodrama as it unfolds, a new phase should never be started until the previous one is finished and the director is satisfied that the next method is an appropriate follow up. This knowledge is based on instinct, but since no two situations are alike, the director will often have to extemporize (*auf dem Stegreif*) and move on the spur of the moment. This is where the director's special talents, those that are based on empathy and tele, can be put to work.

It is a good idea to separate techniques and additional methods into two categories. The first category can be used by any drama pedagogue or specialized therapist working from the modern principle that certain exercises can increase an individual's conscious sensory experience, spontaneity and security in interpersonal relationships. These are elementary exercises which can be learned by persons who have no special training in psychotherapy.

The second category is composed of more complex methods that the director uses to move the enactment forward and shed light on conflicts that the protagonist finds difficult to express. Psychodramatists have developed countless methods based on their own individual qualifications and preferences, for example some directors are particularly successful with hysterical women while others specialize in persons suffering from fear of authority. Whatever fundamental attitudes determine the particular interests of individual directors will not be discussed here. Ideally, a director should be interested in the entire spectrum of human needs.

The techniques and additional methods that are considered most important will be included here; essentially they are based on Dr Moreno's original studies. In practice, a technique will often be influenced by the director's personality. Therefore, the technique in itself might be used in a particular way that Moreno would not have recommended. This condition must be made because the way psychodrama is used as a therapeutic tool depends upon the person who is using it.

We differentiate between role-training, role-playing and improvisation. Although it is not a technique, we have also included role-perception since special exercises can help us study and become aware of how we perceive others (the other's role) and how we perceive our own role through others.

Role-training is going through exercises in simple social functions in order to perform them adequately in future situations. Role-playing involves interaction with others in prearranged situations. Role-perception determines attitudes in interaction with others while improvisation is an advanced form of dramatic technique requiring some knowledge that can be acquired through special methods of training. In this context, spontaneity training provides the most important foundation for the practical training of a psychodramatist.

Role-playing

The most comprehensive technique in a psychodrama is role-playing, but this is a strictly defined form of role playing which is rooted in the reality of the protagonist. A protagonist chooses a situation and selects auxiliary egos. The situation can be a very ordinary part of daily life, such as a discussion between the protagonist and a deputy partner. It can be an imaginary scene in the future or an event from the past.

Although the aim of role-playing is to portray the outer reality as precisely as possible, its content is influenced by the protagonist's inner reality as well as contributions from the auxiliary egos which add surplus reality to the scene. Many different variables are already in place. Primarily, these depend upon the motive of the protagonist, that is which aspects of his inner reality he is trying to elucidate. Further, they depend upon the kind of interaction that develops and whatever unexpected directions the drama might take. Positive and negative transference will influence the result and determine the drama's rhythm and sequence. When the drama unfolds on the non-verbal level, or through symbols, it is not confined by limitations of time and space. On the other hand, it can also become locked into a detailed argument over a kitchen table. Role-playing on many different levels is the most comprehensive element in a psychodrama and it can include reproducing old and ineffective role patterns to daring to step into new worlds and finding unimagined resources. Role-playing can vary from sociodramas, portraying persons in predefined mutual social relationships, to the theatre of the absurd, including dialogues between a protagonist and abstract beings or inanimate objects.

Role-playing has gradually become accepted clinical practice. When roles are assigned and scenes are recreated from a scene in daily life, one could call this cautious role-playing. The individuals are more or less playing their own roles in an attempt to portray situations in the light of their own attitudes and emotional reactions. But a great deal of unconscious material can turn up even in the most banal everyday situations. Therefore, the director must remain alert even during these times since role-playing can overstep its defined framework of cautious testing and bring material to light that requires a complete psychodrama.

In psychological terms, ordinary role playing tries to stay within realistic situations to enable observation of how persons make use of different sides of themselves to achieve their goals, for example these could be unconscious goals – such as in the self-torturing game. At best, role-playing is a process that helps familiarize an individual with himself and his own reactions.

Although nothing could be further from the truth, psychodrama is often mistaken for role-playing. In fact, I can go so far as to state categorically that the way role-playing is taught to drama and psychology students is far more dangerous than when it is practised by a person who has mastered the tools of psychodrama. When role-playing goes into depth, the persons involved are motivated into old patterns of behaviour, defence mechanisms designed for 'survival'. Afterwards, they are often uneasy, thinking they have exposed too much of themselves. This happens often, and often without any proper follow-up discussions. In the second phase of psychodramatic role-playing, 'reality' always belongs to the protagonist. When the auxiliary egos make use of their spontaneity in role-playing, it is only according to the instructions of the protagonist. The director makes certain that the drama unfolds within the protagonist's framework of experience. If the auxiliary egos' reactions conform to this framework, there can be many beneficial therapeutical results. In their interaction, the auxiliary egos are encouraged to play out their own feelings to take the sting out of their often offensive reactions in their roles as mother, father and other important figures in the life of the protagonist. Also, the auxiliary egos have no responsibility for the way they have played their roles.

Improvisation

In contrast to role-playing, improvisation flows more freely, without guidance. Nevertheless, the director can set out small 'traps' to release unconscious impulses. Since these can often result in unexpected kinds of behaviour, improvisation is often used as a warming-up procedure before starting a psychodrama, for example a director could divide the group into smaller groups and ask them to make 'photographs'. The theme could simply be a family portrait or any other photographic composition. The groups assume their positions in front of an imaginary camera and the process will initiate spontaneous dialogue. In improvisation the groups must not be given too much time to choose a theme or assign roles among themselves, otherwise the activity will be more like role-playing.

Improvisations are useful for releasing emotionally charged material that could be the starting point of a psychodrama. The following example shows how quickly an area of crisis can make itself visible.

A woman chose one of Edvard Munch's famous paintings from Åsgård-strand as 'her picture'. She was asked to place the persons in the picture, a man and a woman sitting together by the sea. As she placed herself in the woman's position, her first spontaneous comment turned up, addressed to the man who was to represent the man in the picture: 'The best thing about this place is the silence...(long pause). I don't have to say anything...(another pause while the woman seemed to be struggling to restrain her feelings). Because you never listen to me any more!' Within a few moments, Munch's erotic summer atmosphere became the setting for her personal drama of everyday life.

A director can also insert themes that he wants a group to focus on, without telling them beforehand. These themes might be aggression, submission or the need for self-assertion. The starting point can be relatively innocent but, as the outlines of the theme become more distinct, the director can call for a pause and increase the group's awareness of what the scene is showing.

Another way to use improvisation as a warm-up procedure before a psychodrama is to let some members of the group in on a plan and to keep the others from knowing about it. As an example, picture a man and a woman who are to present a marital scene where the atmosphere is friendly but also filled with disguised aggression. A third person, the 'child', is the central figure. How does the child react to this situation? Most probably, if the atmosphere parallels the one the person has, or has had, at home, the 'child' will use the same strategies that he uses in real life. The simulated scene has a mirror effect. It generates long spontaneous sequences and levels of dynamic action that rarely appear in the more static kind of role-playing. Improvisations of this kind will develop naturally into a full psychodrama.

In groups that are familiar with improvisation techniques there will often be requests for specific built-in conflicts. A woman might want to examine her home situation from the viewpoint of her child. While playing the role of her child, the woman will be surrounded by surplus reality, which will be coloured by the specific situation – in this case, one of camouflaged aggression beneath a pleasant façade in which problems are never discussed. The mother will experience the problems her child might be having in balancing between a mother and father who never speak their minds. The empathy that can be gained through this kind of simulated situation is similar to the empathy gained in role-reversal, a technique we will discuss later.

Role-training

As opposed to role-playing and improvisation, role-training is a separate programme designed for persons who need to rehearse very simple social functions. This might be learning to master an interview for a job or even just taking a bus, going to a coffee shop or the movies or visiting a mother-in-law. Persons who have lived in institutions often feel threatened by life outside the institution. Failure lurks on every corner 'out there' and so many daily things have to be learned before they can feel that they belong to the outside world.

Role-training involves a person going through the same action time and time again in order to function in a particular role in a specific social situation. This kind of training can be compared to an actor rehearsing his role day after day until he has mastered it and made it a natural part of the performance. In Moreno's terminology, actors who cannot incorporate certain parts of their roles into their personal psyches suffer from 'actor's neurosis'. The actor may be caught up in remnants of past roles and this may prevent experiencing deeper empathy in a new role. He makes use of his old successful tricks, just as we all use certain defence mechanisms that have been stored away. We all know some cocky, cynical or sarcastic individuals. These persons might all wish they could discard their 'roles' but they dare not for fear of rejection.

Regression resulting from severe psychological stress is also a form of role-playing. Very little is known about the inner workings of psychotics, but in their personal worlds of unknown components, being psychotic may be the only role they can master. Laing describes a false self-system as a way to *not be oneself*: 'The false self-system described here, exists as a complementary role to the "inner" self. It is occupied in maintaining its identity and freedom by being abstract, immaterial so that it is beyond comprehension, and can never be suppressed, captured and owned' (1960 p.94). Laing discusses the various ways of using self-systems (the schizoid personality, the hysterical, etc.). In a psychodrama it is easy to notice when a protagonist is trying to play a role that he does not feel at home in. He becomes alienated and expresses himself in extremely bizarre ways.

The American psychologist Thomas Szasz is also interested in the ways people conduct themselves when using various dramatic techniques. A patient tries to communicate something but his language is different from the one we are accustomed to (in Sullivan's terminology, this would be parataxic or a parataxic disorder), for example Szasz calls hysteria 'a patient's language of illness', and includes it in his 'proto-language' (compare to Sullivan's prototaxic stage). In the proto-language a patient communicates through body language as well as fragments of an inner dialogue. This is an important consideration in a psychodrama. The body has its own language which can be seen in underlinings when the patient is at a loss for words, such as physical posture, muscle cramps, general fatigue and tone of voice (see Beier 1966). It is these signals that provide the double with his most important information.

Therefore, in a psychodrama, role-training is the technique that requires the most careful attention. It is often used as the first necessary step in simple social training. Behaviourist Joseph Wolpe (1972) uses the expression 'psychodrama of behaviour' in the sense that it is a rehearsal of behaviour. This is an appropriate term for the painstaking approach tried within a fixed and limited situation toward patients who require gradual desensitization in terms of their fears (perhaps simply being able to sit at a table and eat with a knife and fork).

The following example of role-training has been taken from a hospital unit that was established for American veterans from the Vietnam War. In addition to psychological problems caused by the war, these patients were also plagued by problems of alcohol and drug abuse. There were 15 men in the group and they were all day patients, arriving in the morning and returning to their homes in the evening. The director was actually a surgeon (!) but he had also become a specialist in psychodrama. In addition, there were two women: Della, a social worker, and myself.

On this particular morning, Bill was unusually nervous and it was obvious that he had some immediate problems. It turned out that he had invited a woman out to a restaurant that evening and he now realized what a dreadful thing he had done. He panicked at the idea of entering the restaurant, finding a table and ordering from a menu. And then there was the problem of conversing with his date! Bill suffered from sudden anxiety attacks in unusual situations. Before the Vietnam War he had been a rather ordinary young man with a relatively normal relationship to women, that is he was neither homosexual, impotent nor particularly shy. Nor did he have any problems with drugs or alcohol before the war.

A table and two chairs were placed on the stage. Another patient was chosen to play the role of the waiter. He confidently placed a towel over his left arm and prepared to enter into his role. A second patient was assigned the role of head waiter, despite his protests that he had no idea of how to act. Della and Bill made their entrance.

It was easy to see that Bill was already miserable during this first dress rehearsal. The head waiter made an awkward attempt to approach the couple. Bill stared into space, while Della waited modestly in the background. The scene was played over again.

This time, the head waiter, having been instructed by more sophisticated members of the group, bowed and asked if they would like a table for two. Bill nodded affirmatively, said 'thank you', and was shown to an appointed table. As soon as the waiter arrived with the menu, Bill had another attack of panic. His eyes swelled visibly in horror at the sight of the menu (the old magazine that had been thrust into his hands). Della asked whether she could also have a menu. Someone found a crumpled newspaper. She made the comment that there was a great deal to choose from (ironically, there was a war picture on the front page). Bill expressed his pleasure at finding so many choices. Once again we started the scene from the beginning. By this time the head waiter had truly come into his own. Bill made certain that Della was seated before taking his seat (another piece of advice from the group). He was given a menu and he asked the waiter to bring one for Della. The waiter asked whether they would like some wine. 'No', answered Bill, 'beer'. This released a spontaneous reaction from the group: shouldn't you ask Della what she wants?

Indeed. Bill asked Della, and she wanted wine. After the group clued him in, he asked for a wine list. 'Food and beer and wine' appeared on the table. But, with that accomplishment, it was time to converse. Eventually Della broke the silence by commenting on his choice of such a pleasant restaurant (in contrast to the white walls and shabby curtains in our austere room). Bill agreed, it was nice. After a pause, Della asked whether he often came to this restaurant. 'No', Bill replied, blushing as he looked down at his large workman's hands, 'I am out of work'.

This was too much for the group. 'Don't give so much away about yourself. Lie! Say something nice. Charm her.'

It is amazing to experience how strongly the group identifies with the main person in role-training. It is as if they cannot stand even the smallest failure. In a sense, it reflects upon themselves.

Bill tried as well as he could to listen to his peers' cues. He was certainly motivated to learn. Beads of sweat were on his forehead and it was obvious that he was in agony. Finally, he remembered a movie he had seen and began to talk about it. Della was right with him. Conversation flowed for a while until Della asked what his hobbies were. 'Good God', Bill said, turning to the group, 'How can I tell her that I'm just trying to keep myself going from day to day by coming to the Veterans' Hospital?'

Della had purposefully changed the focus to his real situation. It could not be packed away in day-dreams and unrealistic flights of fantasy. It was obvious that Bill's real life did not include fancy restaurants. When the 'waiter' presented him with the bill, scratched out on a piece of toilet paper, Bill suddenly realized that there were some economic realities involved in inviting women to restaurants. Nevertheless, the scene was rehearsed time and again and Bill gradually became more secure in his role. Later, when he told us about a visit to a coffee shop with a woman who had come to be an important person in his life, we were all moved. At least he had not suffered defeat. Bill was encouraged and he felt better prepared to meet life 'out there'.

This situation, and similar ones such as an appointment with an employer, meeting a wife and family after a separation or just plain going shopping, are all important themes in role-training. No matter how elementary they may seem, in Moreno's words, they are still a rehearsal for life. To a person who shivers in anxiety outside a bakery before daring to go in and buy a loaf of bread, this is truly a question of survival – almost literally. The paradox is that a defeat is not experienced in proportion to the difficulty of the task. Indeed, the less the role demands, the greater is the feeling of failure when it is not mastered. For some, role-training has to be based on their youth. The 'youngest' example in this connection was an older man who could not make himself look women straight in their eyes. We traced back to his childhood memories until he, as a 'child', reached up to his mother's (auxiliary ego's) face and tried to turn it toward him so that he could see it. His mother had always been so busy doing other things that the child had grown accustomed to seeing her in profile, her ear and cheek. Training a person to look directly into the eyes of another can be a long, drawn-out process, even among those who have a high level of social functioning.

Role-training is a technique that aims to put the relationship between outer expectations and inner resources into balance. For many, role-training can require a long period of learning. It must never be forced.

In Bill's role-training we saw that he had to be helped step-by-step before his important date. Nevertheless, his sessions covered no more than a fragment of his world and cannot serve as any more than a practical illustration of the technique. Another example of role-training will show how a person can overplay his social role and that he has to learn to play down his behaviour. As a rule, these sessions can be quite pitiful and, rather than leading to successful interaction, they lead to intensive psychotherapy.

While the group was helping to increase Bill's feeling of security in his role as a suitor, the group members revealed their own needs for basic social training. Social situations had become totally foreign to them during their years of combat in Vietnam. Harry, in particular, felt impelled to exaggerate. This was clear in his scornful remarks about Bill's helplessness and how well he himself handled similar situations. Harry would have simply ordered eight drinks at once to save the waiter the trouble of running back and forth. Furthermore, he would have established his social status immediately by telling his date that he was the president of a large company.

It was Harry's turn to visit a restaurant. He swept in and asked for the best table while weaving in a comment about how the service could improve. He then ordered his eight drinks, which the 'waiter' balanced on an invisible tray. 'Put them on the table behind us so you won't be hovering around us all the time', said Harry – whose hands were visibly trembling. 'I'm embarrassed', I said, 'It looks like you're afraid you won't get enough to drink' (Harry had a severe alcohol problem). 'At least the waiter can see that I'm not afraid of ordering!' 'Do you really care what the waiter thinks about you?' 'No, why do you ask?' 'Well, it just looks like you do'.

Harry became very thoughtful. Then he donned his role of president of a large company in California. But he just didn't have the vocabulary of a president and, after a few stuttering attempts, the whole scene fell apart. Harry laid his head in his hands and began to cry. Gone was the restaurant, the head waiter and the waiter. Harry was alone with his problem. He had tried to keep up his game but his meagre resources just couldn't make the grade. All that was left was Harry, talking about his brother.

In his fantasy, Harry lived the life of his brother. But this brother was a figment of his imagination and had no place in objective reality. The 'brother' occupied all of Harry's life. It was he who was successful, he who was lucky in love. There was, as he said himself, 'nothing there that could have been me'. Harry would have fitted Laing's description of an extremely insecure person who uses all of his energy to maintain an existence, even if it is not his own, for fear of being wiped out of existence: 'The ontologically insecure person is occupied in preserving more than satisfying his needs; the mere circumstances of life threaten his low threshold of security' (1960, p.24).

Role-perception

Moreno's sociometry includes, among other things, how we evaluate and judge our fellow human beings and place them in one or another position in relation to ourselves. Sympathy, antipathy, and empathy are inter-human processes in which conscious and unconscious forces join to determine our behaviour and emotions and, thus, how we perform our roles in life (in terms of human interaction).

Role-perception is when we evaluate a person's outer criteria and associate them with social status. The 'letter' is a technique (an inserted scene in my terminology) which was developed by James Sachs (1974), a permanent member of the staff at the Moreno Institute in New York in the 1970s. Many persons see no more than the exterior and react at what the person 'stands for'. A fitting example might be the priest, who is God's representative on earth. Because of this, they want to keep him at a respectful distance. The words of the priest carry extra authority. Many find that projecting authority to doctors, the police, teachers, supreme court judges and others gives an inner sense of security. Idolizing film stars and royalty fills the need of dreaming about the pleasure of living as they do, enjoying success, money, honour and power. These objects of adulation are so revered that they are not even thought of as having normal human functions (children, and some adults, cannot even imagine a king having to use a toilet!).

On the other side of the coin, many persons suffer from not being allowed to 'be themselves'. We read about celebrities' breakdowns, often after many years of substance abuse. The conditions surrounding their lives have forced them into sterotypical roles that thwart their natural impulsivity and spontaneity. In these cases a breakdown might initiate recapturing a lost life. In Laing's words: 'Lose your mind and come to your senses'.

It is even more dangerous when very young children are not allowed to investigate their surroundings: 'Mummy's little boy has always been so good'. 'The visible behaviour that expresses a false self often seems to be completely normal. We see a model child, a perfect husband, an industrious worker. This facade however becomes more and more stereotypical and eventually develops peculiar characteristics' (Laing 1960, p.99).

In a psychodrama one often sees persons who use their routine reactions exclusively. Their contact with an immediate creative fantasy seems to be permanently blocked. Actors who desperately try to stay on top of their careers, or mediocre actors who have never really been creative but only copied character types, can also come to a complete standstill. Their old tricks have gone stale and their lack of an inner life is obvious. The result is a cruel one: there are no roles for them anymore because they cannot interact with their fellow actors and therefore cannot give meaning to their roles.

Even in our daily lives it is useful to be aware of the fact that we are often guided by the way we perceive others and that we react from our own inner needs. We choose some people as friends and discount, or avoid, others. Our positive and negative needs create a response in the other person, who then unmasks himself in the resulting interaction. The starting point of role perception is our own state of mind.

For example, we might see a policeman and confidently approach him to ask for directions. The uniform tells us that he will not steal our money or commit a violent crime. But, in the case of a criminal on the loose, the sight of the same policeman will trigger panic and flight. If the policeman approached this man and asked him a question, the fugitive might react unexpectedly, instinctively attacking him in self-defence.

When mass demonstrations are getting out of control and becoming violent, just the sight of a uniform can incite a desire to fight. Especially in political demonstrations, the uniform is a symbol of oppression, often awakening restrained aggression. The demonstrators fight on behalf of, for example, oppressed groups or races and allow their anger to come to the surface, even though the anger might be caused by something totally different. Occasionally a policeman can lose his self-control and allow his private motives to take over. He sees his opponents as a threat, either to his own life or to everything he stands for. In this way he can justify his aggression and attack on the demonstrators. In reality, he might have been angry because he had not been given a promotion.

Psychodrama has been used by a number of police forces in the United States. An insurance company that had been studying statistics on personal injuries to policemen initiated the idea. The statistics showed that an overwhelming number of deaths and crippling accidents had occurred when the police were intervening in a family crisis. It was obvious that the police force would be wise to look into other methods for making arrests, methods that would help them understand and deal with persons in distress. Often, the very sight of a police uniform caused people to go berserk.

During their psychodramatic training, the police were able to see some aspects of their behaviour that they had been totally unaware of. Members of the police force have all been educated for performing specific functions and, in particular, they are trained to be alert and to maintain keen observational skills. When a policeman is tracking down a criminal, he has to learn about the person's pattern of behaviour while he is also gathering incriminating evidence. In a profession that places so much emphasis on observing others, it is easy to lose track of how one's own behaviour appears to others. There is a good deal of truth in an inmate's remark that he could smell a cop a mile away.

In a mixed group of policemen and prisoners, a friendly officer tried to win the inmate's confidence. For a long time it seemed that his position as a policeman was all that was working against him, until one of the inmates exclaimed: 'Just look at how you walk through that doorway!' The police officer had no idea of how he walked through the door and asked the inmate to show him what it looked like. The demonstration met with mumbles of agreement from the other inmates. One of them added: 'The way you walk is just like the way you push us around'.

Role-perception also concerns how we see ourselves in certain situations. Each profession requires a special role-performance. It is important to be able to understand what the role demands and to anticipate them. Inadequate role-perception can easily lead to misunderstandings. One behaves 'incorrectly' and comes up with the wrong answers. Correct role-performance implies that the expectations tied to the role are being fulfilled.

It is just as wrong when an exaggerated role-perception, being locked into the outer façade of the role, conflicts with the degree of ability to perform the role. This can lead to being incapable of action. The person has set such high goals for himself that he is unable to do anything at all. An illustration of a weak connection between the outer façade and role performance (mask versus performance) is a woman who is totally dependent upon her looks as she sees them in her mirror and who loses her self-control when her hairdo, make-up or clothing are spoiled.

Stuttering and exhibitionism can be examples of behaviour that turn up when the perception of the role is out of step with role-performance. Stuttering is a form of inhibited behaviour, while exhibitionism is a form of exaggerated behaviour, a sort of ludicrous distortion. In both of these instances, the behaviour can be the result of 'over-rehearsing' without trying to pick one's way forward on a trial and error basis in concrete situations. When this is called stage fright, it is often a question of over-rehearsal in which the individual expects too much of himself and overestimates his acting ability. Stage fright or insecurity can also be the results of outside expectations, for example from parents who have a special image of how their child should be – that is, the model child. American psychologist Alfred Baldwin (1960) has proven the relationship between exhibitionism and speech errors. Children with exhibitionist tendencies who are overly self-conscious and unduly concerned about their effect on others are more inclined to develop speech defects than other children.

Sullivan's 'power drive', the desire to dominate or manipulate others, is one of the unconscious motives in role-perception. Sullivan considers this the result of an underlying feeling of inferiority which results in thinking of other people as threatening, whether or not this is realistic. The reaction is an exaggerated need for self-assertion, or even a desire to hurt others. This tendency is often seen in psychodramas in the interaction between a protagonist and auxiliary egos who are representing parents or spouses.

The fact that our perceptions of people are different and that the importance we give them is based on subtle interpretations shows itself in our reactions in many inter-personal situations, for example we approach another person either with trust or suspicion. When a protagonist is asked to describe an imaginary person, he describes how this person appears to his inner eye as well as how the person's proximity affects him. Both of these factors determine the attitude he will have in terms of the auxiliary ego that is called in from the group. Even the choice of the auxiliary ego can often provide information about the motives or strategies of the protagonist. The choice of a specific auxiliary ego is seldom coincidental.

Role-reversal

Role-reversal is a technique used when trying to gain some idea of what one person thinks another person is saying, representing, thinking – in fact, every shading of a person's possible fantasies in terms of trust, apprehension, compliance or dislike of another person. Role-reversal uncovers what Moreno calls surplus reality, that is the proportion of an individual's personal experience that is transferred to another person. In reality, this is a kind of spontaneous projection which the protagonist must either identify with or reject.

In many ways, role-reversal is the opposite of transference. In transference, one person's feelings flow toward another. The protagonist reacts as if the deputy person really is, for example, the stern father. In role-reversal, the protagonist is forced to experience himself in the other person's role and to repeat the words he has attributed to the other person. In this way, the protagonist becomes the performing judge of the situation and is able to intellectually hear and feel how the lines are composed and their emotional content.

In practical terms, role-reversal is performed by having person A change place, literally and figuratively, with person B. For example, A and B might be playing a scene in which A is the protagonist (a son) and B is an auxiliary ego (a father). The son tries to explain to his father why he wants to move away from home and it turns into a heated scene where the son suddenly bursts out with the vital statement: 'When you win, I'm the loser!'

At this critical point, the director breaks in and places the son in the chair of the father. The auxiliary ego (the father) repeats the critical sentence and thereby gives the protagonist the opportunity to react as if he himself were the father. In other words, the son answers the way he thinks his father would answer. The auxiliary ego, in the role of the boy, repeats: 'When you win, I'm the loser'. The son, in the role of the father, replies: 'Yes, you have been a disappointment both in school and when you've been working in my store. I really expected more of you'. The son's fantasies about his role as a loser and his father's opinion of him show up in this dialogue.

Here it makes no difference whether or not the fantasies correspond to objective reality. The protagonist always has the right to his 'truth', no matter how unreasonable it is. This is the only way one can grasp momentary images of a personal reality. It gives important clues to hidden conflicts that can then be worked out in new scenes. Many tragic misunderstandings can be resolved.

In a therapeutic community for drug addicts in New York (Daytop), John, a 16-year-old, was going to have an imaginary conversation with his father. He sat on his chair and mumbled incoherently. It was obvious that he was having trouble expressing the feelings that were surging up inside him. He just couldn't speak. The director asked John to stand up and imagine that he was his own father. John rose from the chair, but with drooping posture and arms hanging limply at his side. The director walked right up to John and asked: 'What does your father say?' John closed his eyes and struggled to keep back his tears. Finally, he broke out and shouted: 'He says nothing! He never says anything! He doesn't listen to what I try to say! He's a bastard, a damn bastard!'

In another group, John's father was one of a group of parents of young drug addicts. He was elderly and hard of hearing, a fact which he had never dared to tell his son. In his words: 'I was so old when he was born and I think he's ashamed of me. Furthermore, *he speaks so indistinctly*'. This marked the end of a deep misunderstanding that had existed for years. The two men had kept themselves in separate rooms and nursed their grudges: John's belief that his father didn't care about him and the father's feeling of shame about his poor hearing and that his son was embarrassed about how old he was. The confrontation was both a necessity and a release. Here we did not use an auxiliary ego. In some cases, an absent person can exist as vividly as an auxiliary ego in the imagination of the protagonist. We will go into more detail about this technique when we discuss 'the empty chair' (see p.122).

Spontaneity training

Human beings all need a certain amount of training in how best to make use of themselves, how to develop the ability to change patterns of reaction and how to become more intellectually and emotionally sensitive in interaction with others. Our daily communication is composed of clichés and meaningless conversation, both of which are influenced by preconceived ideas. Often we communicate through undertones based on what we think other people think of us. Banalities also play an important part in our cultural tradition in that they help us to hide feelings and avoid exposing ourselves to ridicule. This is often seen after a psychodrama when members of the group describe their feelings and reactions. Either they have trouble saying anything at all or their comments sound like they have been rehearsed.

There are many kinds of spontaneity training. In contrast to improvisations on predetermined themes, spontaneity training is full of unexpected surprises. The following is an example from a training session. The director asks: 'Who are you? Don't give your real name'. 'Line Olsen', says Anne Abrahamsen. 'Where do you live?' Line Olsen, who lives in Oslo, replies: 'Bergen'. 'What kind of job do you have?' Line Olsen, who is a social worker, replies: 'A saleswoman'. The director chooses a man from the group and says: 'Here is your fiancée and you are about to break your engagement. You are sitting on a bench in an Oslo park. Take it from there. You can carry on for as long as you wish'.

This kind of spontaneous improvisation can release many unexpected reactions, often absurd and funny ones. At other times they can create deep emotional outbursts.

An effective way to generate more depth into the scene is to 'freeze' the situation. After an emotionally laden statement, the director asks everyone to freeze in their positions. Each member of the group is asked for a spontaneous expression of what he is feeling. This can initiate a discussion about what happened in the improvisation. Or, in another variation, the director can ask the group to give a spontaneous glimpse of a fantasy picture from the past. The 'saleswoman' remembers an episode from her childhood. If she has a vivid imagination, we might be led to a backyard bakery, a shoemaker or an old lady with a parrot. Other members of the group are brought into the improvisation and they bring the baker, the shoemaker and the old lady to life.

Often, a retrospective look at the past can assume very private dimensions. Memory assumes a life of its own and strives to remember more clearly, to understand that which is not understood. 'Flash-frozen' situations, where persons are asked to look forward, will often raise an issue that needs to be resolved.

Another form of spontaneity training is to give two or more persons conflicting instructions without their knowing it. For example, Per is asked to tell Beathe that he has fallen in love with someone else while Beathe is instructed to tell Per that she is expecting his child. The director has Per and Beathe enter the scene from either side of the stage. The situation has been defined, but how will it be resolved?

Moreno constructed spontaneity training as a test which he would record on a tape or video. The duration of the session is registered and points are given for the answers on the strength of their originality.

The person giving the test has chosen a specific subject and everyone is presented with the same opening lines. The point is to answer as quickly as possible and to keep a dialogue in progress for as long as possible. The students enter one by one. The first one is alone in the room, but when he has finished, that is, has no more to say, he takes a spot reserved for the audience and waits to hear how the others do in the test. When everyone has had a turn, the group discusses the different reactions and how the situation could have been settled from other perspectives with more precision and innovation instead of using the time-honoured clichés that so often appear in language. This is not a pleasant test! It requires a certain level of achievement and does not really promote spontaneity. With training it becomes easier. Spontaneity training is a highly effective way to break down defence mechanisms and build up a sense of security within a group. An exercise which is very provocative at first is to instruct the group to split into pairs and ask one another: 'Who are you?' The objective here is to give honest answers and also to keep talking for as long as possible.

The following is an example of how to continue with this exercise after
it has been going on for some time and the most usual answers have been
given: 'Who are you?' 'A person seeking new experiences.' 'Who are you?'
'A person who is afraid of new experiences.' 'Who are you?' 'A person who
wants you to stop questioning me.' 'Who are you?' 'A person who doesn't
dare ask others for help.'

Needless to say, the group members learn more about each other this way
than they would in ordinary conversation. After a while they change partners
until everyone in the group has met in this way. Usually the spontaneity and
honesty is much more genuine at the end of this training than it was at the
beginning.

Spontaneity training is especially important in terms of being a good
auxiliary ego. It sharpens the perception of nuances in the 'opponent' and is
a good exercise in verbal training. It is, of course, also important for the
double to train his spontaneity and flexibility, but the true challenge is the
double's ability to understand emotions with empathy and intuitive understanding.

A very good exercise for training a double's spontaneity is to ask the
group members to arrange themselves in pairs. One of the pair says his name
and the other part says his name in exactly the same tone of voice, for
example, Peter says his name in anger and Mary responds with her name in
exactly the same tone of voice. The second part of the exercise is when Linda
and Andreas 'double' each of their partners. Peter still says his name in an
angry tone and Andreas expresses the feeling in words: 'What got into you?'
Mary's task is to answer this outburst by saying her name in a tone of voice
that gives Linda a chance to express feelings in words, for example 'Don't
talk to me that way!' The exercise progresses in the following dialogue: Peter
(angrily): 'Peter!' Andreas (the double): 'What got into you?' Mary (repeating
Peter's inflection): 'Mary!' Linda (the double): 'Don't talk to me that way!'
This is the start of an interaction that will vary according to the inflection
and emotional content of the first pair, who still only state their names. Using
many doubles will add extra nuances to the interaction. This exercise requires
deep concentration and respect for the person that is being doubled.

In his self-made terminology, Moreno calls what happens during spontaneity training 'creaturgy', in contrast to 'dramaturgy', which refers to the
rules for composing a formal theatrical text. Creaturgy is Moreno's term for
the playful and creative person at work.

CHAPTER 3

Additional Methods

The necessity of warming up the group

The warming-up stage itself is an additional method, or composed of many different additional methods. These can either take little time or become lengthy and they are used by the director to initiate a process, ease pressure within the group and create an atmosphere of warmth.

Some directors may also need to warm up and spend some time talking about a previous psychodrama. In a group that meets regularly this might be a time to discuss problems from other meetings that had not been resolved. Gradually, attention is shifted to focus on the individual group members. This method is called an unguided group discussion.

The association technique is closely related to the above method. The director tosses out a word and asks the group to come with its associations with the word. He might also listen to the group members as they enter the room and seize a chance remark to start a process of discussion among the persons involved.

The theme-related method is not far removed from the association technique. Something has happened and the director has an opportunity to bring up this concrete event or subject. If it is a tangible theme, a protagonist usually appears right away. This method is especially suited for psychiatric wards and helps to prevent pent-up emotions breaking out in connection with other patients. It is the privilege of the protagonist to try out his viewpoint. He has the floor and this allows him an opportunity to present his unqualified version of the subject. If the theme is of a more general character, the director concentrates on any possible frustrations in the group. In this case the person who shows most emotional involvement will become the protagonist, most likely someone who is concerned about a particular problem resulting from something he either did or neglected to do. Sometimes a conflict is triggered by a group member's negative comment when the person the comment was meant for responds. This is especially common within aggressive groups in an institutional environment.

The warming-up stage can also be used as task-oriented training, with the members working in groups of two or more. The task or exercise will then be seen as an inserted scene that can be included in the psychodrama at a later point to intensify the experience of the protagonist.

An efficient method for testing the mood of the group is to pair off the members and to ask them to separate from the group and ask one another the question: 'How do you feel about yourself today?' When the partners have become familiar with each other, positive and negative reactions quickly evolve. When the director is satisfied that the mood is sufficiently heated, he will gather the group in a circle to discuss their experiences. Although the pairing off was coincidental, latent conflicts will turn up and persons with unresolved conflicts will have a chance for direct communication.

Of course, there is a risk of releasing all sorts of conflicts that often result in rather unexpected reactions. When this happens it is the responsibility of the group to decide which conflicts or problems are the most important. The director can only use his authority to choose a protagonist in very special situations, for example, when he knows that one group member has a more critical need than the others. This is a delicate problem since it is a matter of opinion. The ideal situation here is for the person who has a specific problem to inform the director before the session so that the director can prepare a strategy, such as focusing the warming-up stage on that particular problem. A precondition for a successful psychodrama is that the protagonist is supported by the group.

An effective task-oriented activity here could be 'The Unwritten Letter'. The 'letter' is a technique (an inserted scene in my terminology) which was developed by James Sachs (1974), a permanent member of the staff at the Moreno Institute in New York in the 1970s. The person with an immediate problem is always more than willing to get right to work. A letter, which of course has not been written, will be 'read' to the group. In this way the individual can address the group or a specific person directly. Should the person who is reading the 'letter' have weak verbal skills, the success of this activity will be affected. A less concrete method of approach would then be suitable, such as having the group members work in pairs, showing one another an imaginary photograph that has special meaning to them. When the director already knows which person needs special attention, he can show particular interest in this person's 'photograph'. Often, when the individual is in a high state of anxiety, his imaginary picture will be quite uninteresting. It is often difficult to capture the group's interest with such a modest little picture and the director's own imaginative skills will be put to a hard test.

A group of twelve persons met regularly to study the use of psychodrama as a therapeutic tool. The group considered one of its members as a strong and self-assured person to whom everyone could turn in any situation. This individual also had a highly-developed sense of moral values; he was a dutiful individual who could not imagine making a mistake, and who may have rarely done so. Therefore, the group assumed that he could fill any possible role from father confessor to scapegoat.

His 'photograph' was a field of clover, bluebells and daisies. The group was not very interested in this picture but the director, knowing that the individual was tired of being everyone's sounding board, paused at this idyllic summer landscape. He had already intimated that he wanted to withdraw as the protagonist and continue in the role of a loser. In this situation a director must act with restraint and simply guide the individual toward an imaginary crossroad where he can decide either to step up to the stage or remain in the group.

The director asked for the man's associations with the picture, but they were only pretty banalities about the fragrance of summer and a fishing trip. Then the director asked him to project a person into the picture. To everyone's surprise, he described a little boy in a sailor's suit standing beside a little girl with long braids wearing patent leather sandals. When asked to reverse roles with the two children in the picture, the man saw only the girl. An attempted dialogue between the children was a failure since the boy had nothing to say. The director then asked the man, a strong, able-bodied person, to reverse roles with the girl. At this point the man finally came into contact with his feelings. A psychodrama unfolded about an adult man's longing to escape from his image as a little boy in a sailor's suit who was never allowed to cry, how jealous he was of his sister, his feelings of aggression toward his wife and his frustration with the world in general. This outburst of deep human need from such an authoritarian figure changed the whole atmosphere of the group.

The twelve additional methods that follow have been selected from a long list of possible choices. I think they are the most representative and, in my personal experience, they have been the most effective. With the exception of the 'guided daydream', they can all be traced back to Moreno's work. After many years of experience in psychodrama I have gradually placed more emphasis on purely theatrical tools, that is, inserting scenes in the middle of a psychodrama to intensify its content. This seems to heighten the interest and enthusiasm of the group.

The mother/father model and what I refer to as 'psychological so-ciometry' are both my own contributions. In addition, I have included a section about my use of chackras in a conscious effort to evoke different states of mind coming from energy systems in the body.

Soliloquy

A soliloquy can help the protagonist give spontaneous expression to his feelings while also informing the group about his emotions. As an additional method, the soliloquy has a specific function at the beginning of a psycho-drama.

In a classic psychodrama, after a protagonist has been chosen and the situation is more or less defined in terms of problem, theme and conflict, the protagonist is usually instructed to move around on the steps (an intermediate level) leading to the stage before going onto the stage itself. The protagonist has left objective reality. The symbolic introduction has been made. He has a subjective plan of defence when he is on the intermediate level of the steps. We call this intermediate stage the subjective or parataxic level (*para* means next to or above; the protagonist, in a sense, is next to himself). Today a psychodramatic stage is seldom equipped with steps, but marking off a section of the floor will be just as effective.

Subjective reality is met with resistance. Some protagonists become aggressive while others literally arch their backs, constricting their muscles and vocal chords. A protagonist in this state is strongly dependent on having the director or co-therapist at his side for support.

The following is an illustration of a soliloquy with a double – called support doubling when the director stands behind the protagonist and helps him with his lines. In contrast to support doubling, provocation doubling is when the director purposefully challenges the protagonist. The intention is to strengthen the protagonist's engagement in the drama by forcing him to defend himself or explain himself more clearly. Provocation doubling should never be done without the permission of the protagonist. Anyone who wants to double contacts the director and then asks the protagonist. Protagonist: 'When I came into this room, I decided not to utter a single word. And (pointing toward a woman in the group) why did I make this decision? That woman in the red dress said something about daring to face the truth. Somehow, it made me angry. She reminds me of my sister. No one has a monopoly on the truth!'

The director has been given a good clue for a starting point. Without careful help from the director at this point, the protagonist would probably become silent because he is clearly ambivalent about becoming involved.

The director assumes the position of a double behind the protagonist. He has two good words to work from: truth and monopoly. Director: 'The truth is, in reality, that I do not want to know the truth (provocation doubling). That's why I decided not to say a single word. I am always afraid I'll slip up...' Protagonist: 'That's right. I always say too much and it leads to misunderstandings, explanations and arguments'. Director: 'I'm not on very good terms with my sister...' Protagonist: 'She's not all that bad even though she drives me crazy'. Director: 'Yes, she always takes the other person's side...' Protagonist: 'I agree. It's Father who's the worst one. Father always wanted to monopolize the truth'.

By now the protagonist is deeply involved and has forgotten his 'public'. The director asks if he has anything special on his mind. Once again, as in all psychodramas, it is important to move from a simple conflict to a more complicated one, from the periphery to the core. Like a playwright's monologue, a soliloquy serves to give information to the audience and the director.

It is the director's job to expand upon the protagonist's associations. Taking the soliloquy a step further, it can also be helpful for the director to move back and forth from standing behind the protagonist to facing him. While doing this, he should make it clear that this is intentional provocation. The result is a form of Bertolt Brecht's *Verfremdungseffekt* (distancing effect), which aims to focus on an inner conflict by talking about it and giving it a more graphic form. This can be an awakening experience for the protagonist, who then becomes more deeply involved and starts a dialogue with the director (role playing) or continues with the double. After this it is time to go right into the enactment stage.

Therapeutic soliloquy

When the protagonist is 'warmed up', it is time to play the first scene of the psychodrama. The director asks the protagonist to explain what is on his mind in detail. This description should be as clear and graphic as possible, both for the group and to activate the protagonist's memory.

If the first scene has got off to a shaky start, possibly because it burdens the protagonist more than was anticipated, Moreno's therapeutic soliloquy might help it along. This kind of soliloquy is similar to the sideline comments of theatrical plays from past eras. In a classic farce it seems contrived and comical but on a psychodramatic stage its relation to something painful cannot avoid making an impression. In a therapeutic soliloquy the protagonist speaks while turned away from the group and any of the drama's auxiliary egos.

During a therapeutic soliloquy the atmosphere of the psychodrama can be compared to a seance where the protagonist is the medium. Words, which are so all-important, are hard to find. The director's task is to help the protagonist speak. In a way, this is like a secret speech. The protagonist chooses who will be allowed to hear what he is saying. If the protagonist is burdened by an extremely personal 'truth' which he wants to keep from some people and share with others, the director will have to use his insight to determine which members the protagonist truly wants to involve and to help him say so. This can be done by asking, guessing, pretending it is a game – helping the protagonist so that he, like a child, can join in and say 'It's okay for father to hear it, but not mother!'

The protagonist is asked to find a mother and father in the group who will assume the roles of auxiliary egos. As a rule, therapeutic soliloquies are necessary when the psychodrama is dealing with events in the protagonist's past life that have long been suppressed. But what about the 'mother' who is not meant to hear the secret? The woman who was chosen from the group is only a substitute for the real mother, so there is no reason to ask her to leave the room. She is simply asked to cover her ears. In this way, although she hears nothing, she represents surplus reality and can be an invaluable influence on what the protagonist says. This is just one more example of how simply the psychodramatic stage can make use of symbols. We can assume that on a deeper level, the mother is the cause or contributing factor to the conflict with the father. A therapeutic soliloquy is an excellent source of reference for the person who will act as a double.

The director can also make side comments to the group when he wants to point out an important detail. Here he can turn his back to the protagonist to establish the fact that in this case he is not doubling.

The therapeutic soliloquy is an important additional method, especially when working through deep dramas that might have a deep effect on inner conflicts.

The distorted mirror

When a psychodrama has either halted or raced to its start, depending on the engagement of the protagonist and the director's ability to find suitable angles of approach, sometimes it has to be interrupted in order to bring new characters into the drama. The protagonist identifies them and he is asked to give a thumbnail sketch of each character so that the auxiliary egos can have some idea of the person they are portraying. The protagonist can often give very unpleasant descriptions of these persons. Moreno calls this method the 'distorted mirror technique' because the protagonist usually disregards objective reality and presents a distorted picture.

A young boy, showing how his mother acted when he visited her, grabbed a magazine, lit a cigarette and started reading while sucking his teeth, inhaling and absent-mindedly answering his questions. This was a promising role for the woman who was going to play the auxiliary ego because it was a pure caricature.

Again, it is important to point out that the mother may not have really been like this. A psychodrama does not make moral judgments; it makes no judgments of any kind. The crucial point is that this is how the boy experienced her; this is how she appeared to be. The objective of a psychodrama is to shed light on an experience. By reversing roles, the boy can experience his mother 'from the other side'. She may have been tired and fed up with her son (a drug addict) and afraid of police involvement because of her son's constant violations of the law. Despite this, no solution or explanation should ever be forced on a protagonist.

The mirror is used in many different situations, often as a direct provocation to show the protagonist how the group perceives him. When a person insists on being the protagonist but does no more than play the role of a clown, it might be necessary to stop him. The director could ask a group member to imitate his behaviour. If the protagonist leaves the stage, the director should encourage him to return when the situation feels less threatening. We assume that anyone who is willing to enter the psychodramatic stage has something on his mind. Persons who have been 'chased away' often return to the stage to complete what they had so intently wanted to work on but had not dared to express. Although playing the role of a clown is a defence mechanism, a group is rarely tolerant of this and can quickly become aggressive.

The mirror method is an excellent way to show a protagonist his inadequate behaviour. The following example is from a group of Vietnam veterans.

Tony had been released from the hospital but he still returned regularly to his psychodrama group, although he had never presented a real problem that could be enacted. On one particular evening he was unusually aggressive and insisted on being given some attention. Those who knew Tony also knew that his vocabulary consisted mainly of swear words. Tony's problem that evening was that he hadn't been able to control his anger during his appointment at the doctor's office earlier in the day. The doctor had reacted by suggesting that it might be a good idea for him to reinstate himself as a day-patient. Tony became highly indignant. Since it was obvious that Tony needed to be the protagonist, the group selected him – albeit somewhat unwillingly. As we had expected, Tony presented a chaotic picture of his visit with the doctor. The director himself walked up on the stage and started the following dialogue with Tony:

DIRECTOR: Fuck you!

TONY: I, you…what…

DIRECTOR: Fuck you!

TONY: I don't want…

DIRECTOR: Fuck you!

TONY: Shut up!

DIRECTOR: Fuck you!

TONY: Yes, but…

DIRECTOR: Fuck you!

TONY: Please.

DIRECTOR: That's better, do you understand what I'm trying to say?

TONY: Oh, fuck you! (*spontaneous laughter from the group*)

DIRECTOR: Fuck you!

TONY: Are you starting again?

DIRECTOR: Fuck you!

TONY: Stop it! Stop it!

DIRECTOR: Finally. Now you can talk.

The whole group agreed with this picture of Tony. If he wanted to be taken seriously, he would have to cut out his embarrassingly vulgar ways. Tony admitted that he hadn't had any idea that he acted that way and had to tolerate hearing that all he accomplished with his incessant 'Fuck you' was to irritate.

The mirror technique is effective but merciless. It should be used with great care and, preferably, in a humorous setting.

Self-assertion method

Many have never managed to realize their own potential in life because they underestimate their own value and overestimate the value of others. This is especially visible in persons who have been raised by, or lived with, domineering parents, spouses or other important figures. These persons carry their restraint and passivity into their working lives and their interaction with others. Their restraint often conceals deeply repressed feelings of aggression. The following method can help reserved and timid persons to fight back, and it can also help persons with passive aggression to let go of their anger and hatred.

This example describes a young girl who became completely speechless when her 'father' entered the scene. She had been chosen as the protagonist after presenting her problem as steadily increasing nervousness at work. She was a secretary in a large company and was in constant fear of missing sections of her boss' rapid dictations. Unless she was tossing and turning with nightmares or dreaming that she had been fired, she was gradually developing insomnia. She had a deep fear of authority figures and her boss was clearly one of these.

The assertion technique is uncomplicated but the auxiliary ego will require some instruction. The director stands behind the protagonist in such a way that the auxiliary ego can see whatever hand signals he is giving. The auxiliary ego is instructed to harass the protagonist but to stop as soon as the protagonist tries to say something. The director uses a graphic picture of a mouth in action (pushing his thumb toward his remaining fingers) to signal the auxiliary ego to start. As soon as the protagonist starts to speak, the director raises the palm of his hand, signalling silence to the auxiliary ego.

This technique did not work very well for the young secretary. The 'father' was a man who had no trouble being authoritative. In fact, he enjoyed ridding himself of his own aggression without having to worry about a counter-attack (this in itself is a good form of therapy). Seeing the 'child's' defeat only increased his ranting about how self-centred, self-pitying and unrealistic she was. In turn, these criticisms only served to make the young woman even more subdued and overpowered. The director let them continue until the woman finally broke down in tears and the auxiliary ego, who was equally upset, slumped into a chair asking forgiveness for his part in the scene.

The following is an example of one of the many surprising results of a psychodrama. The man who had been chosen as the auxiliary ego was astounded at his own brutality. He said that acting the part of an authoritarian father seemed to spring naturally from inside himself. Of course, the auxiliary ego could have simply refused to continue if he was as upset as he said he was but, since most auxiliary egos are genuinely interested in helping the drama, they rarely interrupt a scene this way. Indeed, it is important to bear in mind that this motivation can also be a way to justify satisfying their own needs. A psychodrama allows room for all participants to unfold. Transference will usually strengthen the drama and activate latent conflicts but the director must make certain that this process stays within reasonable limits.

The same young woman was the protagonist in a later psychodrama that clearly showed the connection between her relationship to a strong and domineering father and her difficulties with her employer. This insight helped her understand that her childhood insecurity was the cause of her feelings of inferiority and anxiety at work as well as her inability to recognize her professional competence as a secretary. In the final stage of the drama, the auxiliary ego who had been her father said that he had been tormented by an uncle whom he spent his summer vacations with as a child. He had not remembered this until after the psychodrama!

The assertion technique is a good method for releasing aggression. The connection between a low and steady voice and the claim of not being able to show anger is a striking one. There is nothing rare about a smiling face concealing aggression. When this finally comes to the surface, it can be a violent eruption. When many years of stored hatred and aggression are released, ending in catharsis and tears, it is experienced as a tremendous relief. In a sense, the assertion technique approaches primal therapy (Janov's 'scream therapy': see Janov 1970). But Janov's scream – as a 'breakthrough to reality' – is the therapy itself, while in psychodrama the assertion technique is an additional method that is followed by switching the focus onto the person's actual life situation and enacting new scenes.

The assertion technique is also similar to an encounter technique which was developed in Synanon and later systematized by Daniel Casriel (1963). Casriel also focuses on releasing aggression, anxiety and pain that have encapsulated themselves in an 'inner fortress'. This method is used in treating drug addicts at Daytop Village, New York. Moreno's assertion technique releases aggression in a different way but the objective is the same.

When a protagonist is having particular trouble expressing repressed aggression, the director can ask one or more persons from the group to contribute verbal reinforcement for his feelings. This type of intensification has a releasing effect in that it allows for an official acceptance of aggression in situations where it may have previously been condemned.

The magic shop

In contrast to the mirror and assertion techniques, which can be rather distressing experiences, the magic shop, a method that originated in India, is almost like a game. Moreno introduced it as a therapeutic technique in 1943 (see Moreno 1959). It has many different applications but, whether it takes place on a symbolic level or is used as a projective test, its conscious aim is to maintain a certain distance to reality.

Not many directors use this method. Some think it runs the risk of reinforcing the protagonist's wish for the magical and thus strengthens regressive behaviour. Schützenberger (1975) uses this argument but concludes: 'When adapted for wise and cautious use, the "magic shop" has beneficial therapeutic results and often evokes a rapid symbolical opening for personal problems'. Others avoid using it because it seems to call for a director with a specific turn of mind. It requires the combination of a highly developed imagination and extreme caution. As a warming-up exercise, the magic shop can be very useful.

The magic shop is used as an additional method when the protagonist shows signs of wanting to change his attitude, that is, when he has gained a certain degree of insight. In this instance, the game is used as realistically as possible.

In the magic shop the protagonist can have whatever he wants in exchange for whatever he is willing to offer. He has to negotiate with the owner of the shop (either the director or a member of the group) and he has to invest parts of himself in exchange for his wish. The 'shopkeeper' should not give the protagonist too much of a bargain. The exchange can take place on a symbolic level, but then it will be more like the procedure discussed later in the 'rehearsal for life'. The following example illustrates the use of the magic shop method.

A young girl had voluntarily joined a programme for drug abusers. In the magic shop she wanted to buy the strength to stay away from drugs. When the shopkeeper asked what she was willing to offer in return, the girl answered: 'My right hand'.

If the shopkeeper were simply to cut off her right hand symbolically, the bargain would lose its meaning. Instead, she should be confronted with reality and asked how she could live her life without a right hand. A confrontation with reality is often harsh. The director has to be careful not to impose his own set of values on the subject.

The rest of the example will be repeated in full and will show how quickly the method got to the core of the girl's immediate problem, even though our only information about the girl was that she was 21 years old and had a long history of drug abuse.

GIRL: You can have my hair.

DIRECTOR: No, I can't accept that, it will grow out again.

GIRL: How about my vanity?

DIRECTOR:	I could take that, but it isn't enough. In exchange for your vanity, I'll give you your self-esteem.
GIRL:	What do you want for it?
DIRECTOr:	Only the best.
GIRL:	I've already given the best years of my life.
DIRECTOR:	There may still be some good years to come.
GIRL:	In exchange for what?
DIRECTOR:	For whatever you are thinking right now.
GIRL:	I'm not thinking about anything much.
DIRECTOR:	Oh yes you are. That's why you're here.
GIRL:	I'm not the only one who should feel guilty.
DIRECTOR:	What would you exchange for your guilt?
GIRL:	Would you really take my guilt in exchange?
DIRECTOR:	It is an easy thing give up.
GIRL:	But what's it worth?
DIRECTOR:	It will get you half-way to your goal. What do you say about trading in your hope too?
GIRL:	I'll tell you something…(*long pause*)…I met a man…
DIRECTOR:	What would you give to have him love you?
GIRL:	Never to use drugs again.
DIRECTOR:	That's not what we're talking about. With drugs you gain nothing. No man, no future, no children.
GIRL:	Will I have children?
DIRECTOR:	Do you want children?
GIRL:	More than anything else.

Women with histories of drug abuse and prostitution are often ambivalent about the future, especially in terms of husbands and children. In the jargon of this institution, the slang word for abortion was 'hook' – meaning the hook where one can hang guilt feelings, that is, as a justification for using drugs to forget. But here the director did not meet the self-pitying guilt so common to young female addicts with repressed aggression towards men because they feel they have been exploited. In this young woman he found a strong, but anxiety-filled, motivation for rehabilitation after being told that she could be a mother.

Rehearsal for life

Like the magic shop, the method of rehearsal for life aims to establish contact with whatever persons, qualities and tools the protagonist needs to achieve a future goal.

If the protagonist is a prison inmate, the future is bound to be uncertain. The same is true for patients who are wondering about their lives after their release from the hospital. And other persons, with or without weighty problems in life, will also want to make the most of their lives and learn to use their time more productively.

For a prison inmate who is hoping for social rehabilitation, the most important and, perhaps, most difficult task will be finding a job. In a psychodrama he can choose his own employer and occupation and accommodate himself to new opportunities. He can explore his abilities and his preferences. The next step is to find out how these ideas can be realized.

Just as it is important to develop opportunities for self realization, it is also important to define their practical and realistic limitations. In role-playing and role-training the protagonist will be able to get a feeling of his future life if he is willing to recognize his limitations and dares to work out some alternatives. The rehearsal for life is combined with 'a look into the future' where the prisoner, the patient and other subjects can be guided into imaginary situations and put to the test. Although they don't always pass the test with the same ease, they are learning adequate responses to different situations, for example, it might be necessary to learn to control a fiery temper – a quality that is not appreciated at a place of work or within a family. It is possible to learn how to anticipate these outbursts and to control reactions. Totally unknown sides of a personality can come to light when the rehearsal for life method is put to work.

Benny was an alcoholic and a compulsive eater whose mother simply thought he was a hopeless case. After he was told that he could do whatever he most wanted to do, it became clear that he could sing beautifully. He played a scene in a psychodrama where he went home to his mother and refused to eat all of the delicacies she had set out for him. Benny was justifiably suspicious that his mother was overfeeding him to keep him from leaving home. Rather than accepting her food, he told his 'mother' that he had found a job in a variety show. The director and the group quickly joined the game and set up a scene where Benny could make his debut, but we all had our worries about Benny. He was so enormously heavy and seemingly charmless.

The director allowed Benny to project two years into the future. Benny had lost forty pounds and had joined a jazz group as the vocalist. When

Benny began to sing the walls shook from the strength of his voice and the sound of the group's applause. He had moved into a modern bachelor apartment, he was engaged and would soon be married and he had just released a new album.

The atmosphere on the stage was infectious and the group was an enthusiastic audience. It will be hard to forget Benny's radiant joy. Whether his dream came true is a separate story, but he had been able to feel the sensation of success. His last line brought the house down: 'Here Mom, you can have your cake and eat it too!'

Looking back and decision-making

A look into the past that forces a decision might be easy for some but very difficult for others. In a psychodrama no problem is too small to tackle. The elderly woman who wonders whether she should get a new pet now that her old dog has died may be experiencing a deep conflict. She feels that she is deserting an old friend that has passed away. In a psychodrama this conflict might give rise to a number of other problems within the group. It might be a question of whether or not to get married for a second time. A widow has many fears and doubts.

In these situations the director needs a general idea of the person's past history. Here the past can be used to understand the present and to foresee what might lie in the future. An effective method here is to work with three empty chairs. The following is from a psychodrama with a 45-year-old housewife.

Bertha was in the throes of divorcing her husband and had recently enrolled in a relatively difficult course at a centre for adult learning. She felt she was doing poorly. Since her husband was constantly turning up and begging forgiveness, she was torn between the desire to return to her protected position as a wife and her need for independence. She tried to resolve her conflict by taking an overdose of sleeping pills.

Bertha was placed in front of three empty chairs, each representing a different version of herself. In one chair she was the housewife, in the second the self-reliant student and in the third she was the Bertha who had successfully committed suicide. By conversing with these three sides of herself, she could get a better sense of perspective. There was little to say to her dead self other than: 'That was stupid, you probably didn't mean to do it'. A hefty duel raged between the two other selves. Bertha reversed roles with them, moving from chair to chair and playing the role of one Bertha and then the other. After a while the director placed two auxiliary egos in the chairs. At first they brought out Bertha's weaker sides, playing the housewife who needed security, and then they started focusing on her stronger sides, her need for independence. Here it is the director's task to support strength rather than to expose weakness, since this could result in an overwhelming sense of defeat in the protagonist. But this kind of shared interaction can give the protagonist a sense of defeat and result in denial and a deep desire to show strength.

In Bertha's case the result was especially successful and her husband eventually joined her in family therapy. Some time later, Bertha told the director that she had passed her course and was living with her husband.

Using two chairs is a key technique in Gestalt therapy, which has the 'hot chair' and the 'empty chair'. Frederick Pearls, the founder of Gestalt therapy, praises Moreno for having inspired him to use two chairs. However, Pearl's technique and results are quite different, especially in terms of Moreno's use of the group. Pearls would probably have protested the use of the word 'technique' in terms of the two chairs. He thought of Gestalt therapy as a psychiatric procedure (Pearls 1966).

The suicidal try-out

A seemingly macabre method to use with a protagonist who wants to die is to allow him to decide how he will die and even plan the funeral ceremony. The aim here is to find out whether the person is really thinking of suicide and how serious the thought is.

Sometimes it seems that the protagonist actually enjoys preparing his own death and funeral. He describes the ceremony carefully and is encouraged by the director to think of more and more details, such as who will be invited and what he will wear in the coffin (in the USA people are often buried in personal clothing with a few personal effects at their side). Through this probing for details, a good deal of information comes forth about the patient's family and friends and the patient provides important clues about how hopeless he feels his world is.

Finally, when the patient climbs into his symbolic coffin – the bare floor – and lies on his back with his hands folded on his chest, the group surrounds him and mourns his death. After a while the group begins to mutter that it is time to leave – after all, life must go on. Someone mentions that he is hungry, another begins to describe his favourite meal. Discussions, all of which are aimed toward the deceased, gain momentum and go into food, drink and what's on at the movies. The group talks about everything that makes life worth living, without touching on family or delicate situations that might be the real reason for his wanting to end his life. It is extremely important to keep personal value systems and religious beliefs aside and to avoid moralizing about one's duty to carry on.

In most cases the protagonist eventually opens his eyes, hesitates for a moment and jumps out of his coffin. Witnessing this reaction a number of times has convinced me that most suicides are actually a frantic call for help in an unbearable life situation. The mere fact that other people are present seems to motivate a wish to continue living.

It is far more serious when a protagonist refuses to return to 'life' after the group has left his side. In these instances the director will try to use a 'psychodramatic shock', which is described later. The director confronts the person with his responsibilities and his cowardice and with everything he hopes to escape. If this confrontation fails, it proves that the conflicts are so deep, and the will to live so weakened, that hospitalization is the only course of action. The 'unaccomplished suicide' method is used as a test at some hospitals. Professor Martin R. Haskell has specialized in the use of this form of psychodrama as a 'suicide test'. Before he passed away, he directed a separate division in a California hospital.

Persons who are handicapped by unreleased sorrow often have to be made to face the reality of death. The 'burial of the deceased' is an additional method. Only after going through this symbolic funeral will the protagonist have a full understanding of the fact that he has lost a person or persons dear to him. Some will have to go through this distressing process in many psychodramas before they understand. It is a process that always culminates in tears – tears that may never have been cried before. In many cases unreleased sorrow lies at the core of deep depression.

Dream enactment

Dreams play a major role in a psychodrama and, when it is possible to reconstruct them in a dream enactment, invaluable information often comes to the surface. A dream must always be reproduced as carefully as possible. No matter how unimportant they may seem, each and every detail should be included. The procedure is to remember one's state of mind just before going to sleep, where one slept, the room, the most recent meal – every detail that might have influenced the content of the dream or activated the recollection of the dream. Reproducing a dream is, in reality, staging a dream. The phantoms of our dreams are figures that are brought to life by role reversal with the protagonist. They represent aspects of his own reality.

A man saw three women in his dream. One was rocking back and forth, holding her hands over her stomach. When he reversed roles with her, he thought that she might be pregnant, but he eventually discovered that she was holding a beggar's bowl. His opening dialogue with the dream woman was: Woman: 'Don't leave me!' Man: 'Let me get away from your eternal subservience!'

The next woman stood with outstretched arms. By reversing roles the man experienced this woman as his mother who was trying to keep him at her side. The third woman was the 'unknown'. She had no face. Working with this figure revealed that the man longed to find a woman who was strong and independent, but that he thought no such woman existed. His basic belief was that women were made for the convenience of men. There was a striking similarity between his wife and mother, both in his dream and in reality, in terms of how he described them. Toward the end of the drama he was asked to choose a woman from the group to represent the third woman in his dream. He chose a woman he did not know very well. One of his comments came to be important in the drama: 'I am actually afraid of you...'

In another dream enactment a woman whose husband had committed suicide appeared tense and restless. Nevertheless, the recollection of one of her dreams made her smile, nearly laugh.

She was in a room filled with sad people who were dressed in mourning. She was particularly interested in her sisters. They were all wearing white capes and resembled 'great restless, flapping birds'. A funeral march was playing and the large room was decorated in red and gold, 'almost like a gala performance'. Suddenly, she saw her deceased husband in a coffin beneath a huge canopy. As if it were a fairy tale, a golden crown glittered beside the coffin. But as she was walking past the coffin to take her place on a wooden stool, she noticed that the crown was made of cardboard.

In the following example, imagine the dream as dramatized through auxiliary egos, doubling, role reversals and other necessary techniques. Sisters and relatives were brought from the group. A man took the place of her 'husband' in the 'coffin'. Since the woman had been seeing a new man after her husband's death and her family knew nothing about this, an auxiliary ego was asked to take a chair on the outskirts of the dream scene.

In a soliloquy the woman reflected over the situation: 'It is strange that I don't feel sad. After all, it's my husband's funeral and I *was* paralyzed by grief. I don't feel anything now'. At this point she turned to her 'sisters', who were instructed to flap around in their white robes the way she saw them in the dream. This time she reacted. 'I can see that you want me to cry. You look like angels of doom, but this is a charade. Look at how *he* is enjoying this', she said, pointing at the 'corpse'. She was asked to reverse roles with her dead husband.

WOMAN (*in the role of her husband*): I am truly pleased to see all of you here. This is just the way I thought it would be. Beautiful grief. A perfect performance.

WOMAN (*as herself*): How strange that I didn't realize what a sham you were until you had died. Day and night I struggled to understand you, and you were wearing that ridiculous cardboard crown. What a pity that I didn't see it before now. You're a damned royal fool if you think you can still dominate me. But I'm not going to grieve. Don't think you can do this to me again!

A WOMAN IN THE GROUP STARTS DOUBLING: I already found a new man.

WOMAN: Yes, a new man. Well, only a lover. What would my virtuous sisters think?

DOUBLE: The problem is, I don't think this relationship will last.

WOMAN (*talking to the corpse*): You are still a horrible nightmare.

DOUBLE: I'm transferring a whole bunch of irrational reactions onto my lover...

WOMAN: No, it's not that. I think he has the same traits. Not that he's a fake, but he gets depressions too and it scares me so much. I'm afraid it's all going to happen again.

DOUBLE: I can't cope with a repeat of the same situation.

WOMAN: I can't do it again.

After a long psychodrama that included memories from childhood and marriage (throwing light on why she was a patient), the drama concluded in a scene where the woman turned her back on the new man and asked him to come back later when she had more control of herself. In the final phase of the psychodrama, the sharing phase, the woman showed that she had gained a good understanding of her previous experiences but that she had never seen her husband as a fake or a fool until she had her dream.

Reconstructing dreams can also provide important clues about a person's physical condition, a fact that a protagonist should bear in mind.

A woman had mistakenly entered the balcony of the Beacon Theatre. As she looked down on the stage, she suddenly remembered a dream. In the dream she is on a high plateau holding onto a railing. She can see a garden or hospital grounds. All of the patients are very ill and they are sitting in bathtubs with missing front panels.

All in all, the dream was absurd and involved a large cast. The director thought that the most interesting aspect was the missing panel of the bathtub. The woman reversed roles with the bathtub, leaning forward and stretching out her arms as if they were the edges of the tub. The space between her hands represented the missing front piece. As soon as she 'became' the bathtub, she felt that all of her vitality left her. She said it felt as if all of her bodily fluid drained out of her, water, blood and strength. The director advised her not to work for a while and to take a vacation. A while later, the woman reported that she should have followed this advice. Instead, she had suffered a total mental and physical collapse that had caused a long period of illness. The body has its own voice, and it is an important voice to heed, even when relayed through a dream.

Dreams, and the different phases of dreams, have the same dramatic composition as a play, moving from the initial exposition of the theme to the problem itself and, finally, to the conclusion. This process is similar to a psychodrama, which moves from a warming-up phase to the enactment and to the final sharing phase.

Another woman dreamed that she walked into a hospital carrying a plastic bag of blood. Tossing her bag into a rubbish container, she said to a doctor: 'I think something's wrong with me'. The doctor confirmed this. When the woman woke up the next day, she called her doctor for an appointment and her doctor later confirmed that she had a blood problem.

The woman then had a dream in three phases. In the first one there were three cats and she was to give them a bowl of milk but a voice said: 'Do not give milk to pedigree cats. At least dilute it with water'. In the next phase she saw a cat clinging to something in the midst of a river's rapids. In the final phase she was at a circus. A man invited her into a magical Chinese tent. The woman's spontaneous answer was: 'No, I certainly don't want to go in there'.

Her blood tests had shown a high level of hydrocortisone and her blood pressure had risen dangerously. After interpreting her dream as a message to stop taking large doses of red ginseng from China without drinking extra water, her hydrocortisone level decreased. When she reversed roles with the cat in the rapids, she associated the image with her high blood pressure. The final scene with the Chinese tent had given her the insight into her ginseng consumption and she understood why, in the first scene, she had been told not to give undiluted milk to pure-bred cats.

Inserted non-verbal scenes

Many lengthy sequences in a psychodrama consist of non-verbal expression. A director can introduce non-verbal methods whenever the drama requires them. For example, the friendly and supportive symbolic greetings like a handshake or a hand on a shoulder are signals to the protagonist that he is not alone.

Many people have trouble with spontaneous non-verbal communication. Psychodramatic training involves daring to make use of physical as well as verbal expression. In itself, touching another person can be therapeutic when it is done with sensitivity and tact, but it requires selectivity. A hug can be an empty gesture when not accompanied with genuine feeling.

As a rule, the group participates collectively in non-verbal scenes. A common method is to give the protagonist the feeling of being surrounded by friends who support him so literally that he can let himself fall and still be held up by the group. The protagonist's sensation of safety may give him the courage to carry on in a difficult life situation. The group could also lift him on their outstretched arms and rock him as if he were in his mother's womb.

The group is useful in just about any symbolic action, whether they represent support or opposition. However, opposition from the group must have a definite constructive objective. A group can represent a 'wall' between two persons who are not communicating or it can represent the distance between persons who are not 'reaching' each other by placing the protagonist and the auxiliary ego at either end of the wall and sending a handshake along the wall from one end to the other. This game can start off being fun but can become very serious.

In psychodramas with alcoholics and drug addicts the group can be used as the source of pressure or temptation that the protagonist is fighting to resist. The group forms a tight circle around him and he has to use all of his strength to break through the ring. King Alcohol could be represented by a particularly able-bodied man who suggests Indian wrestling with the protagonist. In this way, King Alcohol assumes a psychodramatic role for the protagonist to fight against; the group separates into tempters and helpers. The role of King Alcohol must be played by an experienced auxiliary ego and it is important to remember that a psychodrama must never allow violence.

There are other ethical boundaries that must be set. Psychodramas with strong sexual contexts are quite common, and in these cases one must keep to a stylized simulation and avoid realistic imitations. In these psychodramas symbolic or substitute actions, such as the 'symbolic funeral' and the 'symbolic rebirth', become even more important.

Guided day-dream

Moreno was not the originator of the 'guided day-dream', also called a symbolic drama, which stems primarily from H. Leuner, but has been developed and used in different ways by many others. As it is used here, it is a highly effective way to help a group focus on a specific subject, person or situation during the warm-up phase. It can also be inserted into the drama to remind the group of something in a special context. In this sense it might be compared to Stanislavsky's focus on emotional memory. The guided day-dream can be an innocent visit to previous stomping grounds or a voyage into the future. In any case, it is important to remember that even an innocent trip can provoke strong emotional reactions. Therefore, this method should be used with caution.

When the guided day-dream is used in the warming-up phase, the group is asked to lie down on the floor. The director works through a relaxation exercise, starting with the feet, moving through the body and ending with the face and neck muscles. The actual aim of the guided day-dream is optional and each individual in the group can choose who he wants to meet, unless, for example, the director has a certain episode in mind that has created a conflict in the group.

The empty chair is often an effective focusing method after the guided day-dream. When the group has returned to objective reality – the room – some of the members will still be partially in their personal reality, depending on the content of their day-dream. The group member who places an imaginary person in the empty chair will actually be sitting in the chair and using the body language and speech of the person he 'is' and holding a monologue describing that persons feelings. Thus he is expressing his fantasies about the person. After a while, an auxiliary ego can take over and the drama can be set in motion. When there is a strong conflict between two members of the group, it is almost inevitable that one of them will place himself or the antagonist in the empty chair. This allows for a direct confrontation between the two parts. To create a deep and meaningful psychodrama, any conflicts within the group must be resolved. Like crossed wires in telecommunications, conflicts in a group reduce 'tele' and make communication difficult.

When the guided day-dream is used as a warming-up technique, everyone that has a strong desire to present his person and his problem should be allowed to do so. After this, the group can agree on its choice of a protagonist.

When the guided day-dream is used to focus on, and strengthen, the memory of a specific conflict, the person who feels most strongly engaged in the conflict, for example the one with the strongest need to explain himself, must be allowed to speak his thoughts.

If the protagonist is selected before the guided day-dream is initiated, the focus must never be transferred from him to another member of the group.

The empty chair

The empty chair is one of Moreno's most ingenuous techniques and it can be used in many connections. It is especially effective in terms of concentrating the protagonist's attention on specific persons who are important to the drama. This technique is often used as a prelude to a psychodrama, making a lengthy introduction unnecessary. The psychodramatic role that the potential protagonist 'places on the chair' almost always leads to a conflict. It might also simply be an opportunity to say one specific sentence or to train oneself up to a specific role. Here we will describe the empty chair as a training technique, although the empty chair as well as the final empty chair are both additional methods in psychodramas.

The following example, using the empty chair as a training technique for a specific role, occurred with a group of students from a teachers' college. They could just as easily have been social workers meeting their first client or nursing students meeting a person who is terminally ill. Here this technique is not used in the context of role-training but of empathy, reflection and verbal formulation.

In a theme-centred homogenous group the introduction to the empty chair is done intensively through 'a guided fantasy.' The group members are asked to lie down on the floor and the director guides them through relaxation of each section of the body. When the relaxation exercise is completed, the next step is to concentrate on a specific subject. The subject should be as simple as possible, to avoid some group members becoming sidetracked by too many details.

In this example the fantasy was about meeting a student who had rushed from her classroom and was now in an empty room in the school grounds and in an agitated state. The teacher's task was to go to the student and try to get an understanding of the situation. When no one is sitting in the empty chair, the level of surrounding surplus reality becomes particularly high. Each member of the group pictures the pupil in his own way.

Although the empty chair does not require any previous training, the atmosphere in the group has to be a safe one. Some think it is threatening to 'perform'. However, the most surprising aspect of this technique is how clearly each individual creates the fantasy person and how differently these fantasies gradually take on a life of their own when placed in the chair.

After a member of the group has 'seen' his pupil in the chair, he is asked to imitate how the imaginary pupil was sitting. This is to evoke the teacher's inner picture of the person, regardless of whether he experiences his pupil as stubborn, sad, repentant or negative. At the same time, it also provides some clues as to the future teacher's personal attitudes and methods of approach. Without drawing any conclusions, the 'teacher' will have certain built-in reactions from the very beginning, especially in terms of his ability to empathize. This skill is greatly dependent upon training but some people seem to have a natural talent for it. Even though the 'teacher' assumes an authoritarian attitude and looks on the pupil as subservient, this might easily be due to reverting to a stereotypical role of how he thinks a person with the status of a teacher should act (we have previously referred to this as role perception). When this happens, it is often due to a defensive attitude which the individual himself will recognize when he interacts with the imaginary pupil. When he reverses roles with the pupil, he will have to respond in the atmosphere that he himself created. Typical reactions to this experience are: 'It must be impossible to answer that kind of a teacher', or 'Gee, the way I carry on, the poor pupil can't possibly get a word in edgeways!'

There were nine members of this particular group and, with their twelve hours of instruction, none of them were experienced in role-training and doubling. Nevertheless, seven of the group had no trouble creating an imaginary person and eventually reversing roles with it. Two could only see the person's exterior. One of them gave up trying to communicate and the other chose to use a factual event as a starting point, which quickly helped him depict an extremely lively little boy with concrete problems. Since this technique is part of a training programme, nothing is right or wrong, good or bad. Some persons need more time than others, and others create imaginary people on the spur of the moment on their first attempt and seem to enjoy it. In these exercises it can seem as if the persons who are most spontaneous are those who are not unduly worried about what others think of them. There is a distinction here between 'strained spontaneity' and genuine, unbridled openness. Strained spontaneity often belongs to the grouping studied by Alfred Baldwin (1960).

In the group studying to become teachers the fact was quickly revealed that many made use of stored behaviour models. The 'child role' and the 'parent role' were demonstrated clearly – the 'child' when they acted as the pupil and the 'parent' when they acted as the teacher. The exercise pointed out a general anxiety in the group about being able to handle the 'teacher role'. In a similar session with high-school students who reversed roles with an imaginary teacher, many of the same fantasy pictures appeared: 'The teacher probably doesn't care about me. The teacher is too busy. There's no sense in trying to talk to such a jerk!' When they were confronted by a teacher who genuinely expressed his concern for the students, and had personal problems himself, many imaginary barriers were broken down.

An effective way to use the empty chair is to let the protagonist 'warm up' his auxiliary egos by speaking in the first person. For example, the protagonist stands behind the chair and takes the place of the imaginary person, saying: 'I'm quite unsure of myself, but I want people to think I'm in control'. The director or an assistant helps the situation along by speaking in the same 'I' form: 'Am I tall or short?' As a rule, the protagonist replies in great detail: 'I am relatively tall...have a beard...and like to take walks in the woods...' After a while, the group has a pretty good idea of the person the protagonist has in his inner eye. This also facilitates the task of the person who will later be asked to act as an auxiliary ego.

The final empty chair

Although many other inserted scenes could be mentioned, I will conclude with this last symbolic activity – which is often used to give all of the group members a chance to express themselves in cases where the subject has been particularly moving. Often the protagonist has stirred up so many feelings and memories that it is important for each person in the room to add some of his own fantasies about what happened. This is not the same as a direct sharing of experiences.

The protagonist might have portrayed his deep hatred of an insensitive father or mother. There could be persons in the group who have identified with this parent who was under attack and possibly being ridiculed. Earlier we defined the process of identification in a psychodrama as a 'temporary fixation'. No one is meant to remain in this state. The method of the final empty chair is devised to allow everyone a chance to be released from their fixation – either by working it off spontaneously, for example by going to the empty chair and sitting in it, or by defending the absent person while remaining within the group. This method often highlights 'surplus reality' and shows how different people in a group can react to the same experience.

After all psychodramas, the auxiliary egos who acted as negative persons all need to be 'de-roled'. No participant should have to carry any possible negative projections from the group back into their actual lives.

Once again, it is important that no one be allowed to present interpretations or personal attacks on the protagonist. Everyone speaks from personal experience. Therefore, many imaginary persons can end up in the empty chair and most of these are the individual group members' projections of their own guilt and inadequacy. The final empty chair offers room for human consideration and mature tolerance for the absentee person. Therefore, it can be a good source for reflection in the group.

In a heart-rending psychodrama a son who had unsuccessfully tried to get into contact with his extremely authoritarian father, and who finally couldn't even manage to cry at his father's deathbed, a woman in the group said: 'I see a lonely old man, so very alone...' This statement happened to induce deep sorrow in the protagonist. A new scene had to be arranged for a final meeting with the dying man. By completely changing his perspective, it was possible to enact a reconciliation between the father and the son and to work out the deeply ensconced bitterness of the son.

The final empty chair is a beginning for many new psychodramas that can be used in future occasions.

CHAPTER 4

Psychodrama in Practice

Being a protagonist

A protagonist's first appearance on a psychodramatic stage is a frightening experience. It seems overwhelming, standing there and not knowing what to say, just having an inner need to express feelings that need to be released and words that need to be said. Even people who are accustomed to appearing on stage describe their experience this way, perhaps because they feel uncomfortable without a script and often have no idea of what will happen. In the USA professional actors often join psychodramas to adjust to new roles or to release themselves from former roles, and they say that their first experiences as protagonists sometimes upset them more than an opening night in the legitimate theatre.

As soon as the protagonist has left his place in the group, he no longer experiences the members of the group as friends. He catches glimpses of their faces and sees them as an audience waiting for the curtain to be raised. If only for a few minutes, this feeling returns almost every time he enters the stage. It feels like the floor is about to cave in and he is on the verge of losing his grip on the situation. Before words come, hesitatingly and uncertainly, it feels like he is walking next to himself and he wonders where his real 'I' is. Stage actors often have this feeling before they can 'lose themselves in their roles', but in a psychodrama roles are not to be used as a hiding-place. Therefore, it is a tremendous relief when the director starts interviewing the protagonist or encouraging him to soliloquize. The image of the group fades away and the protagonist enters into his own world of reality which he is about to create:

PROTAGONIST: I stood by the window watching my father walk along the road toward the house. I knew he was angry and that I would have to account for what I had done.

DIRECTOR: Does your father come into the room where you are?

PROTAGONIST: Yes, and when he does, I turn around and want to run away.

DIRECTOR: What does the room look like? Describe it in detail. Where is the door, the window? Is anyone else there?

PROTAGONIST: No, but I know my brother is just outside the door.

DIRECTOR: Look around in the group. Do you see anyone who could be your father? Your brother?

(The protagonist points to two persons who then take their assigned positions on the stage.)

The protagonist is usually already involved in his own drama from the very first scene. When the psychodrama has been played to its conclusion, if the protagonist has undergone a catharsis, he will either cry or feel an unusual sense of relief. Without intending to draw any direct parallel to psychoanalysis, which takes place over a long period and involves regular therapeutic sessions, many psychodramas, at irregular intervals and for short durations of time, will be able to solve deep emotional conflicts. Once these are solved, the protagonist can free himself from feelings of pain, resentment and anxiety. Major crises can be worked through in a single evening. Some persons might bury their loved ones, while others might make decisions that will put order into their chaotic lives.

It is not as difficult as one might think to return to the group. The faces that seemed so foreign and curious from the stage now appear warm and friendly. One returns to the group of witnesses and experiences a protective ring of human concern.

The final phase of sharing is calculated to assist the transition from a different level of experience. The built-in solidarity of a psychodrama unites the group members and allows the protagonist to feel that he is not alone. It is important to avoid any time pressure during this phase, but a competent director will exercise discipline here. In a few individual cases the protagonist will need individual follow-up therapy.

Generally speaking, one can say that the protagonist nearly always feels relief at the end of the session. The better the warm-up, the deeper the psychodrama penetrates. This also influences the sharing phase.

Being an auxiliary ego

Sitting in a group of persons who are more or less strangers and suddenly being chosen as an auxiliary ego can be experienced as a great challenge – particularly the first time. The fear may be based on the mistaken idea that it will call for a competent performance. This is why professional students of psychodrama must concentrate on spontaneity training.

Many of the auxiliary egos that are chosen from a group have not had any previous training. Some turn out to be highly competent and selfless because of their desire to help the protagonist. Others consciously or unconsciously concentrate on their own needs for insight into their own problems. As long as the director does not let this go too far (acting in), these persons contribute tremendously because both the negative and positive processes of transference can activate even deeper conflicts in the protagonist. All sorts of dramas take place on different levels. The action moves quickly, jumping back and forth in time and space, while the protagonist leads the drama in compliance with his personal reality.

When groups meet over a long period of time, their members will find it relatively easy to be auxiliary egos – for example a 'mother' or 'father' for certain protagonists who have consistently referred to a mother or father as the 'root of all evil'. In these instances the director and auxiliary ego have to uncover new angles of perspective. Otherwise the protagonist will simply become locked in his own role and the role of the auxiliary egos. In these instances the psychodrama can become detrimental.

Auxiliary egos must distance themselves from their own ambitions. Professional actors are far from the best auxiliary egos, except when a caricature is required – for example in the mirror or in stereotyped roles calling for consecutive performances. However, these actors are good doubles because they are accustomed to perceiving the many nuances of a drama and they know how to fill in the unspoken words.

An auxiliary ego is no more than a subordinate instrument in the drama and must always follow the protagonist's premises. An auxiliary ego must never try to correct the experiences of a protagonist. Through role reversal, the auxiliary ego gathers information about the protagonist's feelings and fantasies about the real person's attitudes. The drama cannot unfold freely unless the auxiliary ego manages to do this.

We have already shown how an auxiliary ego can provoke unexpected reactions from a protagonist. It seems that the presence of a stage and stage lighting influence the progress of a psychodrama. In our daily lives we can also see that certain persons, as opposed to others, have either a positive or negative effect on us; the atmosphere of a stage intensifies this effect. Interactions leading in completely unexpected directions are put into motion, temporary approaches turn up and ambivalent viewpoints pull in opposite directions. Gestures and various physical postures also have their own silent stories to tell. Contradictory signals are sent out, the protagonist saying one thing while acting out another. In these situations the auxiliary ego must be finely attuned to the objectives of the director and allow himself to be guided in his interaction with the protagonist.

A protagonist's explanation of the choice of a particular person as an auxiliary ego can be extremely vague. Many of these choices seem to be coincidental. Numerous undefined needs are involved when one person so intensely asks to scold, love or hate total strangers. Auxiliary egos who are being trained as professional helpers should be relatively robust individuals. If nothing else, they must be able to disregard their personal feelings and opinions while they are involved in the drama. But it is not unusual for auxiliary egos to have strong transference experiences during a psychodrama. They will then need their own psychodramas, whether they are professionals or fellow clients.

Being a double

A description of being a double can sound like a mystic experience. In fact, just what happens when a person assumes the role of another person's alter ego is still a mystery. Systematic research might provide the answer in the future.

The outward behaviour of the protagonist and the double is obvious. They are on the stage either as themselves or as auxiliary egos, regardless of whether they are deities, demons or perfectly ordinary creatures from everyday life. However, the function of the double takes place primarily on an invisible level. This is why spontaneous reactions are often unexpected ones which can change the entire character of a psychodrama in a split second.

Those who have never been a double, but have observed doubling from the group, maintain that knowing the protagonist well will ensure being a good double. This is not true, because the more a double identifies with the protagonist's problem, the less chance there is of possible solutions. Doubles might only see the protagonist's problem in terms of their own ideas and project their personal solutions as suggestions. Indeed, in some cases doubles might evaluate situations correctly in terms of understanding the problem but they are not meant to act as guidance counsellors (in a psychodrama identification is defined as a temporary fixation and should be avoided).

The above touches upon a very difficult and dangerous area. In psychodrama, preconceived ideas about certain issues create a deadlock. A person who evaluates and weighs questions carefully, with textbook in hand or theory on the tip of the tongue, is not complying to Moreno's rule of going *behind* the mask (the role) and living spontaneously from one's own inner resources.

Of the two kinds of doubling, the simplest is based on asking a group member to stand behind the protagonist and express spontaneous opinions about whatever problems the protagonist is struggling with. The protagonist knows he can either reject these statements or take them further and go more deeply into what the double has said. In this sense the double does no more than offer suggestions. In terms of content, the protagonist is free to choose whether or not he will investigate the idea with the double's help.

PROTAGONIST: I was in the garden looking at all of the beautiful roses my wife had planted, watered and nurtured...

DOUBLE: She waters the roses. (*A double must be concise.*)

PROTAGONIST: Yes, she waters the roses...

DOUBLE: She takes care of the garden but neglects me.

PROTAGONIST: That's right. She doesn't see me anymore. I might just as well be the weeds she pulls. Her hand is no longer generous...

Because the double speaks in the first person, the protagonist often relates this to his own inner voice. But the double can just as easily be presenting a private interpretation; he might be in the same situation and also feel that his wife neglects him. There is no way to control the impulses of a double. I have chosen the above scene because it is concrete. 'I was standing in the garden...' becomes the first movement of a miniature symphony played with the double. The second movement is: 'looking at the beautiful roses my wife had planted'. The double may have stood up here. When the word 'watered' is spoken, the double is standing behind the protagonist. The word 'nurtured' strengthens the double's spontaneous inspiration. The protagonist's pause after describing the garden, the beautiful roses and his wife's caring for them gives the double the chance to repeat a phrase with a word that is loaded with meaning: 'She is *watering* the roses' (the opposite of being dry and withered). And the protagonist reacts with a confirmation: 'Yes, she waters the roses...' Here the protagonist reveals an immediate need to be cared for in the same way the roses are cared for, and this need is expressed boldly by someone else. The protagonist reveals his problem: 'Her hand is no longer generous...'

Brief cues from a double often lead directly to the core of the problem. A protagonist can also reject a double, who then returns to the group. If the protagonist had answered the double's provocation with 'No, she does not neglect me', this might imply that the protagonist was not ready to admit his problem. Admittance to a problem may happen at a later stage in the psychodrama. The director must not press the point and the double must not be insistent.

Continuing with the same example, and repeating the double's provocation: 'But she neglects me', the outcome would have been completely different if the protagonist had answered: 'No, she does not neglect me, she smothers me with her silly protestations of love. I barely make it through the door before she is hovering around me with a cocktail and silly prattle. I can't stand it. I wish I could be left alone. Then she could plant, water and care for the roses to her heart's content...'

DOUBLE: I feel tormented.

PROTAGONIST: Yes, damn it! Other things are more important after a tiring day.

DOUBLE: My thoughts are somewhere else...

PROTAGONIST: All I want is peace and quiet...

DOUBLE: All that love makes me uncomfortable...

PROTAGONIST: Well...love. It's not that kind of love.

DOUBLE: I don't want to be one of her damned roses...

PROTAGONIST: I'm a normal man for God's sake!

DOUBLE (*noticing the aggressive tone of voice*): Does that mean I'm supposed to walk around with a bad conscience?

The protagonist is silent. Later, when the psychodrama has progressed further, we might be able to return to this dialogue. Here we saw two different themes coming from the same simple starting point of the roses. If the double had forced his own feelings and interpretations into the dialogue, the protagonist would have lost his personal options. This example of doubling is called 'dialogue doubling'. Usually, doubling only expresses unspoken words or repressed ideas.

The second kind of doubling is the classic one that requires practical training and a strong sense of empathy. Moreno's hypothesis is that when the double mimics each and every movement of the protagonist, he is able to register the inner anxiety of the protagonist. Each time he repeats a gesture, pause, clearing of the throat or any extemporaneous movement, the double acquires information about an inner reality that might not have been gained by standing behind the protagonist. Fingers drumming on the table or a foot tapping the floor, when certain emotional aspects of his life are touched upon, can give the double true insight into the protagonist's repressed feelings and inner turmoil.

The transmission of information from the protagonist to the double is difficult to explain. An inspiration often appears for no apparent reason and, when the sender and the receiver are on the same wavelength, it may seem as mysterious as telepathy.

Empathy and tele are qualities that can be improved by training. When training for a psychodrama, a double has to practice copying the outward behaviour of other people down to the most minute detail. But this practical training is only of minor importance in comparison to the person's ability to maintain the open state of mind necessary for placing one's own self at the disposition of another. The experience of being a double could be described as a temporary absence from one's self.

Being a director

Many directors might say that the first phase of a psychodrama is the most difficult one. Some need to warm up to the psychodrama and use the introductory phase to discuss, describe and make associations. Others claim that provocation in the warming-up phase will create intensity in the group, but this presupposes a clear idea of the quality of intensity one is hoping to achieve. A psychodrama that springs from a director's provocation, for example from direct confrontations in a conflict, can only initiate a positive process when the director does not bring negative projections from the group upon himself. Sometimes it is difficult to set a psychodrama in motion, for example it might get caught up in superfluous discussions. This pertains especially to patients in a psychiatric ward. The warming-up phase is a vulnerable process and the director of a psychodrama must keep a firm hold on the group and be skilled in dealing with strong group processes.

Further, a protagonist might direct his rage toward the director during a psychodrama. In this case the director can make conscious use of aggression methods to bring out the protagonist's repressed feelings. One condition here is that the director must inform the protagonist that he is going to provoke him intentionally, for example the director could say: 'I can see that you're angry but why aren't you answering? Now I'll provoke you. Are you really afraid to stand up to your father? Now you can say whatever you feel like saying'. Provocation shall only be used when there is a mutual agreement to do so. Without trust between the protagonist and the director, provocation will not be therapeutic but will cause the patient to withdraw.

If the protagonist is still evasive but clearly showing signs of repressed feelings that aren't coming to the surface, it might be a good time to introduce the assertion technique – which is in itself a form of concentrated provocation.

A far more difficult situation is when the group becomes aggressive toward the director on behalf of the protagonist. This can confuse the drama, lessen the effect of inserted scenes, cause the doubles to remain silent and auxiliary egos to become insecure. The protagonist will either feel that he can increase his manipulations (he has the support of the group) or become passive. The best solution here is to interrupt the drama and clarify the situation. The following example illustrates this point.

The protagonist was a man in his fifties. He seemed to be very accommodating and agreed with nearly every suggestion about changing scenes. He was positive about the function of all of the doubles, agreeing with even the most conflicting ideas, and he soon had the members of the group feeling like his personal protectors. Here was a man who was genuinely asking for help!

However, the director was far from satisfied with the situation. Despite the mask of modesty and humble behaviour, he saw that the protagonist was a master of manipulation. In the director's opinion, he was a man who was willing to accept anything to avoid his problems. When confronted with this idea, the protagonist admitted that he listened to everyone because 'one of them might have a good piece of advice'. Further, he said that he had not cried since he was five and that he had never loved anyone. He had seen the psychodrama simply as an opportunity to investigate 'why he never felt anything at all'.

Here his honesty was as genuine as his openness in the beginning of the psychodrama and the group's feeling of loyalty to him remained strong. The director based his first question on the man's experience as a five-year-old.

This became an extremely intense psychodrama. Without hesitation, the man immediately reverted to his childhood when, as a five-year-old, he went to his father's funeral. His mother and relatives and neighbours were standing by the coffin. He couldn't make himself cry. He heard his mother whisper that he should show his feelings and his neighbours remarking how strange it was that he wasn't crying for his father.

A scene was dramatized exactly as he remembered it. By now the members of the group craved his tears as conclusive evidence that he had feelings. Often these situations cause the group to forget its function as auxiliary egos and witnesses in a psychodrama and to set out virtually to hunt down its prey. When a tear finally rolled down the man's cheek the director broke in with a cool 'Thank you, that is enough'.

At times like this the group can become dangerous. It unites against the director and forgets the protagonist. Although the group is acting on behalf of the protagonist, it has lost its sense of perspective. This is where the director has to use his authority and break down the power of the group in order to get back to the protagonist's problems. Not until learning that the man had also managed to squeeze out a tear at his father's funeral did the group realize that it had acted just like the mother, relatives and neighbours had acted around the coffin. This became the subject of the man's final psychodrama: his deep underlying guilt for not having feelings and his constant hopeless strategies to make others think that he had feelings. His acute inner stress had led him into compulsive drinking and, as a result, an institution for alcoholics. The fact that the director had not accepted his crocodile tears was a great relief to the protagonist. As he said himself, 'That tear was just a gift to you and the group!'

A director cannot always completely understand a situation. Sometimes a psychodrama can seem like a film flashing by. So much can happen simultaneously. The aim is to concentrate on whatever promotes the protagonist's interests while also listening to the members of the group. An auxiliary ego might have an idea that touches the very core of the problem. The director listens and evaluates – but if he accepts the idea, he will have to ensure that the auxiliary ego doesn't take off on an independent track.

A double might change the entire enactment with a statement that the protagonist accepts. The drama can move in a new direction and the director has to come to terms with the rule that the protagonist should always lead the way. As we saw earlier, sometimes a protagonist can accept any suggestion that turns up and this undermines the contribution of the double. The work of the double is not always characterized by empathy and genuine inspiration. When the protagonist's inner feelings are in turmoil, the double may have to resort to trial and error. In cases when the director cannot come up with a suitable additional method or inserted scene, the best solution is to interrupt the drama and clarify the situation. It is never easy to know the value of a method before it has been tried out. Once again, if it turns out to be unsuccessful, the leader should call the action to a halt. It is important to remember that when a strategy fails, it is not a defeat. A psychodrama has no preconceived objectives; spontaneity and creativity are its true trademarks.

Group psychodramas

The necessity of a group psychodrama usually shows up in the first phase, in situations where the atmosphere is so charged with emotion that many different protagonists become apparent in the group. Group psychodramas should not be encouraged because they are very difficult to control. Every once in a while they can be justifiable, as in the following example where enough therapists were present to care for the patients individually. Under certain conditions, depending on the degree of intensity, a group psychodrama can seem like a play that is unfolding on many levels simultaneously.

The 21 female patients in the following example in which I participated were all drug addicts and alcoholics. The psychodrama was videotaped and later shown to the patients and the staff. Only four men were present, two doctors and two cameramen. The staff members were interested in introducing psychodrama as a new form of therapy, but only a few of them had any experience. A psychodrama director and two assistants from the Moreno Academy in New York were present. The warming-up phase was adapted to find more than one protagonist so that the staff therapists could work individually with a protagonist under the guidance of the representatives from the Moreno Academy. The director would also demonstrate psychodramatic techniques. All of the therapists had worked with their patients previously for at least a month.

The director's opening manoeuvre was a bold one. Seated in the midst of the group members, all of whom had signed a statement that they were volunteers and agreed to being filmed, the director passed out eight rag dolls. Since her intention was to provoke a specific feeling – in this case the mothering instinct – this manoeuvre could be called 'a psychodramatic shock'. There was an immediate reaction. The women either cried and rocked the dolls in their arms, remained still as if they had been turned to stone or lay down on the floor covering their faces. These women, who only a few minutes before had been casually waiting for something to happen, suddenly acted like women in a ritual of mourning – like women grieving over their dead after a war or a natural disaster, almost like a chorus in a Greek tragedy!

Monodrama

A young black woman of huge proportions sat in the middle of the floor rocking herself back and forth – but there was no doll in her arms. She hadn't been given one. She became my protagonist and the next ten minutes brought forth a two-way drama that unfolded on many levels. The woman had never before taken part in a psychodrama. She acted directly and instinctively, driven by deep need. I started right off on my first impulse without knowing anything about the woman:

'Mamma', I said slowly, 'Mamma?'

The woman looked at me for a moment before giving me an immediate clue:

'Don't look at me that way Liz. I couldn't help it...'

'I know that, Mamma.'

'Aren't you mad at Mamma?'

'No Mamma, but are you going to come home soon?'

'They won't let me come home to you yet. It's not my fault...'

'Nothing is my mommy's fault.'

The woman took me in her arms and, a moment later, from her generous bosom, I found myself looking into two large, coal-black, tearful eyes. One of the doctors was standing nearby and suddenly, in the voice of a child, the woman asked:

'Mamma, who is that man?'

Without any instruction, she had reversed roles with me. She was her own daughter, or herself as a little girl. Now I put my arms around her and said:

'It is not dangerous.'

'But why does he come here all the time?'

Again, on instinct I answered:

'Mamma has a good friend.'

'No, he's not good, he's not a friend, he's mean!'

Since I had no information to act on, I reversed roles with her and again played the role of the little girl talking to her mother:

'Who is he, Mamma?'

'Hush now, don't ask so many questions.'

'But I'm afraid of him.'

'I've told you not to pay any attention to him.'

'He talks so loud.'

'Yes, Ernie talks loud.'

'You talk loud too, Mamma.'

Suddenly the woman acted like a small child, but I had no way of knowing whether she was herself as a child or her daughter, Liz. She caught hold of me and began screaming:

'Don't hit me, don't hit me...'

The director had been watching us for a while and whispered that I should try to get her to sleep. I held her gently, but didn't even know her name:

'Hush, hush, little one, close your eyes and sleep.'

'No, I won't go to sleep. Not while that man is here.'

'We'll ask the man to leave.'

The doctor standing next to us understood that he had become part of the drama and that it was time for him to leave:

'See there? The man has gone.'

'Promise he won't come back?'

'He won't come back now.'

The woman opened her eyes and began to speak to her child in her own voice:

'I didn't mean to hit you, Liz. They said...they said you were hurt badly.'

'It doesn't hurt anymore. I'm almost all better now, Mamm.a.

The woman curled up on my lap and sighed heavily. I stroked her hair:

'Now, little one, it is time to rest.'

The camera caught most of this drama. Before falling asleep, the woman put her thumb in her mouth and the room fell silent. The other women had calmed down, some still cuddling their dolls. When we left the institution there was still a good deal of additional work to be accomplished for the remaining therapists.

Psychodrama with a deputy protagonist

It is seldom that a protagonist does not dare to enter completely into the drama. A psychodrama's real advantage is that it allows people to throw themselves into events and participate physically. Inner feelings are put into action. Intellect, memory and feeling are activated through movement and interaction.

Should a person be embarrassed about showing emotions, this has to be respected. A careful approach could be to ask this person if he or she could request someone in the group to present the problem. Noticing the person's quick glance toward 'A', the director suggests that perhaps 'A' could be the auxiliary protagonist. The protagonist's reply might give the first clue of his inner world:

PROTAGONIST: No, 'A' looks too happy. I was looking at her because she is so different from the way I am. I wish I could be happier...

DIRECTOR: Who could you ask from the group?

PROTAGONIST: I think 'B' looks sad sometimes. Yes, I think I'm more
like her...

Hopefully, this has already helped establish some form of tele and 'B' is asked
to represent the protagonist. At this point the director concentrates on the
actual protagonist who stands in the background, giving clues and stage
instructions. The director works more or less as the protagonist's assistant.
When the drama starts, the protagonist continues directing and choosing his
auxiliary egos from the side of the stage. The precision and empathy in the
doubling of the 'background figure' is striking. As opposed to the standard
doubling technique, without moving or being anywhere near the deputy
protagonist, this doubling is virtually perfect because it is always the real
protagonist speaking through his 'mouthpiece'!

Using a deputy protagonist is an indispensable solution when a person
has a physical handicap that prevents him from active participation. A
psychodrama with a deputy protagonist being led from a wheelchair is a
gripping experience, portraying the limitless surplus reality surrounding a
person whose radius seems so bound to physical limitations.

The technical demands on the director of a psychodrama with a deputy
protagonist are no different than those of a regular psychodrama. However,
most of the additional methods are unsuitable because they require a
spontaneity that cannot be achieved when working through another person.
Therefore, a psychodrama with a deputy protagonist is more like a spontaneous dramatization, in this case carried out through the indirect participation of the protagonist.

Theme-centred psychodrama

In a psychodrama it is irrelevant to ask why a person drinks too much.
Reasons and excuses are plentiful and theoretical discussions often lead to
self-defence, guilt, justification, accusation and self-pity.

Family problems, work-related problems, fear of neighbours, the temptation to succumb every time one passes a bar, the fear that refusing a drink
on social occasions will reveal the alcohol problem – all of these can be useful
themes in a psychodrama with a group of alcoholics because of their
relevance to their specific problem.

The following theme-centred psychodrama will be described from its
warming-up phase through the enactment to the conclusion. The theme was
about growing old, what it is like and how old people are looked upon in
general. The example is chosen because it demonstrates how the content of
a psychodrama very often takes on a dramatic life of its own.

The group consisted of eight male alcoholics who were in an institution. Some of these young men were day-patients. The youngest was in his mid-twenties and the oldest was about sixty.

A heavy-set black man finally broke the long and eloquent silence which in itself bore witness to the difficulty of the subject. The man said that recently, on two separate occasions, he had been referred to as 'Sir… And it can't be because I'm so fancy. When I heard the word it occurred to me that it might be out of respect for my age. But I didn't like it!'

In the discussion that followed about whether or not Henderson was old and whether 'Sir' was an expression of respect or a slighting remark to stress his 'Uncle Tom' status, a young white man reacted strongly to the word 'respect'. He worked himself into a rage at the thought that old people should be respected just because they became 'aged and impossible'. He couldn't stand old people, and especially old people who demanded respect.

The director shifted the group's focus to this young man who had just become a day-patient. After a while, the group learned that Paul lived with an old uncle who had been 'impossible' the previous night. A tense and nervous Paul reluctantly agreed to replay last night's scene. Henderson agreed to play the part of the uncle. Paul presented the background for the scene.

They were in the kitchen and Paul was chopping onions for some hamburgers. The layout of the kitchen was carefully described. Henderson fell right into the role of the maligned uncle after Paul had reversed roles and enacted the uncle holding up a bag of chopped onions that Paul hadn't seen in the refrigerator. In a tone of voice that reflected the uncle's feelings about such wastefulness, the auxiliary ego exclaimed:

> 'You could have taken the time to look. It isn't necessary to cut up new onions when we have a whole bag…'

> 'Hey, it's only onions…'

> 'An onion costs money too. You seem to feel right at home.'

> 'I know I'm here thanks to your great charity.'

This was a loaded cue, and the leader asked Paul to walk around on the stage while talking to himself (a soliloquy).

PAUL: Don't think for a second that I like living here. I think you're stingy.

DOUBLE FROM THE GROUP: I have nowhere else to go.

PAUL: I can't stay with my wife, she stares at me all the time, as if I'm hiding a bottle in my pocket.

DOUBLE: That's not surprising, since I went on a binge last week. (*The group knew this was true.*)

PAUL: Of course I drink. Nobody believes in me. I go to night school and try to get an education. Mother just smiles and my wife thinks I should find some real work. They despise me.

DOUBLE: I cheat on the welfare money...

PAUL: That's not true. My wife gets most of the money. But I should get some, shouldn't I? And anyway, I pay my own way at my uncle's...

Paul and his 'uncle' are back in the kitchen. The director asks Paul to reconstruct what really happened. Paul points out his uncle's place at the kitchen table and the director asks him to repeat his uncle's words.

PAUL (*as uncle*): You could be more considerate of an old man.

HENDERSON (*takes the uncle's place and repeats his words*): You could be more considerate of an old man.

PAUL: You get paid. I buy food for you.

HENDERSON (*recalling Paul saying that his uncle is miserly*): The food you buy is much too expensive. And you eat it all yourself...

PAUL (*enraged*): You're an ungrateful old man! All you do is complain. Where were you when I was in Vietnam? Sitting in front of your TV! You've never protested about anything, you never even had an opinion. All you can talk about is a...a...damned onion! (*Paul raises his hand, ready to strike his uncle.*)

In crises like this, when there is danger of physical violence, the director must always interrupt. At this point, there are many ways to continue. One might be to provoke Paul while members of the group hold him back physically. This would be the best approach to make Paul express his aggression. Energetic exercises can also be introduced at this stage, to keep the action within a safe framework.

But, in this scene Paul was clearly showing tendencies of uncontrolled violence. The director had a suspicion that something serious had already happened, so he asked Paul to change places with the 'uncle' and to recreate the scene. Paul was asked to sit the same way his uncle had been sitting and the director said: 'You are old, bitter and tired. Your arms feel powerless, and you are afraid…' Paul sat down at the table reluctantly, but he still showed a strong resistance to play the role of his uncle. Henderson, the auxiliary ego, took Paul's place at the table and said: 'I am stronger than you are. You're just a weak old man!'

To intensify the words of the auxiliary ego, the director began to repeat them. When one or more members of the group give this kind of reinforcement, the protagonist experiences this as intense provocation. He feels that he is alone against all of the others. The fact that Paul protested about enacting the uncle's role was also a warning. An assailant never wants to identify with his victim. In a situation like this the protagonist usually begins to defend himself. Paul assured the group that he really liked the old man, that he was the only person in the family who helped him. He owed him a lot. He hadn't meant to hit him!

It was finally put into words. The admission was out in the open. Paul had beaten up his uncle the night before. Then he had gone to the movies and spent the night at a friend's house. He had no idea whether his uncle was dead or alive.

The media often reports that violent criminals sleep soundly after assaulting someone, that they behave as if nothing had happened. Many of these men use their time in prison to justify their crimes. Rationalization and justification are all-important tools for survival. The prison sentence is experienced as punishment but, to many, the violence in itself has been pushed so far into the background that it becomes no more than a remote event that has nothing to do with them.

Psychodramas with prisoners with long criminal backgrounds are time-consuming and laborious affairs. It is especially difficult to get to the core of the matter because the physical pain that the inmates have given to others frightens them from re-experiencing the crime. This is why it is so extremely difficult to persuade an assailant to reverse roles with his victim.

Since a confrontation between an assailant and his victim is also rare in real life, a crime has a very good chance of seeming unreal to the perpetrator. A psychodrama tries to create a picture of all of the circumstances, the course of action, that led up to the crime. It is not so difficult to get the assailant involved in this and, since he, as the protagonist, is in control of the drama, he will experience a reality that he would never experience in a confession, in court or by serving a prison sentence. Also, the psychodrama gives the person an opportunity to tell his side of the story. In contrast to the reduced reality he experienced at the moment of the crime and during the trial, he is now surrounded by surplus reality – an atmosphere that also includes seeing the consequences of his actions. Psychodramas also focus on the concept of assuming responsibility for one's actions.

In the psychodrama with Paul the director included the final empty chair method. The imaginary person in the chair was Paul's uncle, whom we surmised was either dead or dying but whom we brought back to life symbolically. The whole group took part by voicing its thoughts and accusations. The fantasies of the group were guided toward the 'man in the chair' but their reactions had a strong effect on the protagonist who was barred from defending himself and could only listen to the group's fantasies about the many consequences of what he had done. This is an extremely harsh way of confronting a person with his responsibility for his actions and, to keep it from getting out of control, it must be used with caution.

In contrast to the protagonist, the group members have no trouble identifying with the victim of *another person's* criminal act and they often react by working off their own guilt feelings. In this way, Paul was forced to consider the fate of the old man. It also began to dawn on him that he might be called to account for his actions.

We had learned that the old man was still alive. Two empty chairs were placed in front of Paul. The Paul who had killed his uncle sat in one of them, while the Paul who hadn't yet come home to fry his onions sat in the other. By now he was so accommodating that he was willing to reverse roles with the 'occupants' of the chairs, representing the two sides of his destiny: the day patient who was still a free man, going to night school and living with his uncle and the other, the murderer. In the final scene Paul was on his way home to his uncle's house. This was an artificial situation, but a psychodrama works primarily within the realm of simulated reality in order to focus more strongly on real life. Since the uncle had not been seriously injured, this scene acquired a new dimension. Paul would be returning to his uncle's house – just as he was in the psychodrama – that very evening. He was not a murderer.

The psychodrama had confirmed itself as a rehearsal for real life.

A psychodrama about a murder

The previous psychodramatic process could be considered preventive therapy. Since Paul's uncle was not dead, the detailed process of going through the possible consequences of his action gave Paul fresh insight into his life. This was by no means a guarantee that he would never commit a violent act in the future, but at least he had experienced what it was like to face the consequences. His gradually increasing empathy for the victim had allowed him to experience, and perhaps understand, that all the trivialities and feelings of impotence leading up to his action were interrelated. Often, a

violent act is seen only as an isolated occurrence. While serving a prison
sentence, most prisoners have a hard time facing up to their guilt and their
punishment.

The following example is included because it is unusual, and points out
certain aspects of the need to serve a sentence. Even in the warming-up phase
of this psychodrama we can see some of the irrational feelings that seek out
and discover unknown depths in an individual.

The group was composed of eight male inmates from a New York
penitentiary and ten psychodrama students, most of whom were female. The
inmates, blacks and Puerto Ricans except for two white men, were all
volunteer participants and, among the students, there were a few blacks and
Puerto Ricans, although the majority were middle-class whites. Ages ranged
from 20 to 50. As soon as Dexter, a 50-year-old Southerner, agreed to be
the protagonist, five of the inmates insisted on leaving the room. They did
not want to be witnesses.

The psychodrama started with a soliloquy. With stooped shoulders,
Dexter started walking around the stage:

> I haven't been back home for a long time, some place
> down South… You don't know what it's like to grow
> up down there…as a black. Often you could detect
> the smell of burned…nigger meat. I'm serving a term
> for burglary. I've been in and out of jails for years.
> Guess I'll never get out of this vicious circle. Once
> burned, you'll always smell burned… I hate all of
> society. Hate the whites most. No, I hate my own
> most, for accepting injustice, poverty and
> oppression…

DOUBLE (*a black man*): I really hate myself too, because I'm not doing
anything to improve the situation…

DEXTER: Yes, that too. But what's the sense in trying? You're up
to your neck in shit and shame. I've tried to change,
but after a while I'm right back in the pen again.

DOUBLE: I hate the whites…

DEXTER: It was those damned Browns…

DIRECTOR: Tell us about the Browns, Dexter.

DEXTER: Brown was one of those fat whites, with a fat wallet
and stingy as hell. My father used to work for him
on the farm, and all he got were lousy wages and

four-letter words. Mrs Brown was an old bag who
wished all blacks were dead, or at least that she
wouldn't have to feed them. But Bertram, the son,
he was alright. We hung out together.

DIRECTOR: Do you see anyone in the group who could
                 be Bertram?
                 (*Dexter points at a young white boy.*)
                 Now show us Bertram as he was at the time you
                 want to go back to.

DEXTER: Bertram and I are the same age.
                 (*They walk up onto the stage.*)
                 He's leaving the drugstore. I'm standing there with
                 my bike. Bertram is inviting me to a party that night.

AUXILIARY EGO: Hi!

DEXTER: Hi!

AUXILIARY EGO: Want to come to a party?

DEXTER: Where?

AUXILIARY EGO: Not very far away, a few miles.

DEXTER: How can we get there?
                 (*It was obvious that he was beginning to relive this time in
                 the past. His facial expression changed and he seemed
                 younger.*)

DIRECTOR (*to Dexter*): Did you go?
                 (*Dexter nods.*)
                 How did you get there?

DEXTER: Bertram took his father's car.

The scene now shows a car, made from two chairs. It was a funny looking
couple 'driving' to the party. Dexter, a big, heavy-set man, sitting next to
skinny little Bertram, the driver.

DEXTER: My Mom and Dad don't know about this. They'd
                 never let me go.

AUXILIARY EGO: I wouldn't worry, I never tell my folks where I'm
                 going.

DEXTER: It's different for me. What if something happened?

AUXILIARY EGO: What could happen?

DEXTER: Well, you know, some things have happened...

AUXILIARY EGO: Like what?

DEXTER: You know perfectly well… Don't you remember
                 Jimmy Pierce?
                 (*Here, the director had them reverse roles so the protagonist
                 could give some more information.*)

DEXTER: Sure, I remember Jimmy Pierce. And Sam Oliver.
                 And Harry Stapler. They were lynched by the Ku
                 Klux Klan. They were ambushed. Sam Oliver was
                 killed. And… Jimmy Pierce was blinded.

DIRECTOR (*helping the auxiliary ego*): But that wouldn't happen to you.
                 You're just a kid…

AUXILIARY EGO: That wouldn't happen to you. You're just a kid. Anyway,
                 I know some of the girls. We'll have some fun.

A BLACK MAN FROM THE GROUP STANDS UP AND DOUBLES: But if
                 they're *white* girls? Of course it could happen to me.
                 Those types don't ask to see your birth certificate.

DIRECTOR: Did you meet any white girls?
                 (*Dexter nods.*)

AUXILIARY EGO: The girls are white, but they're okay. Don't worry.

DEXTER: Anyway, it's too late to turn back now.

DIRECTOR: What happened later? Describe where you are.

DEXTER: It's a large meeting-house in the countryside. Some
                 white men are standing around outside the door.
                 Music, they're dancing inside. When I wanted to go
                 in with Bertram, two of the men came over to me.
                 They'd been drinking. One of them asked me to
                 come around behind the house. Want a swig? he
                 asked, grinning. I knew right away that he was
                 dangerous.

DIRECTOR: Do you want to replay the scene?

DEXTER: I think that's why I came today. This haunts me,
                 and back then I didn't dare do anything but go with
                 him.

DIRECTOR: What happened to Bertram?

DEXTER: I didn't see any more of him.

DIRECTOR: Was it dark?

DEXTER: Yes, it was dark, but I remember that there was a new moon. I saw it on our way there in the car.
(*The lights are turned down bathing the stage in a soft, bluish light.*)

DIRECTOR: How many men were there?

DEXTER: Four. When they got me behind the house they put on their white hoods...

Some grey woollen blankets were used to cover the four auxiliary egos. In the subdued light the figures looked like characters from a nightmare, even to the rest of the group. Symbolically, the four men began to strike Dexter until he fell to the floor. His scream was so dreadful and real that everyone in the room felt they were witnessing a scene from real life. Dexter remained motionless on the floor.

Once again, it is important to remember the many strange and surprising reactions that can turn up in a psychodrama. Dexter remained on the floor, seemingly unconscious. After a long pause, he began to breathe deeply and erratically. Suddenly he shouted: 'I can't see! I can't see anything! They have poked out my eyes...'

The director kneeled beside Dexter and spoke to him gently. One by one the group members went up to him, showing their sympathy by touching him softly, letting him know he was among friends. He slowly became aware of where he was. He was trembling and hardly looked like the burly hostile man we had seen earlier. Tears ran down his face and he sniffled like a child. Someone gave him a handkerchief.

DEXTER (*weakly*): I lay there until daylight. Those bastards had glued my eyes shut with mud. I thought I was blind, just like Jimmy Pierce. Then I began to rub my eyes.
(*Dexter rubs his eyes.*)
After a while I caught a glimpse of light. I got up and began to walk home. It was already afternoon.

DIRECTOR: You are on your way home. Think out loud.

DEXTER (*walking around the room*): I'll get hold of you, you bastard. Just you wait. I'm going to walk right in and...if you're there, I'll kill you. I'll have to get my pistol first. I stole it once when someone scared me. I'll have to sneak in the back way...

DIRECTOR: Is anyone there?

DEXTER: Yes, my mother sees me and runs toward me.

DIRECTOR: Do you see anyone in the group that could be your
                 mother?

                 (*Dexter points shyly at a chubby white woman.*)

DIRECTOR: Can you show us what she's like?

Dexter sat down in a chair, crossing his arms (note that even in his agitated
state he can still understand and follow instructions).

DEXTER (*as his mother*): Don't do anything stupid, honey. Remember
                 whites always mean trouble. Be careful, that's all I
                 can teach you...

The woman from the group takes Dexter's place in the chair and assumed
his 'mother's' position.

AUXILIARY EGO: Where have you been, sonny? I've been sitting up all
                 night waiting for you. You know how it scares me
                 when you're not home.

DEXTER: Everything's fine, mother. Don't you worry.

AUXILIARY EGO: But just look at you! Something has happened.

DEXTER: Stay out of this. You have nothing to do with it.

AUXILIARY EGO: You're frightening me. Are you...hurt?

DEXTER: Okay, start crying. 'Be careful!' How the hell do you
                 think I can be careful?

DIRECTOR: Do you want to reverse roles with your mother?

DEXTER: That's not necessary. All she did was cry, just like she
                 always did. But...it's just...that was the last time I
                 saw her.

DIRECTOR (*letting a long pause of silence fall over the room*): Is there
                 anything more you want to say to your mother?

DEXTER: Not now.

DIRECTOR: Where are you?

DEXTER: I'm walking toward the Browns' farm. I can see my
                 father out in the field. His back is bent from hard
                 work and humiliation.

DIRECTOR: Are you looking for Bertram?

DEXTER: The hell with Bertram! I'm looking for every damned
                 white I can find!

DIRECTOR: There's Bertram.
                (*The young white boy stands up and goes to his assigned place.*)
                What are you doing? Are you aiming at him?

DEXTER: Death is too good for that kind of...

The group waits in breathless silence. But Dexter doesn't 'shoot' Bertram. He just stands there looking at him with a strange expression on his face. The leader asks 'Bertram' to lie down and act like he's dead.

DEXTER: Little shit. It wasn't your fault. You're not dead. You probably have problems at home, and may the devil give you some agonizing nightmares. Like the ones I've had, lying in a cell full of a lot of other damned bastards.

DIRECTOR: Where are you now? In jail?

DEXTER: No, it's just the boredom. Miserable boredom, corruption and male whores.

DIRECTOR: Where are you, Dexter? Bertram seems to be dead. Do you want to bring him back to life and talk about what happened?

DEXTER (*almost panicking*): No! Bertram isn't dead.

DIRECTOR: Who is dead?

ONE OF THE BLACK STUDENTS STARTED TO DOUBLE: Stop your questions! Haven't I suffered enough? You damn whites always want the upper hand.
                (*Note that aggression is being transferred onto the director.*)

DEXTER: I haven't suffered enough. Not here.

DIRECTOR: Do you want to continue?

Dexter stood in the middle of the floor, unable to make up his mind. Then a white woman rose. She was in her mid-forties, a hesitant type with a thin small voice. She walked right up to Dexter and began to tell her story:

                One morning, when I was a little girl, I woke up extra early. It couldn't have been much more than about four o'clock. I saw my father riding home. I'm also from the South. He hid something under some bushes. Later, when I got up, I went out to the bushes and found... There was blood on the

clothing. The next day everyone was talking about
it. They (Ku Klux Klan) had lynched a black man. I
never talk to my father anymore...never really. I
think I've hated him ever since then. (*She reached out,
taking Dexter's hand.*) I'll go with you. If you want to
continue.

A MEMBER OF THE GROUP (*gently*): I think you should, Dexter.

ANOTHER MEMBER OF THE GROUP: Is it right to continue? We're
pushing him.

The situation was tricky. Was Dexter's problem something that he had done
time for or was it something 'worse'? Dexter solved the problem himself. He
wanted to continue, but only with three specific persons. The others were
asked to leave the room.

Technically, the scene that followed can be seen as an early insertion of
the psychodrama's final phase. In short sentences, Dexter told his secret, one
that he had never told anyone else. He had not killed Bertram or any of the
men that beat him up so long ago. The victim had been the person who
represented everything that Dexter associated with defeat, his father's
employer. The murder had never been solved and, by now, it was probably
too late to try the case. But Dexter never managed to get away from his
feelings of guilt. No matter how small his crimes were over the years, he was
always caught and sent to jail.

The subsequent conclusion was a strange experience. We had no personal
experiences to share. All we had in common was our understanding of a
young boy who had been brutally mishandled and who therefore became a
murderer. Dexter sat silently, looking down at his hands. Was he regretting
his confession?

At this point the director initiated something that would relieve the
tension, even for those who had been outside during the confession. The
members of the group were asked to stand in a circle around Dexter. The
circle was to symbolize the solid wall of hatred that Dexter would break free
from. It was a dramatic and violent struggle, almost a repetition of his
childhood fight with his four assailants. Dexter struggled to break through,
crying and begging to get through the wall. But the group had inner reserves
of determination and its members knew that it was not kindness that Dexter
needed now. The group members felt their collective strength; they were the
white race, superior and dominating. Feelings of shame in representing
prejudice and hatred gave way to an understanding of the roles we had to
play for Dexter. After a long struggle, Dexter got through.

In the final conclusive phase it was clear that the group had changed. There was a new feeling of togetherness, transversing all lines of race and social status. The blacks had not been part of the circle around Dexter. Using a final non-verbal method, the director asked the group members to walk around the room and shake hands with everyone to strengthen the ties among the group members. Before leaving the room, Dexter expressed his feelings of relief after the psychodrama: 'I'm so happy that I won't have to keep running and looking over my shoulder anymore. It was so exhausting…'

Guided psychodrama with a suicidal patient

The following is chosen as an example of the procedure used to try out whether a suicide attempt was genuine or a last desperate cry for help.

In a group of about twenty women with psychological problems, some combined with histories of drugs and alcohol, the director noticed a young girl who seemed to have shut herself away from communication. Like the others, she had agreed to videotaping the entire session but it seemed like she felt it had nothing to do with her.

In the warming-up phase the group members had worked in pairs, showing each other imaginary pictures of themselves as young girls and sharing associations about their hopes and dreams from their past when 'life hadn't really started'. The theme of youth and hope is nearly always an emotional one, but these feelings rarely turn up during the first exercise. Reactions seem to be stored away and to break out much later in the process. This is particularly true of people who have systematically abused themselves through drugs and alcohol. Their feelings of hopelessness seem to have overwhelmed them.

The members of the group were between 16 and 65 years of age. The young girl the director focused on was 19. Actually, there were three generations of mothers in the group; the youngest was 17, but it turned out that the group was not going to unite on the mother/child level, the feeling of not managing to be a good mother or the generation gap.

The girl had left the group and was staring out of the window. When the director took her hand and led her back into the midst of the group, placing her in an imaginary play-pen, the idea had been to initiate a child/adult constellation. Suddenly the girl was in the middle of the group she had left, either from fear or because she felt rejected by the group. When asked her name, her answer was almost impossible to hear. The leader asked: 'Don't you want to be here with us?'

The long pause that followed indicated a need for contact, although her entire person signalled the opposite.

DIRECTOR (*speaking to her as if she were a child*): What were you thinking about over by the window while the rest of us were talking?

EILEEN (*after a long pause*): That I want to die.

DIRECTOR (*undisturbed*): That's strange. When I saw you standing there it looked like you were reaching for something. You didn't move, but I imagined that you were reaching into space. Have you ever felt as if you kind of have to grasp for your life?

The director had defined the situation and selected the protagonist. In cases like this it is of vital importance that the group become interested in what is happening. Without the engagement of the group, the director can just as well have a monodrama with the protagonist and let the group leave the room. But here the sentence 'Have you ever felt as if you kind of have to grasp for your life?' caught the interest of the group. It was a theme they could relate to. Still holding Eileen by the hand, the director joined the circle of women and made room for Eileen. Eileen was now a member of the group, but she was still the one in focus because the director stayed with her. Nevertheless, it took some time to capture the group's interest in Eileen's problem.

The director looked around the circle of women and continued:

Let us all think that we have our whole lives ahead of us. Not the past, but the future.

ONE OF THE WOMEN BROKE IN SPONTANEOUSLY: That's not much as far as I'm concerned.

ANOTHER BROKE IN QUICKLY: In and out. In and out. This is the fourth time I'm here. When I get home, nothing has changed. After three or four months I'm ready for the hospital again.

DIRECTOR (*in reply to the woman*): If you look into your house, what is the first thing you see?

WOMAN: Levy! *That's* my future. Help yourself, he's all yours!

DIRECTOR: Is that all you see?

WOMAN: How can I avoid seeing him?

DIRECTOR: Let's get rid of him!
                (*She stands up and sweeps the imaginary Levy out the door, closing it carefully.*)

WOMAN (*slightly anxious*): I don't know, it's…now it's Levy who's making the money.

DIRECTOR: What about yourself, can't you get a job?

WOMAN: A job? Sure, but I've got five children.

DIRECTOR: Who looks after them while you're here?

WOMAN: I…they…get help from the social services.

DIRECTOR: But Levy doesn't take care of them?

WOMAN (*angrily*): What are you getting at? You don't get help unless you've hit rock bottom!

DIRECTOR: Have you tried to get a job?

WOMAN: What can I do? Nothing. After working for a while my anxiety comes back and I start drinking again.

DIRECTOR: Is that how you grasp for your life?

Almost unnoticeably, the theme was reintroduced to the group. The director was trying to unite the group around the theme that had shown itself to be the most pressing one in the group. Eileen's wish to die was surrounded by the destinies of burned-out, anguished women who also needed help.

The director introduced a new warming-up exercise. When a group is weak in resources and its verbal communication is limited, non-verbal and symbolic exercises are useful for establishing a group feeling. The women sat in a circle on the floor and, without any sign of stage fright, they performed a simple, symbolical act which was both moving and pitiful. They were stretching their arms into the air above them, trying to grasp a few happy moments in their lives.

This exercise was also important in terms of sounding out the basic mood of the group. A hostile or indifferent group would not be able to tolerate a psychodrama with a suicide patient and, theoretically, a group that is going to deal with a problem like this should not have too many other patients in it. Here there were only two assistants, whose task was to localize opposition and anxiety and to try to neutralize negative feelings by drawing the members of the group into a positive mood. The director's task is to support the potential protagonist. In this group it turned out that the women who were not caught up by the problem were either suffering from severe abstinence problems or so apathetic that they had no understanding of the problem. These were asked to leave the group. Those who stayed – a small, active group – were women who wanted to find something positive to live for. Suddenly, Eileen said: 'There's no point in keeping me here. The others don't like me'.

DIRECTOR: Now I'm going to say something to the group that Eileen certainly hasn't thought about. Very often, when people don't want to live any longer, they think that nobody cares about them and that they might not have the right to live.

EILEEN: Nobody here likes me.

A WOMAN IN THE GROUP: That's not true. But with the doomsday face that you carry around, you can't expect people to run behind you shouting Hallelujah. We aren't angels, and god knows we have enough on our own minds too.

DIRECTOR: Is there anyone here who can show Eileen and me how she looks to others.
(*And to Eileen*): I'm sorry but we don't always think about our effect on other people or how this makes them react to us.

The woman who left her place seemed worried about having to perform, but with encouragement from the director to exaggerate, she seemed to warm up to the role. The following illustrates the mirror technique:

THE WOMAN WALKED AROUND THE ROOM WITH A SULKY EXPRESSION: Don't talk to me. Leave me alone. The hell with all of you. I'm not like you. I'm a winner! Okay, I'm a drug addict, but at least I'm not an old wino! (*Turning to an older woman who constantly pressed a handkerchief to her nose.*) And when I shoot up, I do it systematically. Each trip is one step closer to extinction. I can't stand people like you.

EILEEN: Is that supposed to be me? You haven't understood anything. It's true that I can't stand any of you, but not because I think I'm such a great person! I just don't want to go on. I've felt this way for years!

DIRECTOR: Who do you think it was? Wasn't that like you?

EILEEN: Not me, no. That was Doris, no one else. She has her own hell to live through. She flashes [*a relapse after not having taken LSD for a long time*], so she sees Satan in a coma. But charm, you know all about that, Doris. All

you have to do is flick your behind and you've got
the whole unit behind you!

Doris, who was a voluptuous woman, was speechless. No one had heard
Eileen fight back like this before. Doris looked like she herself needed
someone to rescue her.

DIRECTOR: I'm in doubt here, shall we ask Doris and Eileen to
               reverse roles?

The group was more than willing but Eileen turned away; no more reactions
came from her. She was totally preoccupied with her own thoughts. The
director began to speak to her in a soft voice: 'Well Eileen, you can have your
way. It's alright. It was you who wanted to die...' (Eileen nods, without
replying).

The group maintained complete silence. Without any knowledge of this form
of psychodrama, it might seem like a direct invitation to commit suicide. The
women sat as if they were in a trance. But it is important to remember that in a
psychodrama the group seems to accept anything without technical explanations, no matter how morbid or absurd it seems. No one protested or even moved.

DIRECTOR: I can see that you've made your decision, Eileen. You've
               attempted suicide before, and you don't want to live
               any longer, do you Eileen?
               (*Eileen shakes her head and the director continues*): I think
               it's fair to support your decision. You have our full
               support. (*This last is addressed to the group which remains
               in complete silence.*) Still, it's a shame to allow you to
               disappear just like that. You have looked forward to
               this day. It should be a real event. It's sad to die
               unnoticed. You've made an important decision, you
               know. How will you do it? Morphine? Overdose?
               Sleeping pills? A knife? Or will you hang yourself?

Drugs addicts rarely want to die from an overdose. Eileen flinched at the first
suggestion. Interestingly, there are very few drug addicts who are willing to
admit that being a drug addict can lead to their own death. Others, yes, but
not their own.

EILEEN: I want sleeping pills.

DIRECTOR: Good girl. A knife draws so much blood. And if you
               hang yourself, it will be a tough job to make a
               pretty corpse of you. Not very pleasant for the
               people who find you, either.

EILEEN: That would just serve them right.

DIRECTOR: They say that the eyes are nearly popping out of their
               sockets when people hang themselves. Well, if that's
               what a person wants, it's okay by me. But you want
               sleeping pills. How many do you need?

EILEEN: At least I want to make sure I have enough.

At this point the suicide patient is deeply into the drama. It has been said
that it is lethal to stop at this juncture. Having gone so far, the drama has to
be continued until its conclusion.

DIRECTOR (*opening an imaginary jar of pills*): Here are 50 strong
               sleeping pills. You should take them all at the same
               time. But wait a minute. Do you want to tell us how
               you want the funeral to be?

This fantasy game about one's own death is a grotesque element that is
common in psychodramas with suicidal patients. The director took Eileen
by the arm and guided her to an imaginary coffin. As if she were sleepwalk-
ing, Eileen stepped into the coffin, lay down and made herself comfortable,
crossing her arms over her chest. The women in the group couldn't believe
their eyes. But the director continued talking gently to Eileen, asking what
she was wearing.

EILEEN: My best dress.

DIRECTOR: Please describe it for us.

EILEEN: It's the one I got to wear to the big school concert.

DIRECTOR: How old were you then?

EILEEN: Fifteen.

DIRECTOR: What happened at the concert?

EILEEN: I played in the orchestra. My sister Kate…the one who
               died…sat in the front row…with my mother.

DIRECTOR: It's a beautiful dress, Eileen.

EILEEN: The finest dress I've ever had. Mom never denied me
               anything. Even when I was in jail she came and
               bailed me out.

DIRECTOR: You look lovely in the coffin, Eileen.

EILEEN: I'm wearing make-up, too. Green eye-shadow, and my hair
               is hanging loosely on either side of my face. My dress is
               light blue with embroidery on the neck and arms.

DIRECTOR: How come you looked so unkempt when you were at the institution?

EILEEN: I didn't dare look too good...

DIRECTOR: Who were you afraid of? Yourself?

EILEEN: Everyone.

DIRECTOR: It's a shame if 'everyone' has made such a nice girl get into this narrow coffin. I don't like the thought of the dress, your pretty hair, even your makeup, burning. What if you changed your mind?

EILEEN: I never regret anything I do.

DIRECTOR: No, maybe not anything you've done, but think of all the things you haven't done. And what about the world? Why should you take a jump into the great unknown when you aren't even finished with this world? You don't know what you're going to and you haven't justified yourself.

EILEEN: I don't care.

DIRECTOR: Well, I can tell you that if you leave the world this way, there's not one single person who will understand what you tried to tell them by leaving so quickly.

EILEEN: There's nothing to tell.

DIRECTOR: Good, if that's what you think. But why make such a big deal out of your dress from that concert? The one your mother spent so much money on. How do you think she would feel?

EILEEN: There's not one living soul who cares. At least nobody who would understand.

DIRECTOR: Can't you think of one person who would listen to you?

EILEEN (*after a long pause*): My sister.

DIRECTOR: There. You have a witness.

EILEEN: A witness? What do you mean?

DIRECTOR: A witness who knows the reason.

EILEEN: Why do I have to have a reason?

DIRECTOR: It's time for you to be logical now. Of course you have a reason for not wanting to live. You have every right to make it public.

EILEEN: No one in the public wants to hear.

DIRECTOR: We are the public. Look around you. Aren't you
               surrounded by people?

Eileen raised herself up on her elbows and looked into all of the faces around
her. Some of the group nodded encouragingly, others showed that they were
following carefully. No one turned away.

DIRECTOR: Do you see anyone here who resembles your sister and
               who might be able to be your sister for a little while?

EILEEN (*after a very long pause*): There has been one…she's been here
               for a long time…

DIRECTOR: Will you show me who she is?

Eileen left her 'coffin' and, with a trembling hand, pointed toward a young
black woman. The ceremonial atmosphere was reminiscent of ancient times,
witch hunts. The woman who was chosen was afraid and wanted to refuse
but the director took her hand and asked if she would help Eileen. The
woman nodded, somewhat confused.

DIRECTOR: What is your name?

WOMAN: Deborah.

DIRECTOR: Do you know Eileen?

DEBORAH: We're in the same unit.

DIRECTOR: Don't be afraid, Deborah. What I want you to do is
               to help me find out what happened between Eileen
               and her sister. If Eileen agrees.

Again there was a long, silent pause. And then Eileen nodded. In passing, I
was asked to try to be her double. This resulted in one of my most amazing
experiences in psychodrama, especially because we had so little in common.
We were absolutely different in age, race, socio-economic background, drug
abuse, and finally, a revealing factor: without her knowing it, the girl
probably had lesbian tendencies.

When Eileen met Deborah on the floor, she had returned totally to her
past. She cried out: 'Why did you die? Why did you leave me behind and
alone? Sandy, Oh, Sandy!'

DIRECTOR (*to Deborah*): Welcome, Sandy. We're trying to understand
               why Eileen doesn't want to live any longer. We
               think you can help us. Would you introduce us to
               your sister, Eileen?

EILEEN (*hesitantly*): This is Sandy... She is...was twenty when she
died a year ago.

DIRECTOR: How do you remember her?

EILEEN: In her bed. She was lying in her bed but I didn't know
what was wrong with her. She got worse and worse.
She could barely swallow a little soup.

DIRECTOR (*to Deborah*): Lie down here.
(*Deborah lies down close to where Eileen had been lying in
the 'coffin'.*)
You are ill and Eileen is going to serve you some soup.

EILEEN: The doctor said it was tuberculosis. But I know why
she died. She died from poverty, dirt and hell. And
because my father never brought any money home
to my mother. And my mother, my mother...who
was a whore.

DIRECTOR: What does that mean?

EILEEN: That she took money for doing what decent married
couples do for free...

DIRECTOR: But now Sandy is ill. How will you try to help her?

EILEEN: She just got sicker and sicker every day. How could I
help her?
(*Suddenly she screams.*)
You *wanted* to die, Sandy! And you left me alone. I
will never, never forgive you!

At just this point an intuitive idea occurred to me that cannot be explained.
I walked over to Eileen and asked 'Sandy': 'What was it that you took with
you when you died?' The reaction came as a shock to everyone, including
Eileen's therapist. Eileen walked over to Deborah and kissed her directly on
the mouth. Her movements were suddenly very masculine. Her slight figure
radiated a kind of strength we had never noticed before.

In a situation like this the psychodrama should be interrupted. Eileen sat
down on the floor and hid her face in her hands, while Deborah melted into
the group. The leader knelt down beside Eileen:

There is no reason to hide your eyes from us, Eileen.
I think you should be proud that you managed to
express yourself so clearly. What you just did was a
symbolic action. With a kiss you tried to show us

what your sister took with her when she died. A kiss can mean so very much, for example you were showing us love. Was it love your sister took from you?

EILEEN (*so softly that she is barely heard*): Yes, in a way it was love...

DIRECTOR: When she died wasn't there anyone you loved?

EILEEN: When Sandy died, everything was taken from me. In a sense, I disappeared too.

DIRECTOR: And since then you don't think you've lived?

EILEEN: Yes...no...

DIRECTOR: And then you started with drugs?

EILEEN: While Sandy was alive I never used drugs. They came later. I didn't care about anything. I came to this place because I tried to commit suicide.

DIRECTOR: What if you didn't really mean to end your life? Many times, trying to commit suicide is just a way to call out for help. Could it be that you just needed help?

EILEEN: What kind of help?

DIRECTOR: Help to find out why you are so confused about yourself. I have a feeling you're not quite sure whether you're attracted to boys or girls. No, don't look down. Many people your age don't know. Some never find out either, because they don't dare. There is nothing strange about being attracted to your own sex. And maybe this isn't even your problem.

EILEEN: Then what is my problem?

DIRECTOR: That you don't know who you are and that you don't accept yourself as you are. Do you think these could be your problems?

Here the director brought in the group and asked if there were any others who felt, every once in a while, that they didn't know themselves. The director may have moved away from the theme of homosexuality because Eileen seemed so shocked about what had happened. As a rule, problems in connection with homosexuality are not avoided in a psychodrama. This subject can result in very dramatic scenes. In this case focusing on the feeling of not being in contact with one's true self was a manoeuvre to ease the pressure that had built up. The group members, who had known one another from daily life in the unit, also seemed to be embarrassed. Changing the subject to something most of them could talk about also gave Eileen an immediate feeling of support. Most people in the group were familiar with being their own worst enemies from their experiences from drugs and alcohol and a suicide attempt wasn't anything new to them either. This was a good form and many wise observations were exchanged, based on bitter experiences. The interruption and the premature insertion of the concluding phase was only meant as a temporary pause, an additional method. It was obvious that Eileen was not finished with her psychodrama. She remained sitting on the floor with her eyes cast downward. Her posture was a study of deep depression.

THE DIRECTOR APPROACHED HER CAREFULLY: What are you thinking about, Eileen?

EILEEN: The same thing.

DIRECTOR: What's that?

EILEEN: That I want to die.

In a way it made sense that Eileen kept to her original idea. Many protagonists adhere to the starting point of the psychodrama. Furthermore, rather than receiving help, she may have felt exposed and betrayed. Also, the extent of her depression and whether she really wanted to die were still uncertain.

Those who are not familiar with a psychodramatic suicide will think that the next step is grotesque. However, it is a standard procedure that only changes subtly when it is used. Its objective is to ascertain the depth of the desire to commit suicide.

WHEN EILEEN REPEATED THAT SHE WANTED TO DIE, THE DIRECTOR SPOKE TO HER CALMLY: Why not? It's your own life. Nobody here can stop you, and since we are witnesses we can also help you. After all, it is a very important decision. How will you do it?

EILEEN: Pills. But first a needle and then pills. But this time I'll make sure I take enough of them.

DIRECTOR: Where are you now? Describe exactly where you are.

Once again, it is important to notice how the protagonist seems so willing to become engaged in the drama, even in her own death. This supports the theory that all human beings have an inherent need to engage themselves in their own life situations. In Moreno's words: 'the instinctive will to shape one's one destiny'.

In response to the director's question, Eileen said that she was at home. She described her room, where she wanted to die. Hesitantly, but in detail, she presented a picture of the family's hopeless life in a slum. Gradually she began to prepare for 'the grand event'. Eileen poured pills into her hand from an imaginary bottle and stuffed them into her mouth. Then she gave herself an injection and took a few more pills. Finally, she lay down on the floor with folded arms and closed eyes.

DIRECTOR: What are you wearing?

EILEEN (*trance-like*): A dress my mother bought for me to wear to a
                party.

DIRECTOR: What does it look like?

EILEEN: It's pale blue with lace, knee-length, a tight bodice
               and a wide skirt.

Eileen's description of this feminine dress was in sharp contrast to the tight jeans and T-shirt she was wearing. The director signalled to the group to walk around the 'coffin' and said:

                She's lovely isn't she? (*murmured agreement*) She probably
                didn't know that while she was alive. Otherwise she
                would never have chosen to die. What a waste...

A WOMAN: I bet she was popular with the boys...

ANOTHER WOMAN: She may not have liked boys. You can live
                without men, I know.

THIRD WOMAN: I've never understood why young people want to
                die. That I want to die is a different story. I'm just an
                old shell of a person.

Many similar comments were made while the group wandered around the room. Finally, in a light tone of voice, the director said: 'Of course it's a shame, but there's nothing we can do about it. Anyway, it's getting late. We can't stand around here any more. And furthermore, I'm starving!'

This last remark was a cue to the assistants who were familiar with this strange ritual. Lucille, the other assistant, began talking about a movie she wanted to see. I said something about a party. The point is to concentrate attention on everyday things that might sound tempting to the protagonist. We talked about good food, drinks, shopping and all sorts of other daily pleasures. It is also important to talk about longing for things, things that are meaningful in a spiritual sense without sounding moralistic.

This is a crucial moment for judging the desperation of the suicide patient. A person who genuinely wants to die will not react. However, when the protagonist still feels connected to life, the reaction is always the same: the 'body' doesn't want to be left alone. This might indicate how important it is for suicidal persons to have some form of social contact in their near environment. The first time we caught a glimpse of a smile on Eileen's face was when she stepped out of her 'coffin'. Could it have been in self-irony? Eileen said that she felt better than she had before the psychodrama, but she asked to talk to her therapist.

Psychodrama cannot solve such deep existential problems within a few short hours but it can hasten progress toward improvement. Eileen's case called for immediate follow-up in the form of individual therapy. Had she remained in her 'coffin', she would have been hospitalized immediately and given the intensive care that suicidal patients require.

Conclusion

Psychodrama is a therapeutic method that aims to reduce tension through participation. The protagonist is the author of his personal life, acting in an experimental theatre where he sets his own premises. Members of the group act as stand-ins for persons from his real life. The objective is to provide insight into his behaviour patterns and the ability to control his own life. The group members become co-actors and co-therapists. The director is the stage manager who uses his special skills and techniques to stage imaginary scenes from real life as the protagonist experiences it.

On a deeper level, a psychodrama is an expansion and magnification of a clinical interview. The main difference is that the client does not describe himself and his state of mind, he acts out his feelings in a here-and-now relationship to auxiliary egos from members of the group who then respond with spontaneous reactions created by the protagonist through the role reversal technique. This is a guided acting out which the director controls and has the authority to interrupt at any time.

Two elements are strictly forbidden in psychodrama: physical violence and intellectual interpretation. These fundamental rules apply to the group members, the director and the protagonist. Insight is gained by recognizing and understanding reactions and basic attitudes and by sharing common experiences. Interpersonal relationships can be directly studied in a psycho-drama under the guidance of the director, who can adjust the area of focus according to his objective. This makes it possible to isolate certain vital factors that will throw light on the protagonist's underlying mental dispo-sition, for example his attitude toward authority, or a general attitude toward life. The entire inner life of the protagonist can be brought to life through the fantasies he expresses to an imaginary father, mother or sibling, or toward different professional groups. In this sense, a psychodrama is also a projective test that makes it possible to chart the protagonist's psychological structure and how he experiences meaningful persons in his personal universe. In turn, a psychodrama becomes a method for understanding a person within the context of a family or other important frames of reference. Its practical value is in social training and the support the protagonist receives from the director and members of the group while he is trying to master difficult challenges. Some persons need a certain amount of elementary role training to take on their life roles successfully, while others require many psychodramas to conquer deep emotional conflicts and even others may think that a single psychodrama provides sufficient help in recognizing an inadequate behaviour pattern before continuing in individual therapy. It is impossible to generalize about the depth of help that a psychodrama can offer or how quickly this help can be gained. When some individuals find that one psychodrama suffices, this is usually because they have achieved a spontaneous insight or an emotional a-ha experience about relatively simple problems. These could be problems related to inappropriate reactions at a place of employment or destructive reactions within a family. Others need two or three psychodramas to look at their problems in depth and to find alternative solutions. This is where 'rehearsal for life' can be an important method, because the protagonist is given an opportunity to rehearse for future challenges. By trying out different ways to handle simple, imaginary situations, he might find concrete solutions to actual problems in his life. In many cases a psychodrama will delve deeply into a childhood and bring long-forgotten experiences of anxiety to light. For some, this experience can then become the starting point for in-depth individual therapy. For others, the experience itself may be all that is necessary since the psychodramatic experience in itself has explained something the protagonist had not been able to understand. Regularly scheduled psychodramas with the same people will usually deal with themes that interest the majority of the group. These themes can be enacted by different protagonists and not only benefit the group process as a whole but provide each member of the group with a richer sphere of experience.

People often ask whether psychodrama is individual therapy or group psychotherapy. A psychodrama has to be seen as a whole. It cannot function without a group (excluding the autodrama and monodrama defined in Appendix 2). The group is a necessary life-giving element to the drama, providing energy for the enactment. Groups can be very different and the atmosphere of a group determines the protagonist's feeling of safety and courage. Nevertheless, a psychodrama is primarily a form of individual therapy. The reference to group therapy is based on the fact that the members are involved actively in the psychodrama. Empathy leads to insight and deep, 'forgotten' experiential levels in the group can be activated to bring forth a new level of understanding. Each member of the group knows that in a future psychodrama he may be the protagonist.

Relative to individual therapy, psychodrama's advantage is that it can reach many persons at the same time. Nevertheless, the group should not exceed 16 members and its members should be chosen so that they can be of optimal mutual benefit. Unless the psychodrama is planned to treat a specific theme within a specific professional group, the group should be as varied as possible in terms of age and profession. Fortunately, more and more men are taking part in psychodramas, so it is becoming easier to have more balanced gender representation. Since it can be an extremely difficult task to be the sole recipient of possible projections against men, a group must always have more than one man in its midst.

A psychodrama with one protagonist often leads to a psychodrama with another protagonist from the group. The spontaneous sharing of emotions or attitudes can provide invaluable insights for the protagonist and the group. When working with patients with severe psychological problems, relatively violent spontaneous transferences during the psychodramatic enactment are not uncommon. It is the director's responsibility to protect the needs of the protagonist while also ensuring that the most important needs of the group are taken care of in the concluding phase or, if necessary, in a new psychodrama. A psychodrama should last for at least one hour. When this time limit has been set beforehand by the director and the group, the psychodrama must be structured accordingly. It is best not to have a set time limit since this allows for flexibility in the important concluding phase. Most psychodramas last approximately one-and-a-half to two hours.

The key concepts in a psychodrama are spontaneity and creativity, two elements that Moreno maintains are the very fountainhead of psychological health and personal development. Moreno defines spontaneity as a degree of flexibility and adequate response to a new situation or a degree of flexibility and a new response in a familiar situation. Spontaneity training is based on training people to make the best use of their hidden resources in different situations. In his words: 'Liberate yourself from the manuscript of life and from clichés and stereotypes of a fixed state, to achieve broader dimensions of the personality through new ways of using yourself' (Moreno 1970).

As group members in a psychodrama, patients or regular clients experience being able to help other people solve their problems. The protagonist and the members of the group are presented with new dimensions of experience and thereby gain a more diversified frame of reference to draw from when trying to understand different ways of reacting. This also provides a greater feeling of security in social situations.

Psychodramatic techniques such as spontaneity training are effective in developing a sense of security and self-knowledge. They also improve the ability to perform in a situation that is not seen as threatening (conditions must be adapted to provide the greatest possible feeling of safety in the group). Spontaneity training is a requirement for future psychodrama directors because, as professionals, they must be flexible and sensitive to the nuances in the interaction between a protagonist and the auxiliary egos. Doubling also requires an especially high degree of intuitive, emotional empathy. Professional assistants have to be able to accept guidance from a director without asking for time-consuming explanations. They must be thoroughly familiar with the structure of a psychodrama and know what is expected of them at all times. Psychodramatic techniques are effective in training educators and health personnel in terms of increasing their flexibility and responsiveness. In institutions, psychodrama in its entirety can be used in guidance courses for personnel by illustrating different attitudes and methods of communication.

A psychodrama is a composite of many different approaches. Moreno was a pioneer in areas which were further developed into other therapies, such as Fritz Pearl's Gestalt therapy, Janov's primal therapy, Glasser's reality therapy and Wolpe's behavioural drama. As well as reducing tension and being action-oriented, a psychodrama can also be seen as a learning process or a method for conflict-solving and communication analysis if it is used with these goals in mind. Sometimes, a psychodrama can propel Norwegian participants forward just as rapidly and dramatically as the tension-filled psychodramas in the United States. The conflict itself, the protagonist, the group and the leader are in a reciprocal and interactive dynamic relationship. There is no doubt that the personal temperament of the director is decisive to the staging of the psychodrama.

The American psychologist R.J. Corsini has compared Sigmund Freud, Carl Rogers and J.L. Moreno and placed them respectively in an intellectual, emotional and behavioural frame of reference (1956; see also Greenberg 1974). These then reflect religious and philosophical value systems through 'Know yourself' (intellectual), 'Love Thy Neighbour' (emotional) and 'Work Well' (action and behavioural). Freud emphasized understanding the individual through intellectual consciousness raising. Rogers' person-centred psychotherapy underlines the importance of accepting and investigating the purely emotional aspects of a therapeutic situation, while Corsini has Moreno representing a 'social dynamo' in perpetual action with his magical unfolding and capacity for work.

In Corsini's opinion, and the opinion of everyone else who knew him personally, Moreno was an overwhelmingly dynamic personality. This has influenced psychodrama's form of therapy and may also explain why it has met substantial resistance from psychologists and psychiatrists who have neither had the inclination nor the competence to participate in a dramatic enactment with their patients. The theatrical aspects of Moreno's therapy have been greatly emphasized, not least through Moreno's personal performance in directing the stage for a psychodrama.

Through my personal experiences from numerous groups of different combinations (patients, health personnel in training, research groups) and with advanced psychodramatists with psychological or psychiatric backgrounds and different nationalities (American, German, Danish, Polish and Norwegian), I can state that a psychodrama is clearly marked by the particular individual that is directing it. Therefore, it would be incorrect to look at psychodrama as a form of therapy on the basis of Moreno's personal style. He presented a far too colourful and enchanting personality when he was in the public limelight. On a regular everyday basis, his therapy has many perspectives – including intellectual consciousness raising, emotional empathy and guided acting out and social interaction. Moreno was an astute genius as well as an intellectual, emotional and practical man of action.

However, Moreno's most important aspect may still be his viewpoint of mankind as a cosmic individual with unlimited possibilities for self-realization. With this viewpoint, he expands his therapeutic help to include persons with severe psychotic disorders. A psychosis is considered a retreat from reality and a consequence of a person not being able to live up to the expectations of his surroundings, which results in a damaged ego and a loss of identity. Moreno agrees with the orthodox Freudians that a psychotic patient is incapable of transference, an ability that the Freudians consider necessary for recovery. Moreno ignores transference. Rather than cure a patient by transference and information from dreams and associations from the unconscious, Moreno establishes an entire 'auxiliary world' as a substitute for the actual world the patients cannot accommodate themselves to. In combination with the auxiliary egos the patients need to be able to function in their fantasy worlds. This therapeutic idea becomes a method for understanding patients. By accepting all of his patients' psychodramatic roles, and acting with them, the possibility for contact gradually appears, even on an objective realistic level. Primarily, this happens by showing love and acceptance. Although there is a natural danger of reinforcing their fantasy worlds, Moreno still defends the necessity of 'searching into the deepest level and then rising toward the daylight above'. Moreno was interested in penetrating the hidden universe of his patients even before World War I. Modern psychiatry and psychology have also stated this necessity in their history-making advances of the past 30 years, for example John Rosen's 'direct psychoanalysis', Carl Rogers' person-centred psychotherapy and R.D. Laing's deep and personal understanding of the inner drama of schizophrenics.

John Rosen developed his 'direct psychoanalysis' in the early 1950s. The technique is similar to a psychodrama but he does not use a group. Rosen, in particular, has worked with psychotic patients this way. He avoids professional terminology and concentrates on speaking 'the language of the patient'. The therapist's aim is to establish a direct relationship with the psychotic patient in order to compensate for, as an example, a 'bad' mother. Here the therapist looks upon the patient as a child, one which has to be raised once again with love and safety. To make this 'rebirth' as realistic as possible, an apartment is used to represent 'the home'. Two or more assistants work day and night as members of the 'family'. Rosen does his therapy sessions in front of an audience that can be as many as 100 persons but, in his opinion, their presence has no influence on the therapy (he does not explain why he has an audience). Gesticulations, facial expressions and verbal utterances are compared and analyzed in order to reduce the effect of, for example, the 'bad mother' and reinforce the effect of the 'good' – that is the therapist. The main difference between the approaches of Rosen and Moreno is that Moreno allows the patient far more freedom for development and self-realization. The patient is always in charge of the drama in Moreno's approach, no matter how psychotic he is. With Rosen, one has the impression that it is the therapist's value system that counts and the patients have to live up to this. Nevertheless, both therapists aim at understanding the patient in 'his own world'.

As a far less challenging area, psychodrama can be used in studying observable behaviour within behavioural and social learning therapy. But here too psychodrama can delve far more deeply into the complex pattern of human interactions. A comparison between the sociologist Erving Goffman and Moreno illustrates this point.

Goffmann *describes* the dramaturgical elements of daily life. He is mainly interested in the structure of social interaction. Moreno *uses* the dramaturgical elements in a psychodrama. Goffman focuses on the social situation and how the drama can be *maintained*. Moreno analyzes the situation to find out how it can be *changed*. Goffman concentrates on behaviour as it has *been impressed on the individual* (preserved behaviour) while Moreno's primary interest is in *spontaneous* behaviour, breaking down a fixed pattern of life with new and more creative ways to react. Goffman observes from a distance; Moreno is a fellow player. One might say that Goffman is more scientifically oriented in the established tradition of research in that he remains on the periphery, while Moreno enters into the situation and influences the results (see Goffman 1959; Gosnell 1964; Greenburg 1974).

In combination, Goffman and Moreno are an acceptable team for studying behaviour in experimental situations, if one uses Goffman's model as a starting point and then, in Morenian style, changes the conditions for the behaviour that is being observed.

In today's institutions it should be possible to systematize research studies in connection with the daily therapeutic work, for example psychodramas could contribute by concentrating on very specific themes such as different kinds of drug abuse and its association to parental relationships, the alcoholic and his wife, hysteria, indecisiveness and fear of authority. It might be possible to find some universal common denominators within each area that would be instrumental in gaining new understanding in our preventive work.

By using psychodramas based on special themes or subject areas within an institutional environment, the research could be performed under relatively simple and inexpensive conditions. No matter how primitive the physical appearance of a psychodramatic theatre might be, it is still a workshop where nothing is too great or too small to be considered important. Nothing is moral or immoral, ugly or pretty. If we take Moreno's words from *The Words of the Father* (1941) literally, we might understand why so many have been confused by his work. For Moreno it is as important that the patient can create God, as it is that God is the creator. This is hardly the Orthodox Jewish or Christian view of truth. Tolerance, compassion, love and forgiveness are all by-products of a good psychodrama. Insight, self-control and social adequacy are its practical objectives.

Frozen needs

There are many different reasons for joining a psychodrama group. Many people are interested, although they are hesitant when it comes to themselves. Some arrive with a deep need to solve inner conflicts, others to satisfy their desire to perform, and still others to correct behaviour that they have finally understood is not leading anywhere.

There are also those who maintain that they have no clear need at all, even though they too show up for a psychodrama. The Moreno Academy in New York had an official demonstration of a psychodrama on the theme of bereavement. A woman presented her desperate grief after the death of her husband. Accepting her new situation as a widow was experienced as difficult, if not impossible. Her feelings of inadequacy, inability to reconcile herself to reality and isolation after the death of a dear one are recurrent themes in psychodramas. These subjects are usually of such universal interest that they inspire the group's active participation. However, in the sharing phase there was one elderly man who remained silent.

He was an interesting character, a man who looked like an old tribal chieftain. In a sense, his silence was a challenge. He had certainly had many experiences in his long life. Why had he even come to this meeting if he had nothing to share with the group?

Each and every member of a group should be allowed to avoid pressure. Nevertheless, the protagonist asked this man whether he could contribute at least one word of consolation or wisdom. The man shook his head slowly. A woman asked if he had ever experienced grief or loss. The man still shook his head. In a strange way, roles were reversed and the old man found himself in the process of becoming a protagonist. Hadn't he ever been married or lost a child or relative? Yes…admitted the man at last. But his life had only been a happy one!

The very word 'happy' in a group that had been delving into grief and loss seemed strangely out of place. Furthermore, no one seemed to believe him and the woman continued asking him questions. The director intervened, feeling that the scene was becoming uncomfortably like an interrogation. Everyone's attention was directed toward the old man. The fact that he had never thought about his long life was a provocation to the group.

Eventually, we learned that he had come to the United States from Russia at the turn of the century. His mother had died during the journey; his father was an Orthodox Jew of the old school, a figure of authority who held a strong hand over his seven children. Floggings were not unusual, but the man assured the group that everything had been as it was meant to be.

One day, when he was twelve years old, his father went down to the pier and returned with a Russian housekeeper. Eventually they married. More children were born. More floggings, more discipline. And poverty and hunger were always present. But the man assured us that this was common among Russian immigrants.

By the time he was forty the man had started thinking about getting married himself. He longed for children and, when the woman he had been seeing told him she was pregnant, they set a date for the wedding. On their wedding night she virtually laughed in his face, telling him that she was not pregnant and that she had no intention of ever becoming so. He remained married to her until her death many years later.

And then what, asked the group. The man had lost his interest in marriage. There was so much else to do and he thought it was too late to think about having children.

The woman who had been the protagonist suddenly went over to him and gently stroked him on his head with tears in her eyes: 'But then, you've never lived!'

Her grief seemed to leave her, but the old man sat as if her gentle touch had turned him to stone. After a long pause he took her hand and said in a barely audible voice: 'Your skin is so soft...'

Before the members of the group said their farewells, the man asked awkwardly: 'Is it true that it isn't too late to get something from life? I am 84 years old'.

Many assured him that it is never too late. Someone asked what had inspired him to join the psychodrama group. He had no idea why he had come. Someone had told him it might help...

CHAPTER 5

Norwegian Experiences in Retrospect

Twenty-five years in Norway

Chapters 1–4 of this book, with a few minor changes, were first published in 1978 in connection with my interdisciplinary thesis in theatrical art, criminology and psychology. Most of the examples are from my work in the United States from 1971 to 1972.

My contact with psychodrama has been closely associated with Moreno's theories, philosophy and ideology. I had known Moreno personally and had an insider's knowledge of his version of life in Vienna and, later, the United States. I had become a member of the 'psychodrama family' run by Moreno's wife, Zerka, and was privileged to study under many astute and inspiring instructors. Later, in Norway, I spent two years studying with Dean and Doreen Elefthery and by 1974 I was collaborating with Bob and Ildri Bie Ginn from the Psychodrama Institute of Boston. In many ways these two persons were my most important teachers. The theoretical aspect of psychodrama has changed very little. It is so firmly established in its classical framework that what I learned in the early 1970s is still pertinent today, 25 years later. Of course, I have been continually adding to this base of knowledge and have become more flexible in my use of it. Empirical material has grown and, of course, provided many new aspects of psychodrama. Also, my style has changed.

After arriving home in Norway, and studying further in 1972, I was bursting with optimism and drive. In retrospect, I was foolhardy to start my own psychodrama groups. It soon became clear that I needed more formal education in purely therapeutic studies. This was the beginning of a strenuous period of work to become qualified as a director of psychodrama in Norway. There were many reservations but an intuitive interest in this method soon appeared, making it possible to strike out in new directions. Today we are struggling to retain the creativity of psychodrama rather than letting it become primarily a psychiatric method. The results are therapeutic. I cannot overstate the necessity of a thorough, formal education in psychodrama before starting to lead psychodrama groups. The Norwegian Psychodrama Institute is affiliated with the Nordic Board of Examiners and the Psychodrama Institute for Europe. These three institutions work together to establish the criteria for formal accreditation for three levels of certification for students.

In 1974, two years before I completed my studies in psychology, I was hired as a personnel counsellor at Ullevål Hospital in Oslo, Unit XVI. We worked on attitudes, communication and dreams, and psychodramatic techniques. In September 1976 I was employed as a psychologist in the acute ward in the same hospital under the direction of Henrik Bauge. At that time this was a model unit, equipped to offer environmental therapy, physical therapy, systemic family therapy, art therapy and psychodrama.

Eight important years followed. I used psychodrama for crisis intervention, resolving grief, aggression therapy, working with psychotic patients, 'rehearsals for life' and 'suicide tests'. The latter were to determine whether patients were genuinely suicidal. On one occasion it was used to assess the danger of a possible murder. The man, a day-patient, had acted out his fantasies about how he would kill his fiancée. In a paranoid scene of jealousy he choked her and then became determined to find and kill his rival. The murder was avoided by hospitalizing the man immediately.

In the following section I will describe a few of the many variations of dramas in which people were allowed to play the main role in their lives. I will include the most important and prototypical dramas from Unit XVI and from the Modum Health Care Centre, where I worked in connection with becoming qualified as a specialist in clinical psychology. I will not draw from the year I spent in Unit XVIII, the Unit for Child Psychiatry at Ullevål Hospital, because I believe that clients should be 14–15 years old before participating in psychodramas. In my work with children a psychodrama became more like a fairy-tale where the objective was to find good helpers in a threatening world. I will also describe psychodramas with ordinary clients who were working on personal development. Of course, the identity of these people has been protected. All of the psychodramas resemble one another, whether with psychotic or neurotic patients, or others, in that they all attempt to present inner realities – a theatre of the mind where the main characters strive to stage the dramas of their personal lives.

Naturally enough, the Bauker Course Centre near Lillehammer has played a key role in what has become my long career in psychodrama. I worked there occasionally, at weekend seminars, over a eight-year period. People from all sections of Norway came to the centre. They represented different backgrounds, both socially, psychologically and culturally. We met the lives and activities of coastal Laplanders, farmers from Hedmarken, pious and apprehensive persons from gentle southern Norway with bibles in hand, artists and former psychiatric patients with painful experiences from their daily lives. No attempt is made to find truth with a capital 'T' in their subjective narratives. Their inner dramas force their way into the open in accordance with the rules, techniques and structure of a psychodrama. From my years as an actress, I have often quoted my former boss, poet and theatre director Claes Gill: 'What is Strindberg in comparison to reality!'

After a few intense years of using psychodrama as therapy, my theatrical training began to come to the foreground. Moreno had based his creativity on children's play and the empathy and interpretation of professional actors. He had developed a theory of role-playing by studying the effects of being locked into a system of roles. He made use of his European theatrical traditions when he created his therapeutic theatre in America. He introduced the concept of group psychotherapy and referred to God as a therapeutic actor. Moreno wanted to fill the empty shell of a burned-out schizophrenic with the hope of an innate God – man's own ability to save himself – because godliness is a natural part of the human race. With his concept of 'man as a cosmic being' he broadened the scope of psychiatry's narrow outlook on mankind. But all of this is firmly rooted in our common cultural heritage whether we are farmers, office workers, doctors, priests, housewives or sailors. We are all part of the universe through the traditions, myths and stories that are in our consciousness. Psychology and psychiatry are like newborn children in comparison to our common heritage, which has been compiled by writers and philosophers since antiquity. A return to mythology led to Carl Gustav Jung and, from here, a return to the great Greek tragedians, Aeschylus, Sophocles and Euripides. The subjects of themes such as Electra and Oedipus became combinations of Freudian and Greek texts. A meeting with actress and psychodramatist Ulrike Behrman von Zerboni during the commemoration of the 100th anniversary of Moreno's birth resulted in an exciting collaboration on arranging seminars in Germany. Professional actors, psychologists and dramatists came together and worked on creating new plays based on the endless interaction between men and women, sons and daughters of the era of Agamemnon and Clytemnestra. Having pre-viously used the theatre as therapy, I now began to envision bold possibilities for using therapy as theatre – that is, moving therapy back to the stage as a form of artistic expression. The results are therapeutic here too. They are far from the 'canned theatre' so strongly disdained by Moreno since the play is created on the spur of the moment by skilled professionals who later stage it according to dramaturgical standards. Not until actors begin to memorize their lines is there a danger of becoming what Moreno scornfully referred to as the 'cultural conserve'. But then, modern dramas have all been written in this way!

I began using this approach as early as 1985 at The Open Theatre in Oslo, where I worked with playwrights suffering from 'writer's block'. Later, we also experimented in studying the Jungian models and archetypical roles in plays by Henrik Ibsen and other classic dramatists. The magic of the stage often allows a psychodrama to achieve its best results, not because stage effects have an intrinsic value but because, in Moreno's words, they provide a new dimension in which fantasy can 'set the soul free from the darkness and from its ignorance of itself'. By using theatrical effects, spontaneity and creativity bring the psychic material to catharsis. Even though we are often forced into the dark chambers of childhood, we do not have to stay there. Moreno's genius is that he allows the unknown to burst forward and take form. Ordinary men and women acquire a glimpse of their inborn significance. Moreno's psychiatry is related to the renewed interest in spiritual values that has appeared in recent decades.

Aggression in crisis

Directly translated, the word psychodrama means 'soul action', that is, spiritual content that is converted into action. Therefore, it was natural for me to seek contact with patients as soon as possible – preferably the first morning after their admittance. Although rest is part of their treatment, persons in crisis do not have to rest all the time. It is often important to chart the patients' networks immediately to find out whether there are any useful resources within their circle of family and friends or whether they have been living in social isolation.

Even though many patients arrived in a sorry state during the night, I saw how important it was that someone sat on the edge of their beds, greeted them and offered a few words of encouragement. I gradually developed a procedure for handling these patients when they turned their backs to me or refused to say anything at all. After a little while, I would get up to leave and say: 'I feel that you are rejecting me. I am not rejecting you. But I am leaving now. I will be back in ten minutes. You can either talk to me then or continue to reject me. You might need me more than I need you. And I am willing to take another chance'. After ten minutes I went back to them and, in most cases, the patient was facing the door when I walked in.

Moreno's most important theory is that all human beings have an innate need to be involved in their own lives. This is often the straw we reach for in the realities of psychiatry when a patient seems to have lost all hope for a new life: 'You will get another chance...'

What I had to offer was a cellar room, a spooky but alluring world waiting at the bottom of a steep stairway. It had a mouldy smell and, at one point, we had to set out rat poison. Numerous Strindbergian dramas unfolded in this simple room. When we were working with patients from the acute unit, we usually made use of monodramas. In such a hectic unit it was hard for the personnel to find time to join us but the nurses and younger doctors did what they could to work in the cellar. It was reassuring to have a male staff member there because the dramas often dealt with treachery, aggression, fantasies about revenge and the wish to kill someone. Even so, these situations were easier than when the patients had no feelings at all, when the course of their illness had ended in exhaustion and despondency.

Anton was a 29-year-old man who was married and had two children. He was admitted to the hospital under dramatic circumstances. After a call from his neighbours, the police had seized him in the middle of the night. On his first morning he simply lay in his bed and seemed totally apathetic. I suggested that he come to our cellar sessions and intimated that he just might have had real reasons for being so out of control. Psychodrama in itself is amoral. It is not that we have no morals but that when we are trying to understand another person's reality, we make no moral judgments. Of course, this does not mean that we are not ethical – ethical responsibility is something completely different (the Norwegian Psychodrama Institute has its own professional ethics committee).

Anton admitted that he had been furious but he couldn't understand why he beat his wife and children. The reason I have chosen Anton as an example is that he is the most angry man I have ever met. With his frail and pallid façade he was the picture of calmness. He was the son of a famous figure in Norway, had a good educational background and was in the midst of a successful career.

Usually, people are afraid of their own violent aggression and, after making a solemn pledge not to hurt anyone, many need to be provoked into action. Making this commitment is a kind of ritual between the patient and the director. Provocations and techniques were not necessary for activating Anton. He literally flew at the walls, beating his fists and banging his head. After allowing him to continue for a while, we finally found something that could be used as a scene in a drama. It had happened the day before he was admitted. After years of frustrations with his employer, something happened that made him feel he had been completely humiliated, discounted and placed under suspicion. We played the scene and another burst of anger appeared. But this time it was more explicit. Even further into his volcanic outburst we found the root of his tortured fury. Indeed, it was deeply hidden but it came out: a picture of a father who had abused him, humiliated him and – in his words – castrated him ever since the day he was born.

Anton was released three weeks later. He recovered quickly. His wife appeared loyally for clinical discussions. When he was leaving, he said that he remembered nothing from his first round in the cellar. It had been like 'that dreadful night when the world exploded'.

Unresolved grief

In many psychodramas deceased persons assume a place on the stage as if it were the most natural thing in the world. This is a proven resource since unresolved grief, and all that has not been said, are closely related. When feelings of loss are finally expressed, tears come quickly. In the concluding phase, when bitterness has been released and there has been some form of reconciliation, a veil of solemnity falls over the group as it shares its feelings and experiences. Very often, if we can get the departed persons on the stage, and the protagonist is willing to work within the dimension of death, the entire group will experience recovery.

Birger's father had died in a hospital, but Birger had never visited him. He was extremely bitter about his father's treatment of him in comparison to his brother, the favourite son. In Birger's words, there was a 'block of ice in his stomach'. The appearance of his 'father' on the stage had a paralyzing effect. Through role reversal, Birger was able to see that his father also had some dark sides in his life. He had felt like a failure and had been unable to communicate any thoughts or feelings. Birger understood his father's lack of words.

First of all, negative feelings must be brought to the surface. When they have finally been expressed, tears are not far away. Birger was able to say how much he had longed for his father and how helpless he had often felt. It might seem strange when a protagonist, in the role of his dead father, says that he wants to hug his son. When this occurs, the auxiliary ego can hold the protagonist in his arms and bring about a scene of reconciliation based on a deep longing rather than sentimentality.

A death can often bring on strong feelings of guilt. Here the director can bring in the greatest of all of Moreno's actors, Jesus or God himself. By allowing the protagonist to play the role of God, who can see the world and all human beings, the director can ask whether he (God) thinks it is fair for one person to suffer so much. In this role, the protagonist will usually answer that it is not fair. Then, when the protagonist returns to his own role, and an auxiliary ego takes over the role of God, the protagonist hears in his own words that he is allowed to forget his guilt feelings. Once again, these scenes might seem absurd, but they are deeply important.

The first incest drama

In the 1970s incest dramas were rare. The concept was unknown. Many women were imprisoned in their desolate night-time secrets, with low self-esteem, repulsion for their bodies and unspoken guilt.

Randi had been admitted to our unit many times and she was usually in a psychotic state when she arrived. She knew about the cellar and its possibilities but had always remained reserved about participating. I had seen glimpses of strange relationships in a few monodramas but the idea of sexual abuse had never occurred to me. When Randi was admitted this time, she was more down-and-out than usual. A few weeks passed before she was offered a chance to do a monodrama. But one day she told me that she had met a man. She had never had any feeling for romance or falling in love before. Her obesity was a good physical camouflage and she had adopted a sarcastic tone that was meant to keep men at a distance. I think I may have had a vague suspicion of incest but I was inexperienced with cases like this at that time. Rape was different; it was something we knew about. Rape scenes were enacted by forcing a mattress over the woman until she could gather the strength to fight back and overpower the 'rapist', thus releasing her emotions of justified rage that had been pent up for so long.

But in incest the drama has to revert to an early age, often to the age of two or three or even earlier. Randi was also physically handicapped, so the scene had to be enacted by a deputy protagonist. In these cases the therapist must use extreme care in assessing the clients' physical limits. In addition, when incest dramas turn up in mixed groups, a woman should direct the scene of the act of incest when a woman is the victim and a man is the abuser. In the case of men, if the abuser is a woman, an man should direct the scene. Sometimes it can be a good idea to include men to provoke the situation, since their genuine disgust for the perpetrators provides a good source of support for the protagonist.

At first, Randi only wanted to work on the possibility of meeting her Hans. The scene was set in a restaurant. They ordered roast beef and beer, but Randi did not enjoy her meal. She just sat there dreading '…what would happen afterwards'. The scene that gradually unfolded was one of Randi as a seven-year-old. She had polio and her lameness made walking difficult. Her upper body and small hands were strong but not strong enough to ward off her father's advances in the barn. Two assistants played the scene of the father raping her in a pig-pen while she watched it from her chair.

As mentioned earlier, when the protagonist is feeling extreme anxiety or is physically handicapped, the scene is enacted by a deputy protagonist. The most traumatic scenes are riveted in the minds of the protagonists. Pictures from a very early age can be reproduced and felt as intensely as they had been in the past.

When the scene was enacted the first time, Randi kept her eyes closed. During the second enactment she watched with gritted teeth. The third time she lifted herself from her chair, limped over to the 'pig-pen' and beat a cane against a chair until it was shattered. A 30-year-old secret had finally been set free. We were the witnesses and, after her outbreak of rage, Randi could finally cry as she had never cried before.

More about incest

By the mid-1980s incest problems appeared more often in psychodramas (Randi's drama was in 1977). In the 1990s there are many dramas with incest at the root of an un-lived erotic life. There could also be many incest themes within the same group, although some of them turned out to be 'false' – that is, after looking at them in depth, it became clear that they were fantasies about forbidden eroticism. It is important to support the protagonist's erotic feelings as a child. It is, after all, the adults' responsibility to define the limits. Genuine male incest problems are also becoming more common. Oedipal conflicts and their after-effects are recurrent themes in psychodramas, both for women and men. These persons have feelings of guilt without knowing why. In a sense, psychodramas become catalysts in the process of distinguishing between real and imaginary abuse – often to the great relief of the protagonist.

In addition, unconscious competition with one of the parents can be clarified and settled. In the desire to be daddy's princess, many daughters have competed secretly or openly with the Queen Mother for the attention of the Father King. And many sons have wanted to marry mummy and later had trouble with feelings of inferiority: for example, Stein remembered having been in the bathroom with his father. They were both urinating and his mother had come into the room, seen them and smiled. Afterwards, he had always felt inadequate; even as an adult he thought that his penis was far too little. In a sense, he had forever lost to his father.

The incest scene that will be described here is a more recent one from a group of women. Inger is an unusual woman in our day. Not only does she look like Solveig in *Peer Gynt*, she also sings 'Solveig's Song' beautifully. Even so, Solveig had never dared sing anywhere but in the forest. She was burdened by feelings of guilt and shame and had trouble finding pleasure in anything at all. And she certainly could not take any pleasure in her husband, whom she loved but whose advances she always rejected. The marriage was developing into a tragedy. Inger knew very well that she had been abused by her father; her mother had silently accepted this fact. Inger felt that she had been forced to take her mother's place. This abuse went on from the time she was four years old.

A scene including sex with children must be very carefully prepared. In a total state of helplessness, the woman has to surrender herself and return to the memory of how this had felt, experience it once again and feel how her body recoils in disgust. Extreme reactions often follow. In some cases the protagonist has vomited, been unable to speak or broken out in a terrible rash. These are temporary reactions, lasting until the worst is over. In this drama we quickly came to a scene that always repeated itself. The mother had left the house. Inger was alone in her room. Her father often entered her room with the same words: 'Now you can be daddy's sweet little girl'. Strangely enough, a man's voice is not necessary in the enactment. At the very sound of the familiar words, Inger crouched into a ball as if she wanted to shrink away from adult treachery. With the utmost care, the director gradually guides the scene into the offensive act by relating how it was done. The therapist spreads the girl's legs while assuring her that she is not the father. The protagonist remembers the act while her emotional trauma is being protected by the calming presence of the therapist. The protagonist is then encouraged to fight against her father and told that this time it will work. After numerous seizures of vomiting, Inger started fighting her father. Soon she was screaming and shouting words that she had been carrying inside her throughout her life.

But then her behaviour suddenly changed. She remained on the floor, lying perfectly still. Her body trembled and tears ran down her face. She whispered: 'This is my body. It is mine. I own my body. No one else'. She stroked her body and said suddenly: 'My body is alive'. But just as suddenly as the first change had appeared, a new change came over her. She began to wipe her mouth. It was clear that there had also been oral sex. Later she told us that she had never remembered that before. Inger vomited as if she had something huge and disgusting in her mouth. The psychodrama went on for a long time. She wanted to meet her mother and tell her how she had felt deserted. In a role reversal with her mother, the drama took another surprising turn. Inger said suddenly: 'I can understand why you couldn't have sex with him. You must have been very disappointed and unhappy. But why didn't you leave him? Oh, Mother, I feel so sorry for you. You didn't have anyone to turn to either...' This was a drama that could have been entitled 'The Impotence of Women'. One of the most dreadful incest dramas I have ever participated in was where a father placed his five-year-old daughter on a stove burner, saying he was going to eat her up. She was so delectable! Fortunately, the psychodrama showed that the stove could not have been turned on. The body has a very good memory!

A lost world on Christmas Eve

Naturally, there were many psychotic patients in Unit XVI. Most admittances involved persons in acute crisis with substance abuse problems or severely depressed women and men who had given up living. Many therapists would maintain that psychotic patients and psychodrama do not belong together. Moreno never hesitated in meeting his psychotic patients with the offer of helping them back to the world they had in common. St Elisabeth's Hospital in Washington D.C. has been a model clinic for psychotic patients since the 1970s. Here all of the patients have their own auxiliary egos during their sessions – strange performances which I never felt particularly attracted to. Even though in Washington they had their co-existing auxiliary egos with them, hand in hand, I still do not think that psychotic patients should work in groups.

The monodramas in Unit XVI were all aimed at putting the psychotic's confused world together again. Following the patients through their mazes of chaotic pictures was like working on a jigsaw puzzle. It is often said that the neurotic's inner world is in conflict and chaos while the world of the psychotic is fragmented. Anxiety has taken over. The outside world has become dangerous. A patient can often react by fighting back in self-defence. Sometimes it is best to refrain from physical contact and other times it is called for. Intuition is all-important.

Asta was one of these unusual persons who was searching for a lost world. It was two days before Christmas and the scene was a Christmas Eve from her childhood. Many imaginary gifts were unwrapped. One horrid animal after another crept into an atmosphere of hatred and fear. A bird sat and screeched from the top of the Christmas tree but, when we lured it down to us, it became the patient's father and hands that would strike her. Asta had a dismal Christmas in a closed unit. She did not improve until some months of the new year had passed.

As a rule, psychotic patients came into contact with reality after relatively few weeks. Of course, this pertained to the reactive psychoses. In mono-dramas with psychotic patients it is usually possible to follow their disconnected symbolic language toward some form of understanding. The most important factor might be to stay with them and to give them the feeling of being in a safe environment.

Looking from a bird's nest

Berit was a day-patient who was working with another therapist. But every once in a while the therapist sent Berit to psychodrama, especially in periods of anxiety and obsession. A trip to the movies to see 'E.T.' had convinced her that a creature from space was trying to contact her.

Berit and I had a good relationship. In her better moments she had a rich sense of humour. But this time she was afraid, cringing like a wounded animal. To strengthen her feeling of safety and create a bridge for communication, I suggested that we pretended that we were a baby bird and a mother bird. We had played this game before. We made our 'nest' in a corner with a blanket and a pillow. Then we crawled in and waited for something to happen. After I while I encouraged Berit to come with me to take a look around outside. I told her that as soon as it got dangerous we could simply draw back into the nest. She gradually gained courage. But then a large roll of paper suddenly became dangerous. It was the creature from outer space! We returned to the nest and waited. Eventually I suggested that we talk to it. I crawled out first. Berit waited in breathless excitement. I returned and told her that it was a sad, frightened creature who had lost its way. Berit was only vaguely interested, fear was something she already knew about. I finally persuaded Berit to reverse roles with the creature. Asking psychotic patients to reverse roles is not very common. They have more than enough trouble keeping control of their own selves in this world. Nevertheless, in this case role reversal worked – perhaps because she was a bird and I was her protective mother. When she exchanged roles with the creature, she exclaimed in triumph: 'Now I am the one who is dangerous'. 'Maybe you are fear', I said. I will never forget her words while playing the role of fear: 'There's nothing to be afraid of, Berit!' She had conquered 'the dangerous' – maybe the self-destruction within her own being? She made an amazing recovery.

The victims of Nazism

By the 1970s relatively few patients were still carrying shades of their past from World War II. In their journals we often found tragic family destinies that were rooted in Nazism but they could not bring themselves to talk about this in monodramas.

It had all become too much for Ruth to handle. She was having recurrent dreams that she found her father dead. As a five-year-old she had actually found him after he had been shot or knifed to death. The way he died had never been clarified. In her dreams his head, arms and legs were strewn over the ground. After some work it became possible to enact the dream and to put the father back together so that he could become a person she could talk to. A pillow served as the father and she could cry and tell him how she longed for him.

Another disturbing drama was when a Nazi father was hanging on a cross in repentance for all of the Jewish people who died during the war. Psychodrama does not recoil from the strangest rituals as long as they can help free a protagonist from a painful past.

Karl was his mother's little protective knight. His father had been killed in 1945. The mother fled with her four-year-old son and hid from the Allies in a hut in the woods. Every night, before going to sleep, the mother asked her little son: 'If the enemy comes and tries to rape me, you will protect me, won't you?' One morning the boy awoke to find that his mother was dead. She had taken too many sleeping pills. Karl was alone for many days before he was accidently found. As unbelievable as it may seem, the protagonist experienced tremendous relief after enacting a scene where he defended his mother against the enemy. This was what he had wanted to do during all of his adult life.

The alarming red light

Bjarne was a person with the sad tendency to fondle young girls. Preferably, they were about eight years old. But Bjarne was deeply determined to overcome his inclinations. He joined a psychodrama group while he was under special care after his unsuccessful suicide attempt in a prison hospital where he had been serving time. There was a lovely young sixteen-year-old in the same group, a long-term patient with severe problems of drug abuse. The two of them were a strange pair as they enacted a scene from Bjarne's childhood. It was during the war and Bjarne, who lived in an orphanage, had made friends with a little girl who lived nearby. His playmate's mother was a friendly woman and she invited Bjarne into the house for waffles – a kindness he never forgot. The two children were playing together in a woodshed. In the midst of their game, which was of a sexual nature, little Brita was called home by her mother. Brita left and Bjarne heard a car's screeching of brakes. He was seized with a sense of warning. This was the punishment for playing a forbidden game. And he was right. Brita was killed by a large truck. The psychodrama dealt with how Bjarne came to want to fiddle with little girls. In the drama, each time he was about to do this we focused a red floodlight on him. It was almost like an example of a Pavlovian reaction from our days as psychology students. Bjarne gained insight into the relationship between the game in the woodshed and his constant fixation on eight-year-old girls. He had been eleven, while Brita was eight.

I went off on vacation. Bjarne had been released before I left. When I returned, Bjarne was the first person I saw in the Unit. He looked ashamed but he took me by the arm and said: 'I didn't do it really! I almost did, but then I remembered the red light'. But still, Bjarne had been caught in the act and had to serve more time. Today, many years later, he is married and still holding down a permanent job. The red light had worked.

The mirror or window technique

I will now leave Unit XVI and the acute cases in this crisis unit and return to more ordinary individuals, the neurotics. We are all more or less neurotic – struggling with inner conflicts and problems that keep us from living our lives wholly and fully. And we certainly are experts at making messes of our lives in all sorts of ways. The following psychodramas are from different places and with persons from very different backgrounds. First, I will give some examples of using the more common techniques.

The technique I will describe here is also very helpful in individual therapy. Mrs Olsen and I had regular discussion sessions while her husband was hospitalized and a member of a psychodrama group. Mrs Olsen had a habit of rolling her eyes whenever she talked about her husband. After a while, I asked if she would let me 'mirror' her. Since being 'mirrored' can seem quite brutal to the person who will experience it, it is important to explain that the aim is not to make fun of the individual but to show how she might appear to other persons. Therefore, it is emphasized that the mirroring will be exaggerated. Sometimes, if the atmosphere permits, this technique can turn into a caricature. I took my time and repeated some of what Mrs Olsen had said, making sure that I rolled my eyes every time I came to a well-chosen point about how impossible her husband was. Mrs Olsen protested strongly. She certainly did not see herself in the same light. But then, she did get something to think about.

A while later we accepted Mrs Olsen into a psychodrama group. In family therapy it is important that the spouses are each given a chance to show how they see their partners before they are confronted by the group. In a scene enacted by Mr and Mrs Olsen, Mrs Olsen forgot her good intentions and rolled her eyes. She was then removed from the stage and an auxiliary ego was chosen to play her part. Mrs Olsen protested again and looked im-

ploringly at me: 'But I didn't do it now, did I?' We all replied: 'Yes you did'.
Mr Olsen interrupted and exclaimed: 'Yes, is it so strange that I've gone nuts?'
Releasing peals of laughter from the group reduced the painful sting of hard
reality.

The doubling technique

To double is to sink oneself into the undertones of what is being said. The
technique requires practice. It can become something approaching art. There
are many categories of doubling. Provocation doubling is used with the
permission of the protagonist and is meant to act as a strong stimulation for
the release of blocked feelings. Support doubling is used to provide the
protagonist with the confidence to continue talking about difficult subjects.
And there is the co-therapist's doubling, which is often simply to remind the
director about something that was said earlier that might be important.
In-depth doubling has to do with intuition and timing. If doubling is used
too soon, it will not work, and if it is too late, it becomes no more than a
piece of commentary and wasted time.

Personally, I have virtually stopped using the classic doubling technique
where the double sits beside the protagonist and imitates all of the protagonist's movements. This slows down the drama. However, sometimes it might
be important to give the protagonist a permanent double throughout the
entire drama, depending on the style of the director. I myself prefer a flexible
drama with the group being able to become involved and perform doubling.
At its best, doubling is performed with profound human wisdom.

In-depth doubling can also be extremely effective in individual therapy
as long as the patient agrees that it be used. Otherwise, in-depth doubling
can seem like an invasion of a patient's private life.

Pettersen was an unusually quiet patient. In fact, he did not say a single
word during our first meeting. The next time Pettersen came for an
appointment and placed himself on my sofa with the same silent suffering
expression, I asked permission to sit next to him. I explained what I was
going to do and he nodded silently. Of course, I knew his history from his
medical journal. Therefore, my plan was more like support doubling. I spoke
quietly about my loneliness, how unfairly I had been treated and how afraid
I was of people after everything I had gone through in my private and
professional life (I made sure to go into detail). When I finished, Pettersen
sighed deeply and said: 'Oh, it feels so good to finally say it!'

An example of in-depth doubling is when another patient, Tom, was
finally going to confront his mother but remained in his chair without saying
a single word. A double stood behind him and said softly: 'I cannot be your

husband anymore. You have to turn to father!' Tom began to weep and his life history came out between gulps of despair. Although he had felt abused and exploited, he had never had the heart to turn his mother away. When we advanced further into the psychodrama it became clear that more than tears were necessary. Mother turned out to be a clever spider and Tom had been caught in her web for years. In Tom's case, we had to find the strength of his virility.

The use of the voice is an important factor in doubling. When using in-depth doubling, one has to listen carefully and find the inner drama, the sub-texts that reveal the true nature of the problem. In provocation doubling a strong voice is usually best. Auxiliary egos can often find it hard to play their roles with sufficient strength, particularly when they haven't had any training. After two years of study at a psychodrama institute, they are expected to be 'professional auxiliary egos', but some of them aren't bold enough. In these instances the director has to enter into the drama and take over the role of the auxiliary ego. There is always the danger that a protagonist can come into a transference relationship with the director, but this usually solves itself when the leader is careful to define the role he is playing.

Fortunately, in the drama with the spider mother there was a professional auxiliary ego who could play her role well. She asked permission to provoke the protagonist and then, suddenly, threw her arms around her 'son' and begged him never to leave her. At first Tom remained perfectly still, seemingly frozen in place. But then his anger exploded. 'Mother' came a hair's breadth from being thrown from wall to wall. After a while, three women were called in. It was his task to free himself from them. Drastic measures were called for. His spider mother had the strength of at least three women.

Seldom is the atmosphere of a psychodrama group as happy as it is when a protagonist throws off the yoke of parental burden. But this does not mean that the problem is solved. Conflicts of loyalty and feelings of guilt are comrades in these psychodramas and they must be thoroughly worked through before the release is whole and genuine.

Psychodramatic shock

About the worst thing that can happen is a drama becoming stuck in meaningless role reversals without making any progress. This is a particularly difficult problem in dramas with pent-up aggression based on poorly developed self-images: persons who don't dare fight back no matter how unjustly they have been treated. This is when it is beneficial to turn to psychodramatic shock, but this method must be used with extreme precision and care.

Bente was a typical protagonist, having trouble expressing her needs. She had been ridiculed throughout all of her school years, not just by the students but also by a teacher who appeared as a veritable sadist in the psychodrama. A scene was enacted in the classroom, but when Bente met the teacher, she just smiled and accepted everything. The whole group fidgeted in its chairs with impatience. As the scene continued Bente not only accepted everything, she also submitted to all of the teacher's suggestions. It became a true display of humility and went so far as to be characterized as 'identification with the aggressor'.

Bente was sent out of the room and told that when she returned, a scene would be enacted and she was to react spontaneously, no matter what her feelings were. In turn, the 'teacher' was instructed to play a scene where he was to repeat the same scene he had played with Bente, but this time with an auxiliary ego who would represent Bente's daughter. When Bente appeared and understood that it was her own daughter who was being treated so badly, she reacted spontaneously. She threw herself over the teacher, swearing, beating with her fists and kicking. Years of anger were released as she acted in defence of her daughter, in fact in defence of herself. In the language of psychodrama, psychodramatic shock 'goes behind the resistance'. Bente had never learned to react for her own benefit, but when she saw her 'daughter' in the same situation, she could finally allow herself to fight its injustice. This procedure is also effective in cases of incest, rape and all kinds of abuse.

The mother/father model

A very effective model for rapid analysis of a spontaneous emotional relationship to parents is to have the protagonist choose group members to represent mother and father. They are then told to stand in front of the protagonist, who closes his eyes and tries to sense which of them should be placed at his right side and which on the left. In any case, the director should probe this point many times to be perfectly certain that the protagonist has chosen carefully. Experience has shown that the father is placed on the right and the mother on the left. If the protagonist is convinced that the father should be on the left, this usually implies that the father has been an absent figure, weak or, perhaps, a distracted artist. If the mother is placed on the right side, she has been the dominant person. Without being able to explain it, this has proven itself true time after time – it might have to do with the concept of energy, but this idea bears no scientific significance. We usually ask the protagonist to try to feel the energy flowing from 'mother' and 'father'. On the whole, I have stopped using the role concept except as it is used in sociology or in theatrical terminology. I find it more dynamic to talk about states of mind, for example you can easily have a role in its sociological or theatrical meaning but the moment you enter into interaction, you enter into a state. In addition, a state is extremely complicated and changing from moment to moment. Good directors must never lose their close contact with the protagonists and they should not plan too far into the psychodrama.

In the mother/father model the protagonist reverses roles with the father and mother and tries to feel what kind of energy – or message – they project. This is both an excellent way to prepare for a scene and an effective inserted scene if the protagonist needs to go more deeply into spontaneous feelings for his parents. It is amazing to see how quickly latent feelings can be activated, even with just a single sentence. Kåre hears his 'father' say: 'You're not good enough, son'. He feels an icy stab of contempt and defeat. Mother says: 'Don't worry about father. Stick with me'. From her comment, he feels his hands becoming clammy. It is not particularly easy to grow up in this family. Kåre answers: 'You've never been there to help me, Father'. And to his mother: 'If you could only stop hassling me. Do you always have to be in control?' Needless to say, this mother was standing on the right side.

The above does not have to last for more than a few minutes before a psychodrama is in full swing, maybe about a difficult childhood.

Finding the psychic atmosphere

A suitable method for charting a group and finding out where the members are in terms of their psychic atmosphere is to let them walk around in a circle. The director makes a special kind of compass where North represents depression, South aggression, East sorrow and West fear. Between each of these poles there are transitional states and the centre of the circle represents pure joy. After having tried out different areas of the circle, the group members are asked to place themselves in the spot where they feel they belong. Not much time is needed before the group is warmed up. Some try out different positions carefully and lengthily, while others go directly to the feeling, or state, where they feel their reactions are strongest.

Many scenes can be played out between the North-South axis of depression and aggression, such as when the aggressive are given permission to 'harass' the depressive. By reversing roles so that the depressive have a chance to harass the other side, the mood becomes more intense. There will also be a good deal of laughter and when it is time to chart the group a second time, many of the depressive members will have come into contact with their reserves of energy and move closer to the other side. A more difficult task is when many members of the group stand on the side of sorrow. Copious tears and pent-up feelings of loss will abound when this happens. When many are drawn to depression, it might connote shifting feelings of depression and aggression, as well as temporarily undefined feelings such as having a poor self-image, fear of authority or other emotions that need to be worked out.

Charting a group like this cannot be called sociometry because sociometry pertains more to the reciprocal interrelations within the group. Nor can it be called psychometry, since this is part of parapsychology and refers to the energy released by a physical object that can give information to a psychic medium about the history of an object. Finding the psychic atmosphere can be effective as a warm-up at the beginning of a group process or as an inserted scene within the process itself, when the general feeling of safety might be greater.

The social atom and the inner scene

Both Moreno's 'social atom' and 'the inner scene' (Røine's model) are well suited to gain an overview of a patient's social network or to chart the potential resources of a protagonist.

In the social atom the protagonist sits in a chair in the centre of the stage. He places other chairs around him to represent the people in his personal universe. Persons who have died are also included in order to find out who is, or has been, meaningful – whether in the positive or the negative sense. This can later be drawn out like a map, for example as part of the nurses' patient journals (the patients' social network).

The more chairs, and the closer they are to the protagonist, the more substantial is the network. If there are very few chairs, one can assume that the protagonist is a very lonesome individual, for example Reidar's social atom consisted of four chairs placed quite closely to his but it turned out that all of the persons they represented were dead. Reidar was a drug abuser who had been admitted after an overdose. His four pals had died in the same way. The chairs 'outside the room' belonged to his father, mother and sister. By reversing roles with a person who was placed on his sister's chair, Reidar finally managed to present some information that was positive.

Gradually, as the game gains momentum, the chairs are replaced with deputy persons from real life. Thus the protagonist's world is mapped out. Even the dead can be reached and often, perhaps because they are dead, it is possible to repair some fragments from a ruinous family life. Feelings, and even possibilities, can be placed on the chairs and thus initiate a 'rehearsal for life' or a new perspective of the future.

Nevertheless, the model 'the inner scene' is even better suited for seeking deeper emotional content. Here the director chalks out a space on the floor and then asks the protagonist's permission to join him in his 'inner scene'. Feelings and experiences are reawakened. Bitterness and jealousy become voices that can communicate with the protagonist. Pain also 'speaks' and its physical location can be discovered. Relationships between physical symptoms and psychological causes can be revealed.

Lise often felt a pain in her breast, which she thought had to do with heart problems. By giving the pain a voice, it said. 'Why can't you forget a rejection from so long ago?' This led directly to a psychodrama about Lise's deep distrust of all men after her betrayal by one. The wedding was cancelled a few days before it was to be held, the gifts were all returned and Lise thought she had been ruined for life. The voice from her heart showed her a new path to take, with new opportunities.

When Tormod went into his inner room, he felt an oppressive darkness. Only in one corner was there a patch of light. His inner room was populated with defeat. Disappointment was his strongest feeling. By reversing roles with disappointment he said: 'You can't count on getting any more out of life. It is too late. You can never be the musician you once were'.

This was a realistic statement because Tormod had hurt his hand and lost two fingers in an accident with a chain saw. Here the director's task was to make some room for feelings other than failure and disappointment. As the light spread from the 'small patch in the corner', it shone on Tormod's little daughter. A touching interaction representing hope and meaning between father and daughter followed.

A pillow of hate

In psychodramas involving strong aggression it is often best to use symbolic figures. Peder had long been a member of the group but he had never shown much more than a bout of rage against his mother. This was a violent paroxysm of rage, followed by a long period of crying. He fantasized that his mother wanted to strangle him. His father had also been physically violent but distant, and his mother switched between being a traitor and an aggressor. The whole scene was dominated by the presence of an insatiable thirst for love.

But Peder never seemed to get beyond his hatred of his mother. One evening, after getting Tormod's permission to use provocation, the director tossed a pillow on the floor and said firmly: 'Here is your hatred of your mother. Instead of raging at your mother, you should get rid of all these unending negative feelings that have made you physically sick. You've almost stopped breathing!'

At first the protagonist just stood there, looking in astonishment at the director and the group. The director continued: 'Are you trying to avoid positive feelings by clinging to your hatred of your mother?' Understandably, it is very important to ask for permission to provoke the protagonist in a situation like this. Peder didn't know how to react. The director gave him full permission to keep his hatred but this time he was to be aware of what it was doing to him. Some protagonists find release in simply blasting out a spontaneous flood of pent-up aggression, only to build it up again. Also, something like hatred of a mother can be a good excuse for avoiding taking responsibility for one's self. After a long period of provocation, Peder began to get a hold on his perpetual hatred and he cried out: 'I hate my own hatred. I want to get rid of it!'

After a session where Peder beat on the pillow, he started crying in a different way. His breathing was deeper and less encumbered and he was encouraged to breathe even more deeply and to fill his lungs as fully as possible while the director said: 'Now, Peder, breathe in good feelings. Make room for your longing for love. Until now there has not been enough room for any other feelings than hatred...' After a long pause, Peder lay down and cried quietly. Then suddenly he smiled and said: 'There is actually more room in my chest now. Maybe...maybe there is room for love?' He got up from the floor, saying: 'Thank you. It was about time'.

It was an emotionally moved group that took part in the final phase, the sharing of experience. There is always an atmosphere of solemnity when genuinely negative feelings are transformed and find their positive expression in a catharsis or a quiet insight. This is something that most persons in the group long to experience. One year later, Peder was married and had a child.

Searching for a reason

In monodramas the director often has to carry the burden of projections and transferences from the members of the group. In psychodrama groups it is possible to maintain a certain amount of clarity because the processes occur between the participants or on empty chairs. A constructive technique is to ask who it is that is influencing a group member when unreasonable reactions turn up. As a rule, the answer is usually a mother or father. Direct conflicts between group members must be handled with confrontation methods or role reversals.

It was obvious that Laila was beginning to be irritated by Aud. She had played the role of Aud's mother earlier and, although we are careful about 'de-roling', that is, ritually removing the negative roles of the participants, we are not always fully successful. This particular process was further complicated by the fact that Aud reminded Laila of her own mother. As she said: 'You remind me of my mother and how she walked around sighing while waiting for father, for the potatoes to cook or for the news on TV to start'.

Aud was not aware of the fact that she sighed all the time. She wanted to look into why she did this and what its cause might be. By going into her childhood, she remembered a scene from the kitchen. Her mother used to hide chocolate in the kitchen cupboard and Aud had found it and was just about to eat it when her mother appeared. This mother was more than normally frustrated and, at the end of the scene, she was furiously beating her daughter with a coat hanger. Aud had reverted to the time she was five. She was lying across her 'mother's' lap being beaten symbolically with an imaginary hanger, just hard enough to be a little painful (violence is not permitted in psychodrama). Suddenly she remembered that whenever she was being spanked by her mother, she held her breath. This was what she had been doing here too, until the director asked her to walk around the floor and consciously repeat: 'I'll never let her hear me cry!' It became clear that in Aud's later life, whenever she felt stressed, rejected or under some outside threat, she held her breath until she eventually drew in a deep breath and released it in a deep sigh. Without her being aware of it, Aud had been doing this for twenty years. She also had a number of physical symptoms that were rooted in her habit of suppressed breathing. The laughter of the group lightened the atmosphere when Laila said: 'Now I have to find out what my frustrated mother did to *me*...'

Transpersonal psychodramas

Transpersonal psychodramas are relatively rare, but when they occur they are colourful and fascinating stories. The protagonist leaves himself and enters into a different time. One of these strange dramas was enacted out in the woods on a bright summer's day. Ole suffered from obsessions and compulsive actions he could not control, for example his knife and fork always had to be arranged in a special way. He even treated a roll of toilet paper in a ritualistic way before it could be used. Otherwise, he became overly anxious. Before the psychodrama, he had gone out and found a scene by a small pond in the woods. On our way there, Ole became a totally different person. He had always been large and strong but now he was truly awe-inspiring. He pointed out two members of the group who were to be the King and Queen. He chose a frail and timid teacher from western Norway for the male role and the female role was to be played by a middle-aged housewife from northern Norway. Unintentionally, there was a sense of humour around her because she always referred to her depression as 'my despression' – a mixture of desperation and depression which clearly reflected her state of mind. Ole folded his arms and stated that he was a rebellious farmer who had come to kill the King in front of the Queen! For obvious reasons, the teacher from western Norway lost his interest in being King for a day and the Queen also distanced herself from the scene. But the rest of the group waited for the drama to begin.

A psychodrama appeals to a protagonist's theatrical tendencies to rewrite reality and this provides the strength to resist blockage when dangerous material turns up from the unconscious.

Having arrived at the pond, I used a large stone to replace the teacher. Ole had hidden an iron crowbar behind a tree and he presented it to one of the male participants who was to be second-in-command to the rebel farmer and in charge of weapons. At this point Ole had become the commander of a peasant army in the Middle Ages.

The two men made their entrance onto the scene. Ole grabbed the crowbar and went to work on the stone. With his enormous strength, he chopped it to bits. When he had finished, he stepped back proudly and looked at the results. It was at this point that I was inspired to ask Ole to throw each of the small pieces into the pond while calling out each of his compulsive actions by name. Ten of the larger fragments of stone ended up in the pond. One by one he symbolically rid himself of his compulsive actions. We concluded by holding a burial ceremony for the King, describing his oppressive hold on the farmers. The drama was over and done with. Ole became himself again and we went back to the group's meeting room. A few weeks later, he called me to report that he had got rid of all of his compulsive actions but one. He was not willing to tell me which one this was.

Another drama from the Middle Ages took place in a different group, and it appeared just as unexpectedly as Ole's. Signe had portrayed her inner room as a castle in southern Germany. When she started to play her role from this picture, she became a young and poor maiden who had been taken in and abused by the lord of the castle. Later in the drama she went to a lake where she gave birth to, and drowned, a child. As she was returning from the forest, the lord of the castle appeared, riding toward her on a black horse. During the enactment of this scene, she fell to the floor and fainted. Those of us who were watching this scene could practically hear the beat of the horse's hooves. The man who had played the lord of the castle spontaneously jumped from his 'horse' and ran to her side in horror. In a weak voice, she whispered: 'I have killed your child and I did it on purpose. You will never be able to touch me again!' I have often wondered whether this was an incest drama, since there was nothing else in her background that could be seen in relation to the murder of a child. In later years I have often been presented with sudden glimpses into other realities. There does not seem to be any immediate explanation for this.

Marital conflict and allergy

This psychodramatic method is an excellent way to investigate how a married couple responds to one another. Primarily, it has to do with communication. Neither spouse understands what the other person is trying to say or communicate. If this method takes a truly bad turn, it can bring about physical symptoms. One man presented himself in deep seriousness, saying that he was allergic to his wife. This was especially tragic because he loved her very much.

In marital conflicts it is important that each of the spouses appear separately before meeting one another in a joint psychodrama. It was decided that Karen would come first. She was a beautiful woman, stately and proud, and she had high ideals of how a man should be. The ideal man was her father and it was clear that it was probably difficult for Arne to live up to this man. In Karen's home life a central possession was a bench for massage. It was here that she satisfied her sensual needs. Karen's two cats, Nefertite and the General, also had a key role in her life. Arne thought that the cats might be the cause of his allergy but he had his doubts because the allergy – or itching – also came when they were on vacation and away from home, particularly when his potence was being tested. The scene was being played in a hotel room in a Southern country and he felt that he had been castrated. Attempts to find reasons for this in his childhood and parents were unsuccessful. Arne, in the age he really was, sat on his 'hotel bed' and cried.

The cats made it possible to understand the inner dynamics. In Karen's psychodrama the cats reigned as key figures. When she was playing Arne's role, she kept trying to chase them away. When she reversed roles with the General, she showed her contempt for Arne. He was not good enough. Her aristocratic behaviour came to light. Against this, with his working class background, Arne was relatively defenceless. While playing the role of Nefertiti, Karen showed her sensual needs on the massage bench – which Nefertiti usually chose to lie on. Here there was no problem with her strong sexual attraction to Arne. But between the attitude of the General and

Nefertiti's demands, the situation became intolerable for the husband. Later, in the joint psychodrama, one of Arne's replies was: 'Damn it, I'm not just a sex machine!' Through the mirror method, Karen was able to see what the scene in the hotel room looked like from the outside. The two sides of Karen, represented by the cats, got onto the bed and played out an absurd scene that had the group in fits of laughter. Nefertiti meowed and purred and snuggled up to Arne while the General sat properly on the side of the bed and criticized him. Arne's new spontaneous reply was: 'I even have your father in my bed!'

Some of the best insights in a psychodrama occur when a protagonist has a humorous 'a-ha experience'. By reversing roles with Arne, Karen understood how seriously she had contributed to Arne's impotence. Further into the psychodrama, the focus shifted onto a very complex father/daughter relationship.

An ordinary routine psychodrama would have only focused on the spouses' communication and this could have led to that unbearable moment that happens in purely technical psychodramas when the drama becomes stuck in its tracks. The magical potential of the stage and the numerous chances for role playing are a psychodrama's most important contribution toward creative release.

Trivialities, whether comic or tragic, must be brought to light in a way that allows the protagonist to see himself from new perspectives – in this case from the perspective of two cats.

A child's loyalty and 'repair work'

Loyalty is deeply related to a child's inborn sense of dependence and love for parents. Regardless of the quality of the parents' ability to provide care, there is a sense of longing behind feelings of helplessness, hatred and rebellion. For this reason, a protagonist must never be forced to renounce a parent or force a parting from them. The very first task is to help the deepest level of the child's consciousness to realize that in most cases only some aspects of the mother and father were bad. This also pertains to incest problems. Even if a father overstepped a boundary and was brutal and unreliable, he is still father and he might have been good in other areas. Even in cases where the father or mother were apparently only evil, the child's feeling of longing for what he never received will always exist. This is where it is important to heal old wounds by doing some repair work. This part of a psychodrama will always seem absurd. How can one explain a forty-year-old woman sitting on the lap of her 'father' and getting the hug she never managed to extract from him in real life or explain seeing the same woman with glowing eyes and joy because she has finally made real contact with her father? The very body seems to undergo some kind of structural change on a molecular level. Something is added that has been missing throughout the person's life. We can observe backs straightening and voices strengthening.

In Grethe's drama we saw how she tried to reach her father who was always hidden behind a newspaper or in front of a television. Grethe's schoolwork became increasingly worse, although she was a bright girl. By playing a scene with her father it became obvious that her arithmetical problems were not her most pressing problem. She had initiated a regular ritual of interrupting her father while he was reading the paper and, just as regularly, she was turned away. A vicious circle developed with a bad self-image, dependence and tears. In addition, she never got along with men because she had been programmed to expect disappointment and rejection.

But Grethe's father was basically an emotional man. He shut himself into a room and played his violin. Grethe's mother went to another room and sang arias. Father, an engineer, had wanted to be a musician. The mother, a housewife, had dreamed of a singing career. They went into their separate rooms with their cooped-up 'melodies of life' while their daughter was left out and alone. By asking her to try knocking on her father's door and asking to enter, she was also working up the courage to open her mind to men in general. When she knocked on the door this time, her father said she could come in and he let her sit on his lap. A long tearful scene followed before her smile appeared.

Grethe had been caught in an incomplete interaction between her mother and father. She had submitted to their desires, been loyal, played the role of mediator and always felt that she was the loser. Maybe it was her own fault. Not until she was finally allowed to sit on her 'father's' lap and he had played his favourite sonata for her was she willing to share him with her mother. A test for finding out whether or not this is a genuine feeling is to have the protagonist sit on the laps of both parents. In Grethe's case it was real. It seemed that she did not become truly whole until she saw her mother and father sitting next to each other on a couch and she could sit with both of them. In other cases the reaction can be one of disgust and the protagonist can only sit with one or the other parent. These situations require a great deal of further work, since it is the mother and father 'in ourselves' that have to be united.

Sometimes a mother or father has to be separated into a good side and a bad side. We often start off with two chairs, using one of them for father's bad, and even awe-inspiring, qualities and the other chair for his positive sides. The strict separation of the chairs makes it easier to work out the negative sides.

However, when working with the same group over a long period of time, using the same techniques becomes boring. It is important, therefore, to learn additional creative methods that can give some variation in the psychodramas. Once again, the many potentials offered by a stage are at our disposition.

Liv had been in a psychodrama group for a long time. The group themes always dealt with a strict father and an indulgent mother or a dominating mother and a weak father. Everyone in the group had taken part in the mother/father model.

Liv had been abused as a child but she did not know whether it involved incest. One fact was certain: she had been given many beatings. Liv had the same characteristics as Grethe. She was afraid of closeness and had a poor opinion of men, a fact which is always caused by previous rejections. 'It is better to turn someone away than to be turned away'. She remembered a time when she was in the barn as a six-year-old. Her father had been angry and, as usual, beat her up. Liv coiled up and became a little girl but the drama foundered because her feelings of anger, longing and loyalty had worn her out.

A method for avoiding resistance is to 'play on a team' with others who also have reasons for being angry. Here the dog Passop was a good team-mate. Passop often went to Liv when she was hiding in the barn and Passop had also been a random victim of the father's temper tantrums. An auxiliary ego was brought in as a funny Passop. At this point the director joined forces with the dog to plan revenge. Since the protagonist had a good sense of humour, they suggested that Passop would sneak in to her father while he was taking an afternoon nap behind the barn and piddle in his ear. At first Liv became stiff with fear at the thought of what could happen but Passop, the director and the group encouraged her adamantly. Wide-eyed in fear, Liv watched as a six-year-old (she was almost forty) while Passop lifted a leg and piddled into her father's ear. Just as the leg was being raised, the father broke out in a natural sneeze. The timing was so perfect that the protagonist, the father, the dog and the entire group fell apart in roars of wonderful, healing laughter.

Revenge had been taken, but the psychodrama was far from being over. First, the protagonist had to articulate her anger about being treated so badly. Now, with Passop at her side, she was ready. But after her anger came the heart-rending cries of childhood longing. The director gave her a match box with three matches left. Each time she lit a match she could make a wish and when she had used the third match, something unexpected would happen (a form of psychodramatic shock). In this version of Hans Christian Andersen's 'The Little Match Girl', Liv solemnly used up the first and second matches. When she lit the third match, a new father appeared (as he had been instructed) and sat down next to her, stroking her hair. In a mild tone of voice he began to say how proud he was of his little princess. When Liv heard the word princess, she cuddled into the crook of his arm and started prattling like a child. Her father began to tell a story and, before we knew what was happening, we were all carried off to a world of baby foxes in the woods and singing dolphins. Liv had started using the dialect of her childhood. Later that summer, Liv sent a postcard saying that 'the new father was beginning to have an effect on her'. It was a wonderful summer!

From psychoanalysis to psychodrama

Many turn to psychodrama after other forms of therapy, usually such as talking to a therapist or psychomotoric treatment. The aim can often be to break free from temporary emotional blockage. Other times it might be to rebuild the necessary defences. If the previous therapy has been psychoanalysis, the ground might already be prepared for a breakthrough – and usually one of a Freudian nature. Some patients come on the recommendation of psychologists or psychiatrists.

Alvilde had been in psychoanalysis for two periods of time, with different analysts. The therapy had taken place in classic style – by lying on a couch with the therapist sitting behind her head – three to four times a week for a total of eight years. A great deal of time, pain and money is invested in this kind of treatment.

Alvilde's problem was sexual anxiety. She had been married for many years, without any children. She detested everything that had to do with sex. Her husband was reasonably upset. Alvilde had given up. She came to psychodrama 'for her husband's sake'. Neither of them wanted a divorce.

At her very first psychodrama Alvilde was asked to lie down on the 'analyst's sofa'. She lay there tensely with closed eyes while the minutes ticked away until almost 20 minutes passed. The group fidgeted restlessly. Alvilde's body became stiffer and stiffer until she jumped up from the couch and cried out: 'I can't stand it anymore'. The fear and panic she had been carrying for almost 30 years forced itself forward from her unconscious. In the physical reality of the theatre, her drama took concrete form. As a four-year-old, she had been awakened by frightening sounds. She crept out into the winter darkness and sought refuge in her parent's room. But what she saw was her father raping her mother in a particularly brutal way. Alvilde remembered her exact age because she could place the experience at a time before the family had moved from its house by the sea and the sound of crying seagulls. 'Strangely, I have always felt this fear whenever I hear the shrieks of seagulls.'

Alvilde worked out her problems in many psychodramas. She was out of touch with us for a long time, but then I heard from her: I received a Christmas card with an idyllic family picture of a mother and father and a baby.

The Chakra system as metalanguage

As mentioned before, I have gradually stopped using the concept of roles except in a sociological and theatrical connection. I think that in psychodramas we are working to a much greater degree with the concept of states of mind. The concept of roles is too limiting. This is best illustrated when people find themselves in conflict, either with different role expectations or with external role perceptions, for example a woman can come into conflict with her own expectations of herself as a mother and wage earner. On an external level this can be described through a conflict between father and daughter – father thinks his daughter should act in accordance with what might be his patriarchal expectations of marriage rather than allowing his daughter to study or become an artist.

Otherwise, psychodrama moves forward in terms of the mental states in the relationship between a director and a protagonist and between a protagonist and auxiliary egos. Therefore, it is of utmost importance that the director maintains sensitivity to the protagonist's progress from one state to another, for example when a person leaves the group and becomes a protagonist, that person shifts from a role to a state. There is also a clear difference between the director's role and the role of a group member before they enter into a mutually interactive relationship. And this is where the concept of energy appears. Sensitivity to all levels enables the director to arrive at the essential relatively quickly. A good double can also find inspiration through this kind of sensitivity.

The chakra concept is relatively new to the Norwegian language. The word is derived from Sanskrit and means 'wheel'. The body has seven major and innumerable secondary chakras. The major chakras are placed vertically in the body. The lowest is the root chakra at the base of the spine, and from here they run upward from the root to hara, to the solar plexus, the heart chakra, the throat chakra, the third eye and the crown chakra. Ancient Indian wisdom associates each chakra with a specific colour of the rainbow. Chakras also have different speeds. The lowest is slow and their speed increases as they approach the fastest of them all, the crown chakra, which rotates at a tremendous velocity.

Moving from the lowest chakra, which is red, we assign it a symbolic meaning by saying it represents security – what Eric H. Ericson would call 'Basic Trust'. Thus those who have no basic feeling of security are not securely 'grounded'. Quite simply, their legs can be unsteady. This might not always be in the literal sense but the members of a group quickly understand what the director means by this instability.

The hara is two finger-widths beneath the navel and its colour is orange. This psychic centre represents a man or woman's sensuality and individuality, as well as their identity as a man or woman. The solar plexus is in an area of the body that most people know about. This centre is yellow and represents will or power. Anxiety and fear of authority is often found here. The heart chakra is slightly to the left of the heart. Its colour is green and it stands for growth and love, but also rejection. An amazing number of persons come into contact with their problems of rejection when we work in this area.

The throat chakra is blue and represents communication. Here too, many communication problems are uncovered when we work in this area. The two highest chakras are associated with intuition and inspiration. By working on the lowest chakras, the individual's 'aura' is cleansed and this increases access to intuition and inspiration. An excellent warm-up before a psychodrama is to draw a spectogram with the entire chakra system on the floor. The group members then choose the area where they feel they have most blockage. Some go immediately to their insecurity (the root chakra), while others work out their male or female identity or choose to work on controlling their fear of authority, rejection or communication problems. Just as a fastidious, sophisticated and skillful psychologist uses the Rorschach or other projective tests, chakras can be used just as advantageously to initiate a creative dialogue with a group. Afterwards, one can simply move right into the psychodramas.

Epilogue – 'sickodrama!'

Christmas greetings and letters with good news are always a pleasure, as are short meetings that bring specific psychodramas and protagonists back into recollection. There have been some meetings like this from Unit XVI and with persons from all over Norway who visited the Bauker Course Centre near Lillehammer in the years before the Norwegian Psychodrama Institute found its permanent centre in Oslo.

One day, two men delivered a refrigerator to my home. One of them smiled broadly and asked whether I remembered him. There was something familiar about him but I couldn't place him. 'Sickodrama', he said, 'down in the cellar in Unit XVI. I beat up a pillow with a cane. That's all I remember'.

Another time, I met a man who was cementing a wall in the back yard when I went out to empty my trash. 'I saw your name on the door', he said, 'you were my sickologist when I was in the XVI Unit. Those were quite the days. Are you still doing that?'

I also had a happy meeting in a restaurant. A man appeared suddenly at my table and asked whether I recognized him. I saw a familiar smile but his previously toothless smile now revealed bright and shining teeth. 'I just wanted to thank you. I was that crazy bank robber. My mother committed suicide because of me. At that sickodrama I was allowed to cry'. He looked at me with tired eyes in a relatively young face: 'The most important thing is to forgive oneself…'

Most of the people in the dramas from Unit XVI pronounced 'sickodrama' by accenting the first syllable of the word instead of the word drama. It always touches my heart when I hear someone say it this way. It reminds me that there is hope for everyone, including the most disadvantaged. They too can learn to play the leading role in their own lives.

Psychological Viewpoints on the Theatre of the Absurd

Examination Lecture for Magister Artium Degree in Psychology, University of Oslo, 1976

The title includes a hidden contradiction. I will systematize some viewpoints in order to elucidate that which by definition remains apart from any relationship to concepts such as space, time, reality, truth and identity. But, nevertheless, it is precisely in the absurd that psychology and theatre actually approach one another!

In *Madness and Civilization* (1965), Michel Foucault shows how society, throughout history, has isolated the weak and mentally ill. This made it easier to forget their existence. In Latin, absurd means 'conflict'. The absurd is discordant. It brings disturbance and apprehension into the safe and customary.

As long as Galileo could renounce his belief that the world was round, to escape being burned on a stake as a heretic, the bounds of space remained undisturbed and the Pope could maintain his monopoly on purgatory, salvation and eternity.

In his book *The Opposing Self* (1955), literary critic Lionel Trilling compared Shakespeare – Galileo's contemporary – and Kafka, one of the most important forerunners of the Theatre of the Absurd as it first appeared in the 1950s.

Shakespeare's characters see themselves as real and living, even though they both doubt and suffer, and usually die violent deaths. In contrast, Kafka's personae are alive without feeling they are alive. Shakespeare's questions of guilt and personal identity are not the shapeless concepts that Kafka presents. Shakespeare's personae usually die in the midst of action. In a sense, even Ophelia chooses madness and death as the most beautiful solution to a total breakdown. With Kafka, something dreadful has happened long before judgement is passed. His personae are wholly disrobed, in the spiritual sense,

right down to their naked skeletons. All that remains is the abstract idea –
humanity.

It is tempting to make a second comparison. Sigmund Freud's world
consisted mainly of the middle class in Vienna. And even though his sexual
theories caused a revolution in the *petit bourgeoisie*, with few exceptions these
people were determined to maintain solid walls around the values of the
middle class. The persons in Freud's world were safely anchored in their
concepts of morality and immorality. Like Shakespeare's persona, they could
feel that they were alive because their conduct was based on something
definite that had not yet lost its substance.

R.D. Laing is Kafka's opposite in a time when issues such as guilt, morality,
identity and reality have become vague and without contour. In the race
against death, the body maintains its lead. '

Laing also refers to Kafka as an example of a person who cannot feel his
own identity without feeling it through angst. Therefore, Kafka does not
want to be without angst because it at least confirmed that he was alive. Far
worse is the icy gust of nothingness, the great vacuous void that the Absurdist
writers offer as the framework of human existence. One of Samuel Beckett's
favourite quotations was from the Greek philosopher Democritus: 'Nothing
is more real than nothingness!' In his book *The Divided Self*, Laing (1960)
explores the world that Beckett creates, where nothingness seems to soothe
fear, despair or the boredom of existence. The two shabby vagabonds in
Waiting for Godot have no apparent aims and are sentenced to life. As Pozzo
says at the beginning of Act I, 'Man is born on he road to the grave....'

The more recent trends in psychology and psychiatry, and the Theatre of
the Absurd, have common roots in existential philosophy – primarily in
Søren Kierkegaard and Martin Heidegger. Both of these men present angst
as the most basic category of human existence. In the concept 'naked angst'
we have an intimation of a person facing the question of the meaning of his
life – and his death. This is where discordance enters and mankind meets
the absurd.

First, let us establish what this existential psychology and psychiatry try
to comprehend in order to help a patient and his angst. Ludwig Bienswanger
and Rollo May express it this way: 'The endeavour to take part in the patient's
reality, in the way reality appears to the patient'. Of course, this does not
imply the greatest absurdity of all: that a doctor identifies with the patient's
angst. To the contrary, the quotation means that it is the patient who speaks,
no matter how incoherently. The fragments of his distorted reality are the
diagnosis. The therapeutic help is in the acceptance that the way reality
appears to the patient is the way it is experienced. Concepts of reality in

themselves have become relative and they are the starting point for treatment. Thus the patient's experience of his own world becomes the framework of a structure that will be raised, but its foundation walls must be solid enough to hold up the building.

In Eugene Ionesco's earliest plays we can see the same tendency to remove all social, individual, political, moral and philosophical dogmas from the theatre. What he is trying to show is the basic structure of theatre. The result became grotesque robots and mankind reduced to mechanical organisms in which the use of language as a form of communication suffered a complete breakdown in screams and disjointed sounds or there were only empty clichés, spoken solely for the purpose of saying something.

One of Laing's patients starts noticing his mechanical answers to his wife's regular morning greetings. Would he like a cup of warm milk? Yes please. But does he really want the milk, and why did he smile, why did he say thank you? Eventually he felt that his thoughts were no longer his own. They were simply 'social mechanisms'. That was the day he began to feel that he was dead.

As a starting point, the psychotic patient's seemingly incomprehensible flow of words, or lack of words, and the Theatre of the Absurd's lack of message are no more than an introduction to our universal desire to maintain life because, in the words of Albert Camus, 'in the arid desert area where thought reaches its ultimate limits' we do not, strangely enough, commit suicide – most of us. 'When the spirit has arrived at the limits it must pass judgment and draw its conclusions. Here is suicide and the answer', wrote Camus in *The Myth of Sisyphus* (1953). But then he adds: 'The absurd appears when the longings of a man meet the senseless silence of the world.' Rather than ignoring this fact, we should embrace it as one of the foundations of life. Since the three characters in this drama – irrationality, human desire and absurdity – all appear at this point where longing and silence meet, the drama 'must end with all the logic that this condition can muster....'

By this logical necessity, Camus means that Sisyphus is *happy* when he returns to the valley and the stone that the gods declared he would have to roll up the mountainside for all eternity

Like writing and psychology, all philosophy has tried to understand life. In reality, 'to structure' means no more than to establish factual evidence. Theories and hypotheses are clues – theses, antitheses and syntheses. We structure in things, both valuable and worthless things. In distances – in what is near or far. We establish horizons, draw parallels. We orient ourselves in space by learning more about it. Only in this way can we keep space under control. Otherwise, the dreaded consequence might occur: space can invade us, possess us in the sense of Laing's concept of engulfment, being swallowed up, absorbed. Or implosion – being filled with something external the way gas, for example, fills a vacuum. Or petrification – that which petrifies and kills life and dehumanizes, transforms a person into a thing.

One of Laing's patients says in desperation: 'This is intolerable! You are arguing to triumph over me. At best you will win the discussion. At worst you will lose. Haven't you understood that I am arguing so that I can maintain my very existence?' These could easily have been the concluding lines in one of Ionesco's Absurdist dramas.

The absurd shows itself when there is a collision between universal, objective reality and an individual's subjective or personal experience of what others have defined as objective. Fellowship not only presupposes a common world but a common interpretation of the world.

The absurd shows itself in space, where things are distant and without validity. Man is no longer in control. Walls crumble. Space becomes endless. Space contracts. Or it becomes filled with things that no longer have any meaning.

The absurd shows itself in time that disallows thought. While a thought itself crosses into the past and the future without any restrictions, the present can never be held in place. If waiting is no more than destroying time, does death then become the final destruction or the very cessation of the destructive? One of Laing's patients maintains that his life began before birth and stretches beyond death, and Laing admits his helplessness. He cannot prove anything.

The absurd shows itself in language when there is disparity between the content of the words and the situation the words are meant for. Søren Kierkegaard presents an example that can be used as a worthy contrast to Galileo's knowing silence while the Inquisition declared in Latin that the world was flat. Kierkegaard describes a man who wants to prove that he is not crazy – at whatever cost. Therefore, his point of departure was a statement that everyone had to agree with. But to emphasize the effect of this unique truth he placed a ball in the lining of his jacket and every time his legs bumped into the ball he said: 'Boom! Boom! The world is round'.

I will have to limit myself to space, time and language in the Theatre of the Absurd. The difficulty is finding the best examples of plays that can be explained from a psychological viewpoint. The psychological common denominator is angst – the nameless fear of annihilation that follows the threadbare hopes and longings that make it possible for man to keep on living.

I will start with Harold Pinter's earliest play, called, quite concretely, *The Room.*

The main character is Rose, a person who never leaves her room in a house that she does not know the exact location of. She knows just as little about who the landlord is or how many rooms there are in the house because the landlord, Mr Kidd, does not know either.

Rose lives in her little private room surrounded by a large exterior space. There is a door that leads out to this great unknown. Attention is gradually focused on this door. It becomes a threat to a life that has been lived without looking at the familiar and near. When knocking is heard at the door, Rose's fear is intense. An ordinary young couple are on the other side of the door. They have heard that there is an available room in the house. Room number 7. Rose's room!

The play is filled with many obscure symbols that can be interpreted in Freudian terms. I will refrain from this and discuss only what we see – a slice of daylight forcing its way into the darkness. An individual's meeting with a bit of reality, which is not dangerous in itself but which is experienced as the destruction of an entire basis for existence. The young couple become intruders who threaten to obliterate Rose, take her place. And where should she go? She knows of nothing other than her small dark room. In Laing's terminology, Rose is an extreme example of ontological uncertainty. But what do we actually know of a psychotic patient's dark haven of refuge? And yet it is here, right here, that we have our starting point for therapeutic treatment.

Laing has described a psychosis as a voyage into the interior and he asks why so few return from this voyage. He also answers the question by stating that there are far too few institutions and therapists offering the patient the opportunity to complete the journey.

In *A Stroll in the Air* by Ionesco the concept of time is compressed into a voyage that runs right through the apocalypse of fear. Without having taken LSD, Berenger, the indomitable everyday hero in many of Ionesco's plays, takes off on a trip through space – a voyage through a sort of fulfillment of a dream of merging with the salt of the world and finding meaning in all that is beyond thought. Here we have an example of joyous euphoria ending in depression! But Ionesco carries out his journey with Berenger. He has said that the meaning of his play, among other things, was to achieve an inner restoration with the help of fear and the paralysing confrontation with destructive forces in our superficial era. Berenger, on his way down from the heavens, sees the downfall of the world. Annihilation and obliteration.

Originally, Berenger's final line as he crashed into the English tea-drinking middle-class was: 'No more just now thank you'. But Ionesco changed the ending before the play's opening night. Instead, he let Berenger's daughter have the last words: 'Maybe the fire will die, the ice melt, and the voids will be filled again. Perhaps the gardens...gardens... In the voice of a child we hear the echo of belief in a lost paradise. A cautious compromise between a rose and a thistle becomes an illusion of a garden...

> 'I am the prairie.' (Laing 1960)

> 'She is the ruins of a city,' says the young girl in Laing's study of a chronic schizophrenic entitled 'The ghost in the weed garden', 1960.

> 'She is only one of the girls who lives in the world. Everyone pretends that they want her, but they do not want her. I myself simply live the life of a cheap whore.' (Laing 1960)

This existential death, death-in-life in Laing's terminology, is described as a way to live. To uphold existence. But beneath this, he said, was the belief that something was buried deep inside her, undiscovered by herself or anyone else. And Laing concluded with a wish: 'If one could just travel far enough into the darkest interior of the earth, one would discover "sparkling gold". Or, if one could get to the deepest fathoms, one would discover "the pearl at the bottom of the sea (Laing 1960, pp.204–5)".'

It is worth noting that even when Laing is in, to quote Camus, the 'ultimate desert landscape of thought', his language is poetic. In reality, he is saying what Karl Jaspers wrote in 1955 when he started the importance of focusing on the freedom of the patient. Both men are actually optimists. Ionesco is not optimistic in his final and most important play, *Exit the King*, when he lets us see death itself and the decomposition literally occurs before our eyes. All that is left is the stage shrouded in a mist in which nothing, absolutely nothing, is left. He is not optimistic when he allows the break-down of language and the loss of all connection with the world either.

In his first play, Ionesco seemed to amuse himself by researching the platitudes of language and showing how words had become inflated; conversation literally killed with a kitchen knife in *The Bald Primadonna*, a play that had nothing at all to do with a primadonna.

Ionesco's inspiration came while he was learning English and being instructed in what 'the Smiths and the Martins' did for entertainment. When the banalities of language are dispersed into their separate factors and taken out of context in certain situations, language ceases to be language. It turns into nonsense syllables, not worth anything other than measuring memory on a scale of oblivion. In the one-act play *The Lesson*, a professor develops such a delirium of words that he finally rapes a student, literally, with words.

Here he presents the unpleasant consideration that words can become instruments of power. Authority, with its magical words, cripples both life and health, as can happen with the doctor and the patient. In *The Lesson* it is the simple servant girl who summarizes the situation: 'Arithmetic leads to philology, and philology to crime...' In *The Chairs* language collapses totally. The play ends with the guest speaker, who is to present an important message, bowing and simply standing on the stage with gaping mouth. There is no message, only emptiness – 'a void in nothingness'.

The absurd appears when space has no orientation, time becomes non-descript and indeterminate and language does not communicate anything that the receiver can understand.

But, in reality, these are conditions that psychology must try to under-stand. In a pathological sense, the starting point is the collapse of space, or the limitless present which is both the past and the future, and language that is regulated by something that is beyond common understanding:

'How old are you?'

'I am as old as the centuries, Sir.'

'How long have you been here?'

'I can't say precisely because we are pulled up by the air at night-time.'

'Where is this place?'

'It is called the Star.'

'Who is the doctor in charge of this section?

'A body like yours, Sir. They can make you black or white. People die and the microbes take over. Prestigites send you to another world. The government in Washington sent me to a different star. You look like a prestigite.'

'Who are the prestigites?'

'You are one yourself! You can well be a prestigite. They get you to say ugly things. They can read inside you, and they bring Negroes back from the dead...' (p.549)

This dialogue could easily come from an Absurdist playwright, but it is a patient's answers to a doctor's questions in Robert W. White's (1948) book, *The Abnormal Personality* ('prestigite' is a word the patient has invented). The patient is diagnosed as a paranoid schizophrenic and White points out the patient's apparent logic and coherence, despite his disorientation in time and space, and the fact that his language has no concrete meaning. This contrasts, for example, with the disorganized schizophrenics whose thoughts jump from one subject to another or the catatonics who say nothing, but who can tell you later that they still carefully followed everything that went on around them. White comments on the catatonic's 'silent inner drama' as a process that often ends in an answer to one or another hallucination. Everything that seems meaningless has the common factor that everyone is trying to communicate something. If we interpret these attempts as a way to give structure to a world that has become absurd, without the coherence that we others see, then we might be able to understand something of what the great French theatrical poet Artaud meant when he wanted to break the mirror to see what lay behind it, and seize his thought in flight to avoid perishing from fear. Artaud had been committed to a hospital and diagnosed as schizophrenic but he was released through the efforts of Jean Paul Sartre who understood his existential need: the human obligation to gain insight into all forces of evil that comprise the spirit of the times.

None of these Absurdist authors wrote for fun, even though comic elements are interwoven with the tragic. This is Life itself. Even Plato wrote that tragedy and comedy are unified twins in the great drinking feast in *The Symposium*. The narrator had collapsed under the table but heard Socrates' words to Aristophanes, the comic poet, and Agathon the tragic poet – the only two guests who hadn't fallen into a stupor: it is the same man's task to write both comedies and tragedies. Not separately, but in the same work!

Charlie Chaplin and Buster Keaton, the Marx Brothers and the circus clown are all forerunners of the Theatre of the Absurd. The secret of their success is that they touch upon the heart-strings of the audience. They find a sounding board because humans recognize themselves in the tragicomic, in the grotesque and in the absurd. In this sense, the figures in the Theatre of the Absurd are archetypes. Even though space, time and language are distorted and changed, man is permanently associated with space, time and attempts at communication. Man does not exist only in relationship to himself. He lives, to the highest degree, in his relationship with others.

Let us revert to space. Space is not only defined by us in terms of how we experience it. The limits of both inner and outer space are part of us. Therefore, freedom and reality become very relative concepts.

In *Self and Others* Laing illustrates this relativity with the example of a young boy who has run away from home. He ran around the block time and time again, and when a policeman finally stopped him and asked what he was doing, the boy answered that he was running away from home. But his father had forbidden him to cross the street!

The conscience, or the internalized Super-Ego, is as much man's loyal companion as the thought of death or whether or not there is a meaning in life. We would prefer to be able to drive this persistent trio out of our consciousness, into a corner the way Boris Vian pushes it aside in his play *Le Battisseurs d'Empire*. He creates excitement in the contrast between the harmless life of a middle-class family and a sinister creature that is growing larger and larger inside their house. Everyone pretends that nothing is happening but they have less and less room in the house. Finally, the members of the family disappear one by one. The daughter lets out a scream when she disappears but the father continues talking in a conversational voice: 'Oh yes, the children are flying from the nest...' When the husband and wife attempt to flee from the ominous Schmürtzen (at least they gave the creature a name) into the attic, the man forgets his wife in genuine egotism. At the end, it is his turn. Schmürtzen has taken up all the space. He throws himself out while saying: 'Excuse me!'

Interpretations can be manifold. Let us look at the play from the perspective of people who never discuss problems or those who lose their identity because they never assert themselves in relation to another person. The identity-less person might be the most sinister aspect of the Theatre of the Absurd, where people have neither a past nor a future and where the present is confused with what one might have been or might come to be. That is, unless everything is already hopeless!

The feeling of a real self can only be experienced in relation to persons and things that are real. Like Shakespeare's characters who lived and died in relation to someone or something, even if only to an old man's insanity on an isolated moor, at least King Lear raged against the weather and his destiny. And the voice of the Fool sounds sorrowful with its scattered grains of truth:

> He that has and a little tiny wit
> With heigh ho, the wind and the rain,
> Must make content with his fortunes fit,
> Though the rain it raineth every day (Act II, Scene II).

Kafka's characters feel they are just as unreal and without identity as Laing's do. In *The Divided Self*, Laing describes Peter as a person between parents who never really paid any attention to him – that is, they treated him as if he was not there. In order to survive existentially, Peter developed what Laing called 'false self-systems.' For example, if Peter was in a situation where he felt vulnerable, he imagined a role in which he was not himself. This uncoupling saved him from angst. But he had to be constantly on guard so that he would not be surprised by someone looking at him because then he

would, in a sense, be real and a part of the world. He would be someone
who could be seen.

Arthur Adamov's professor in the play *Le Professeur Taranne* was just the
opposite. Here his identity relied upon being recognized. The scene is played
in a courtroom where Professeur Taranne has been accused of appearing
naked on a beach. He denies this and refers to his spotless record and fame
– the man who has, among other works, written *La Parodie!* A few persons
in the courtroom, whom Taranne recognizes from his lectures, look at him
with surprise. A woman is called to the stand who knows him, but it is still
a mistake. It is Professeur Mesnard she knows. Gradually it becomes clear
that Professeur Taranne does not exist. He has no identity or he may have
even stolen someone else's identity. As a person, he is not himself. He is a
different person. The man who wrote *La Parodie!*

The individual who might have given the most intense description of
false identities and the interdependence of roles in what Laing calls 'iden-
tity-for-the-self' and 'identity-for-others' is Jean Genet.

In Genet's play *The Balcony*, the world is a bordello, a temple of illusion
where everyone can change identity at will. But even here the roles depend
upon 'the other person'. The Bishop needs his Sinner, the Executioner his
Victim, the Judge his Thief and the General his Mare. In this case the Mare
is a red-headed prostitute who is also a thief and the Judge informs this girl
that he needs her to be able to maintain his identity as a judge. And this is
not all. He says: 'You have to be a real thief so that I can be a real judge. If
you are just a pretend thief, then I will be just a pretend judge. Do you
understand?' And to the Executioner: 'Without you I am nothing…' And
turning to the Thief again: 'Nor without you either, my child. You two are
my perfect opposites. Oh what a delightful trio we make!'

Only one person remains in his own identity: the Chief of Police, whom
no one wants to identify with. He suffers in his isolation because all of the
people are his opposites, that is, they are all playing complementary roles.
He has no desire to identify with anyone else but life will not be complete
until someone wants to take his identity. Finally, a person appears, a defeated
rebel from the Revolution. As he abandons himself to fantasies of power and
torture, he exclaims: 'If I play the Chief of Police… I will also be allowed
to lead the person I have chosen to the outer limits – no, to *my* outer limit
and let his fate merge with mine' (Act III). He then draws his knife and
castrates himself, while the real Chief of Police smiles happily over the fact
that he has finally become a part of the dreams of the people.

It could be tempting to embark on a discussion of Freud's principle of
submission, the castration complex – the Proto-Father or the highest

authority who forces his sons into sexual abstinence and latent homosexuality. Jean Genet was homosexual. Let me just state that it was the Police Chief, the highest figure of authority, that he identified with at the moment of castration.

Ionesco focuses on submission and identification with the assailant in a different and equally unpleasant way in *The Killer*. On the way to the police station to inform the police about the murderer, Berenger, Ionesco's everyday hero, finds himself face to face with the murderer. But the murderer says nothing and Berenger has to answer for himself as well as his opponent. Finally, he has to admit that every once in a while he has his doubts about the value of life. He kneels in front of the murderer and asks for forgiveness. We are free to interpret the murderer as Death, Guilt, Berenger's Shadow or his other self.

Rose, one of Laing's patients, says of herself: 'Here is an I who is looking for a me'.

I have tried to shed some light on the psychological perspectives of Absurdist theatre in terms of disorientation in space, time, language and identity. Their point of convergence is angst. And it is so absurd that if we were to take away angst, the *psychologist* would lose his complementary role – the *patient*.

Nevertheless, psychodrama and Absurdist drama have only just touched upon one another so far. In conclusion, I will discuss an area in which psychology and the Theatre of the Absurd join forces and become a therapeutic treatment. This occurs in Jacob Levy Moreno's psychodramas, a subject I have treated in depth in my thesis. Here I will only mention one important aspect that the Theatre of the Absurd lacks totally, with the exception of one of Samuel Beckett's plays, *Waiting for Godot*. This is probably the only Absurd drama that will survive as a literary work, even though it examines only one static situation in two acts. Godot, who never appears on the stage, functions like the thread of Ariadne, connecting the absurd to life. Godot could be God, Death, Everyday Habits, or Life's Unreasonableness. But there is a certain *something* that captivates. Without this, each and every psychological treatment is just as meaningless as it is in Beckett's *Endgame*, where the people have ended up in urns and trash containers.

Psychodrama is the Theatre of the Absurd as a therapeutic instrument – where also God Himself or Jesus are included as co-therapists, wholly in accordance with the need people might have for relating to them. Psychodrama is also the Theatre of the Absurd in that it accepts that everything is relative in space, time, reality or truth and that the world is the way it is experienced by the individual.

Moreno can be considered a religious person, an atheist or a blasphemer. If we take his words literally in *The Words of the Father*, it might not seem strange that people are horrified. For verily, verily, Moreno says: 'Take a place by my right hand or my left... What would there be to create if there were no God to be created, and if *you* could not create *me?* (Moreno 1941, p.108).'

When Moreno includes God or Christ as a co-actor on the human stage – or in the play that is a psychodrama – his argument is that since God exists as an image in every single human being, he should also be able to be gestalted from the expectations of every human being's qualifications, whether they are lame, blind, naïve or afraid, rich or poor, epileptic, schizophrenic, prostituted.

As Moreno says: 'God exists in us all. Let Him therefore make His entrance on the stage, in the light, instead of isolating Him or repressing Him to the darkness of the garret'. Not only does Moreno include God and Christ as co-actors, he also invites role reversal with them. They are the cosmic forces which are also in human beings, on the strength of the existence of human beings as cosmic creatures. Through role reversal humans can draw upon the enormous resources they have within themselves, but which are repressed or scorned in the habitual living of everyday life.

God is not the stringent Hebrew God, HE-GOD! God is all that is spontaneous and creative in the Universe, a power or source of energy that is within human beings because they themselves have taken part in creating him. This is what Moreno means in his expression 'I-GOD' – an expression that many have found difficult to swallow and that has given him many enemies.

But in the way that God or Jesus appears on the stage of a psychodrama – whether in a skirt and blouse or in blue jeans – he becomes something that it is possible to relate to. The psychodramas where God or Jesus perform usually deal with unresolved sorrow, an overburdened conscience or aggression. As absurd as it may sound, aggression might be the most common emotion when meeting God the Father – the stern Super-Ego who has had the effect of a stranglehold throughout a long life. The therapeutic objective is to remove the God that is experienced as judgmental or unjust from his high throne and bring him into communication. Absurd? Yes, but still perfectly possible.

Personally, I agree completely with Moreno when he says that a psychotherapy that blocks out the enormous resources that all human beings have only meets the patient halfway. For, in the final analysis, Moreno says, man can only redeem himself:

Play yourself as you never were, so you can begin to be what you could have been. Be your own inspiration, your own author, your own executor, your own therapist and finally, your own Creator. (Speech to the International Conference on Psychodrama and Group Psychotherapy, New York 1972)

Moreno's Terminology

ACTING IN: When the auxiliary ego, the double or the director include personal motives which run counter to the protagonist's motives. In psychoanalytical terminology, acting in was introduced by J.N. Rosen (1962), who sees it as an 'inward reaction' – especially in reference to the inner world of the psychotic.

ACTING OUT: Moreno's use of this term has a much broader meaning than when it is used in psychoanalysis. Acting out is the fulfillment of all impulses and thoughts, that is, an enactment. Acting out in the more general understanding of the word, for example physically or violently, is channelled into constructive action through psychodramatic techniques.

ACTION INSIGHT: When a person spontaneously acquires a new insight or has an emotional 'a-ha' experience during an enactment. Moreno also uses the term 'working off' as a spontaneous emotional release.

ACTOGRAM: The course of events during a psychodrama in which one keeps track of what happens within the group: the members' relationships to one another, their rhythm, choice of auxiliary egos and positive and negative transferences.

AUTODRAMA: A drama in which the protagonist alone plays all of the roles.

AUXILIARY EGO: A deputy person from real life whom the protagonist needs for the enactment of his drama.

CATHARSIS: Moreno used this term in two ways: as primary/active or as secondary/passive. The protagonist experiences a primary/active catharsis while the group usually experiences the secondary/passive – unless they have been directly involved, so that their own problems have been touched upon and given an emotional release or an 'a-ha' experience. Actually, Moreno also uses a third type of mental catharsis by introducing the 'healing effect', which applies to all members of a psychodrama: 'The healing effect is produced…in the producer-actors, who produce the drama and at the same time liberate themselves from it'. (1970a)

COSMODYNAMIC: This expression is especially directed toward Freud's deterministic viewpoint and implies that man is a cosmic being not limited by forces within the individual psyche. Man is a cosmonaut who, like an astronaut, can travel freely in inner and outer space. See also Psychonaut.

CREATURGY: When a person creates spontaneity from inner resources. In reference to Darwin, Moreno said 'Survival of the Creator!' The person who creates, survives.

DOUBLE: Like the auxiliary ego, the double also plays a role in a psychodrama. The double's function is to help the protagonist express thoughts and feelings that often exist on a pre-conscious level. With the support of the double, a protagonist finds the courage to express what is often the very nucleus of the problem.

EMPATHY: (German: *Einfühlung*) Insight into the other person. Moreno uses empathy and tele in the direct I–you relationship which he seeks in the concept 'Encounter' (German: *Begegnung*).

HISTRIONIC NEUROSIS: The actor's neurosis. When portions of the actor's own psyche block out deeper understanding of a role or when the actor falls into a rut and is not able to renew his habitual acting techniques.

IN SITU: At the place where thoughts and impulses are given expression. Originally used to describe Moreno's psychodrama in Vienna, a kind of seeking-out activity in streets and parks. Drama in situ is also called Austrian psychodrama or existential psychodrama.

LOCUS NASCENDI: The point in a psychodrama where an action is 'born', that is, the starting point of a meaningful moment which is important to recreate in the psychodrama. Moreno also uses this expression when referring to the embryo in the uterus.

MONODRAMA: A psychodrama which is enacted without the group and with only the director as a co-player for the protagonist (not to be confused with autodrama, see above).

PSYCHONAUT: This designates, like the cosmonaut, man as a cosmic being. Here, like the astronaut, the psychonaut moves freely through time.

SOCIAL ATOM: The smallest part of the social structure of human society. The total sum of all choices and experiences that an individual has made in his life.

SOCIODRAMA: This focuses on social relations between human beings and on attitudes. For example, as a starting point, a sociodrama would investigate attitudes about abortion, race or religion, or shed light on patterns of gender roles. A sociodrama also shows relations among groups, especially in terms of conflicts.

STATUS NASCENDI: The creative moment. That which becomes tele. Moreno translates this word into German as *Zweifühlung*, as opposed to *Einfühlung*. In tele, the empathy is reciprocal, having 'two receivers and two senders'.

THEATROTHERAPY: This is the opposite of psychodrama and refers, in particular, to the work of Das Stegreiftheater in Vienna, when Moreno worked with professional actors and improvised on the basis of newspaper texts and current events. This is an incomplete psychodrama because the individual does not live out his own life in a spontaneous drama.

Bibliography

Adorno, T.W. *et al.* (1950) *The Authoritarian Personality*. New York: Harper and Row.

Anzieu, D. (1973) *Le Psychodrame Chez l'Enfant*. Paris: Editeurs EPI.

Artaud, A. (1967) *Det Dobbelte Teater*. Fredensborg: Arena.

Aubert, W. (1964) *Sosiologi*. Oslo: Universitetspelaget.

Baldwin, A. (1960) 'The mode child: the relationship between exhibitionism and speech errors.' *Journal of Abnormal Social Psychology*.

Bateson, G. (1970) 'Towards a theory of schizophrenia.' *Haagse Post*, 25 November.

Beier, E.G. (1966) *The Silent Language of Psychotherapy*. Chicago: Aldine Publishing Company.

Berne, E. (1961) *Transactional Analysis in Psychotherapy*. New York: Ballantine Books.

Berne, E. (1967) *Games People Play*. New York: Ballantine Books.

Bienswanger, L. (1958) 'The existential school of thought.' In R. May, E. Angel and H.F. Ellenberger (1967) (eds), *Existence*. New York: Simon and Schuster.

Boss, M. (1963) *Psychoanalysis and Daseinanalysis*. New York: W.W. Norton.

Camus, A. (1953) *The Myth of Sisyphus*. Oslo: Cappelen.

Casriel, D. (1963) *So Fair a House. The Story of Syanon*. New York: Hill and Wang.

Cleckley, H. (1964) *The Mask of Sanity*. Saint Louis: C.V. Mosby Company.

Corsini, R.J. (1956) 'Freud, Rogers and Moreno: an inquiry into the possible relationship between manifest personality, theory and methods of some eminent pscyhotherapists.' *Group Psychotherapy IX*, 4, pp.274–281.

Dragnes, A. (1967) *Empathy: Reflections on a Tradition of Research Material, Supplied with Examples from Own Investigation*. Unpublished dissertation paper, University of Oslo.

Dymond, J.R. (1949) 'A preliminary investigation of the relationship of insight and empathy.' *Journal of Consult. Psychology 12*.

Else, G.F. (1965) *The Origin and Early Form of Greek Tragedy*. Cambridge, MA: published for Oberlin College by Harvard University.

Ericson, E.H. (1968) *Identity, Youth and Crisis*. New York: W.W.Norton.

Foucault, M. (1965) *Madness and Civilization*. New York: Pantheon Press.

Foudraine, J. (1971) *Hvem er av Træ? En Vandring gjennom Psykiatrien* [*Who is Made of Wood? A Journey through Psychiatry*]. Copenhagen: Borgen.

Frazer, J.G. (1963) *The Golden Bough: A Study of Magic and Religion*. London: Macmillan.

Fromm, E. (1970) *The Crisis of Psychoanalysis*. New York: Holt.

Freud, S. (1941) *The Psychopathology of Everyday Life.* London: Imago.

Freud, S. (1963a) *The Collected Papers of Sigmund Freud.* New York: Collier Books.

Freud, S. (1963b) *The Complete Introductory Lectures on Psychoanalysis.* London: Allen and Unwin.

Gatheru, R.M. (1964) *Child of Two Worlds: A Kikuyu's Story.* New York: Traegn.

Glasser, W. (1965) *Reality Therapy: A New Approach to Psychiatry.* New York: Harper and Row.

Goffman, E. (1959) *The Presentation of Self in Everyday Life.* New York: Doubleday.

Gosnell, D. (1964) 'Some similarities and dissimilarities in the psycho- dramaturgical approaches of J.L. Moreno and Erving Goffman.' *International Journal of Sociometry and Sociatry IV*, pp.3–4, 94–106.

Greenberg, I.A. (1974) *Psychodrama, Theory and Therapy.* New York: Behavioral Publishing.

Grotowski, J. (1973) *Teatret og Riten: Teatrets Teori og Teknik* [*Theatre and Ritual: Theory and Techniques of the Theatre*]. Holsebro, Germany.

Guntrip, H. (1973) *Personality Structure and Human Interaction.* London: Hogarth Press.

Haugsgjerd, S. (1970) *Nytt Syn På Psykiatrien.* Oslo: Pax.

Heidegger, M. (1976) *Sein und Zeit.* Tübringen, Germany: Niemeyer.

Hunningher, B. (1961) *The Origin of the Theater.* New York: Hill and Wang.

Janov, A. (1970) *Primal Therapy. The Cure for Neurosis.* New York: Dell Publishing.

Jaspers, K. (1955) *Wesen und Kritik der Psychotherapie.* München: Piper.

Jung, C.G. (1933) *Modern Man in Search of a Soul.* London: Kegan Paul.

Kahn, E. (1931) *Psychopathic Personalities.* New York: Basic Books.

Kierkegaard, S. (1963) *The Concept of Dread.* Copenhagen: Begrebet Mgst.

Klein, M. (1937) *The Psycho-Analysis of Children.* Second edition, London: Hogarth Press.

Laing, R.D. (1960) *The Divided Self.* London: Penguin Books.

Laing, R.D. (1962) *Self and Others.* London: Penguin Books.

Laing, R.D. and Esterson, A. (1964) *Sanity, Madness and the Family.* London: Penguin Books.

Lawrence, E. and Weissman, S. (1965) *Acting Out.* New York: Grune and Stratton.

Leeuw, G. van der (1969) *Mennesket og Mysteriet.* Oslo: Cappelen.

Levy-Bruhl, L. (1935) *La Mythologie Primitive.* New York: Grune and Stratton.

May, R. (1966) 'Eksistensiell psykologi.' In R. May, E. Angel and H.F. Ellenberger (1967) (eds), *Existence.* New York: Simon and Schuster.

Mezurecky, A.W. (1974) 'Psychodramatics – the genealogy of a clinical modality.' *Group Psychotherapy and Psychodrama XXVII*, pp.1–4.

Moreno, J.L. (1941) *The Words of the Father.* Boston MA: Beacon Press.

Moreno, J.L. (1970a,b,c) *Psychodrama I, II, III.* Boston MA: Beacon Press.

Moreno, Z. (1959) 'Survey of psychodramatic techniques.' *Group Psychotherapy and Psychdrama XII*, pp.5–14.

Nietzche, F. (1969) *The Birth of Tragedy*. Oslo: Pax.

Pearls, F.S. (1966) *Gestaltterapi*. Copenhagen: Munksgaard.

Rogers, C. (1949) 'The attitude and orientation of the counselor.' *Journal of Consult. Psychology 13*.

Rosen, J.N. (1963) 'Acting-out and acting-in.' *American Journal of Psychotherapy*, pp.390–403.

Sachs, J. (1974) 'The letter.' *Group Psychotherapy and Psychodrama XXVII*, 1–4, p.184.

Schactel, E.G. (1963) *Metamorphosis. On the Development of Effect, Perception, Attention, and Memory*. London: Basic Books.

Schubart, W. (1969) *Religion and Eros*. Copenhagen: Haase.

Schützenberger, A.A. (1966) *Précis de psychodrame*. Paris: Editeurs EPI.

Slök, J. (1963) *Det Absurde Teater og Jesu Forkyndelse* [*The Theatre of the Absurd and the Preachings of Jesus*]. Copenhagen: Gyldendal.

Stanislavsky, K. (1937) *An Actor Prepares*. London: Geoffrey Bles.

Stone, L. and Church, J. (1957) *Childhood and Adolescence: A Psychology of the Growing Person*. New York: Random House.

Sullivan, H.S. (1947) *Concept of Modern Psychiatry*. New York: W.W. Norton and Company.

Sullivan, H.S. (1970) *The Psychiatric Interview*. New York: W.W. Norton and Company.

Szasz, T. (1970) *Psykisk Sykdom: En Myt* [*Illness of the Psyche: A Myth*]. Stockholm: Aldus.

Trilling, L. (1955) *The Opposing Self*. London: Secker and Warburg.

Vian, B. (1967) *Les Batisseurs d'Empire*. Paris: Pauvert.

Weiss, E. (1950) *Principles of Psychodynamics*. New York: Grune and Stratton.

Westcott, H.R. (1968) *Towards a Contemporary Psychology of Intuition*. New York: Holt, Reinhart and Winston.

White, R.W. (1948) *The Abnormal Personality*. New York: Ronald Press.

Wolpe, J. (1972) *Adferdsterapi i Praksis*. Oslo: Cappelen.

Wolstein, J. (1964) *Transference: Its Structure and Function in Psychoanalysis Therapy*. New York: Grune and Stratton.

Subject Index

Name Index